VIC KEEGAN'S

LOST
LONDON 2

SOUTH BANK EXHIBITION. FESTIVAL OF BRITAIN 1951
FROM THE RIVER

LAMBETH WALK SE11

First published in 2023
by Shakespearesmonkey
174 Ashley Gardens
London SW1P 1PD

ISBN: 978-0-9540762-8-3

Cover illustration Christopher Keegan
www.chriskeegan.co.uk

Formatting and Compilation by The Amethyst Angel

Victor Keegan's blogs:
OnLondon.co.uk (Lost London section)
LondonMyLondon.co.uk
victorkeegan.com
Instagram - vickeegan
Flickr - Flickr.com/shakespearesmonkey
Twitter: @vickeegan
@BritishWino
@LonStreetwalker
@ShakespearesLon

Contact: victor.keegan@gmail.com

First Edition

CONTENTS

OTHER BOOKS BY VICTOR KEEGAN

Non-Fiction:

The Guardian Year, 1999 (editor)

Lost London (1)

Poetry:

Crossing the Why

Big Bang

Remember to Forget

Alchemy of Age

London my London

Selective Memories

Duelling Poets (with Michelle Gordon)

LOST LONDON MAP

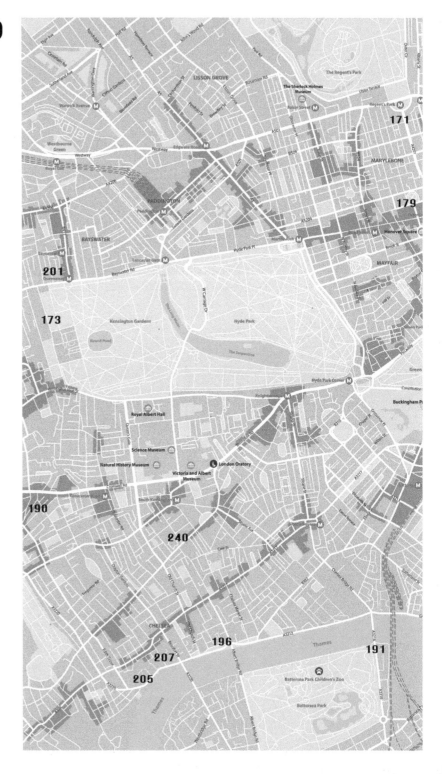

Numbers are placed in approximate places. Those on the very edge indicate locations off the map.

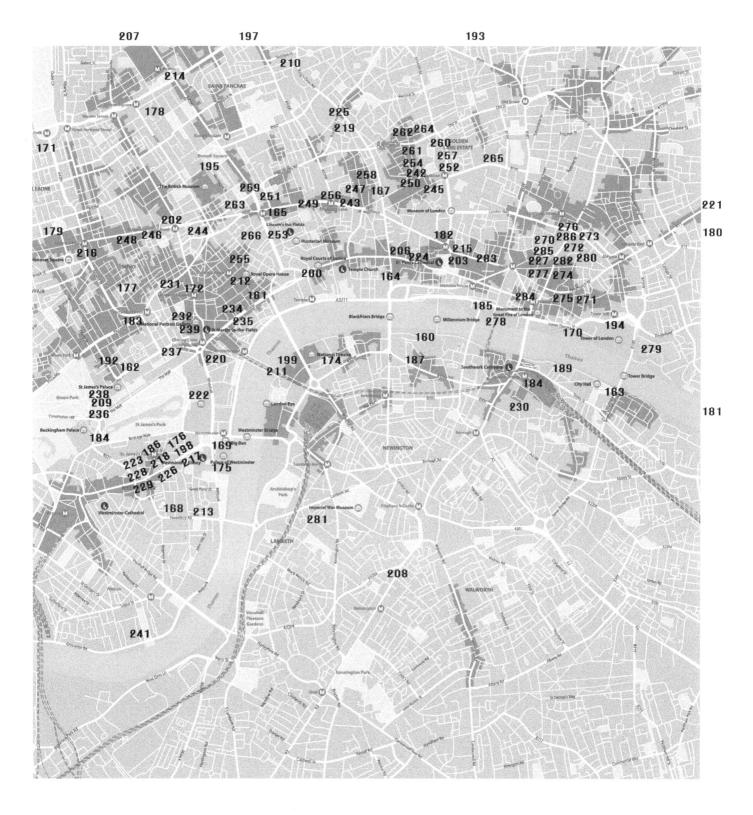

INTRODUCTION

Before starting my previous book, Lost London (1) there were doubts I would ever get to 100 entries let alone the 160 that somehow emerged. I had grossly underestimated the fascinating layers of infrastructure and memories that lie beneath the surface of this stunning city. Long lost buildings still tell their tales. An early wake-up call was Salisbury House in Finsbury Circus in the City. I worked there for several years in the financial office of the Guardian. Over 40 years later looking at an old map I saw to my amazement that it was on the exact footprint of the second Bedlam asylum designed by that great polymath Robert Hooke. There was no plaque then to indicate anything and there still isn't.

This book has provided numerous surprises. I had no idea that the mundane Highbury and Islington station used to look like an Italian palazzo before it was shamefully pulled down, nor that there was an extraordinary cricket match in Walworth between a team from Greenwich with only one leg and the other from Chelsea with only one arm, or that in 1810 a black bare knuckle fighter was swindled out of being world champion by white subterfuge. There are dozens of similar tales which I hope you will enjoy.

The main sources apart from books and the internet (thank you, Wikipedia!) have been old maps and the amazing number of archaeological excavations that have taken place over the years. Sadly, too many have been built over and the foundations of new buildings are too deep to save any remains. But at least the findings exist in numerous archaeological surveys which will preserve the memory of these historic layers of London.

I am grateful to Michelle Gordon for her publishing help, and Dave Hill, founder of OnLondon.co.uk, for much needed editing advice, and to my wife Rosie and sons Dan and Christopher for their support. Christopher, a professional illustrator, has created lovely covers for all eight of my books.

My thanks to two Business Improvement Districts (the Central District Alliance and ECBID) who supported over 40 entries through a deal with OnLondon.co.uk (where they first appeared as a weekly column). The idea is to provide historical background to areas they are trying to attract business to. I continued to write completely freely but the need to research their areas intensively, meant I uncovered lost history I might have missed.

I was deeply moved by the reactions to Lost London (1) and I would like to thank everyone for their heart-warming comments which have prompted me to attempt a second - and, surely final - tribute to this unique city. The more I delve into its past, the more I realise I am still only scratching the surface.

Vic Keegan

161: BEFORE THE STRAND PALACE HOTEL

At 11 a.m. on Monday, 1 June, 1840 Prince Albert entered a building (above, left) which stood where the Strand Palace Hotel is today and, according to a verbatim account, said, to rapturous applause: "I have been induced to preside at the meeting of this Society from a conviction of its paramount importance to the great interests of humanity and justice." (Cheers.). "I deeply regret that the benevolent and persevering exertions of England to abolish that atrocious traffic in human beings, at once the desolation of Africa and the blackest stain upon civilised Europe, have not as yet led to any satisfactory conclusion." (Cheers).

It was the first meeting of the Society for the Extinction of the Slave Trade Trade and it was held at the Exeter Hall, whose three large rooms could accommodate over 5,000 people. Largely because of this meeting, the words "Exeter Hall" became a byword for abolition. Albert's speech was a defining moment, even though it came over 60 years after the pioneering efforts to end slavery had got underway in London.

Exeter Hall was but one iteration of this site in the Strand, which has fascinating links with London's history. It was situated at the eastern end of what had once been called Lundenwic, an area between the Strand and the Thames, recently excavated, that was colonised by Saxons. Lundenwic was part of a network of international trading ports that existed between the late 7th century and the mid-9th century.

The first known house on the site was begun by a diplomat, Sir Thomas Palmer who was executed in 1553 before it was finished. That is what often happened in those days. The house was completed by Elizabeth I's chief of staff Sir William Cecil, who became Lord Burghley. It is said that when Elizabeth visited him there when he was ill, her headdress was so high she could not get through the door. It was succeeded in 1676 by the very large Exeter Exchange building – popularly known as the Exeter Change – which had a narrow entrance that jutted out on to the Strand.

Exeter Exchange contained an arcade of almost 50 small shops, such as drapers and hosiers, but is most famous for hosting a zoo on its upper floors for over 50 years, which was dignified by visits by William Wordsworth and Lord Byron. The menagerie included lions, tigers, monkeys and a hippopotamus, all locked in small iron cages. There was also an elephant called Chunee, which was shot in its cage in March 1826 by soldiers from Somerset House when it started rampaging. Chunee's skeleton was later exhibited at the Hunterian Museum in Lincoln's Inn Fields. When Exeter Exchange was pulled down in 1829, many of the animals went to London Zoo in Regent's Park and Edward Cross's new venture at the Surrey Zoological Gardens at the Elephant and Castle.

Exeter Hall, where Albert made his speech, was the next building to appear on the site. Other events held there included a seven-hour meeting in 1834 to support the establishment of a free colony for South Australia and, in 1846, meetings of the Anti-Corn Laws League. It also served as a musical hall, where Hector Berlioz first conducted concerts. In 1880, Exeter Hall's lease was acquired by the YMCA, which sold it in 1907 to the J. Lyons catering empire.

The Hall was torn down soon after and the Strand Palace Hotel built in its place. It opened in September 1909, and has remained there ever since and will do so at least until the next transformation takes place.

162: THE MANY FACES OF SCHOMBERG HOUSE

Observe 80-82 Pall Mall and be bemused by this brazen anomaly interrupting the architectural calm of London's clubland. It has no parallel in Britain, according to the architecture writer Ian Nairn. That is partly because it is a floridly designed "beery" 17th century Dutch building, but also because what you see is not what you get.

The house dates back to 1698, when it was built for Meinhardt, the third Duke of Schomberg, who commanded the right wing of William of Orange's Protestant army against the forces of the deposed James II during the controversial Battle of the Boyne in 1690.

The right-hand side of Schomberg House is as it was originally, except for one thing – it is only a facade. The left-hand side is also a facade, but a fake one. It was reconstructed after going missing for a hundred years. It was a fine piece of invisible mending, as it is impossible to see where the fake facade starts and the original ends.

That is not the case with the beautifully preserved classical statues supporting the portico. They are made of the hardwearing artificial Coade stone made at Eleanor Coade's manufactory, which was across the river where the Royal Festival Hall now stands.

A VIEW from Mr COSWAY's BREAKFAST-ROOM PALL MALL,
WITH THE PORTRAIT OF Mrs COSWAY.

The house has its origin in war, but its later history is a chronicle of art and sex. Its artistic renown began when John Astley, a fashionable portrait painter, took over the lease in 1769 and built himself a studio on the roof overlooking St James's Park. He rented one wing to Thomas Gainsborough. When Gainsborough left, many of his paintings were sold at an exhibition held at Schomberg House and the rest at a later auction held by Christie's, whose business was started in Pall Mall.

Richard Cosway, another fashionable artist and miniaturist, lived in Schomberg House from 1784 to 1791 with his artist wife Maria (see above) and a former slave, Ottobah Cugoano, who was their servant. One of Cosway's paintings shows a servant in attendance. It is almost certainly Ottobah, who became an active abolitionist in the Sons of Africa group.

It is interesting that two of the rare paintings of former slaves at that time were by artists associated with this house. After he moved to Bath, Gainsborough painted Ignatius Sancho, the black African who became a distinguished man of letters. Cosway also painted a miniature of the Prince Regent's "wife", Maria Fitzherbert, which the Prince wore for the rest of his life.

In 1794 Shakespeare made his presence felt when James Woodmason moved his New Shakespeare Gallery from Dublin to Schomberg House to provide competition for James Boydell's Shakespeare Gallery in the same road at No 52, which contained over 180 paintings specially commissioned from contemporary artists.

It was not all high culture at Schomberg House. In 1781, a Scottish quack doctor called James Graham opened a "Temple of Health and Hymen" there. Advertisements for it boasted of "medico-electrical apparatus" and a "grand celestial state bed" supported by 40 pillars of brilliant glass with near naked "goddesses" in attendance, including Amy Lyon, the future wife of Sir William Hamilton and mistress of Nelson.

The "temple" was covered by a dome lined with mirrors with coloured sheets, and played music. It later turned out to be a high class brothel that was closed by the police. Let's go no further.

Schomberg House was eventually returned to the military in 1859, when all three sections were occupied first by the War Office and later by the Director of Barrack Construction. Since then, despite being dominated by offices, Schomberg House has remained a rare example of a 17th century town house. Or at least the facade of one.

163: THE ORIGINAL GREAT FIRE

What was known for centuries as The Great Fire of London killed 3,000 people, almost 7.5% of the city's population. Not the famous Great Fire of 1666 that started in Pudding Lane and sticks in everyone's imagination. That caused huge damage to property, with over 13,000 houses destroyed, but hardly anybody was recorded as being killed. The original Great Fire happened over 450 years earlier, in 1212, in Southwark.

No-one knows how it started, but it swept through Borough High Street ravaging most of it. It completely destroyed the historic church of Saint Mary Overie (site of today's Southwark Cathedral) and then was blown across the recently re-constructed London Bridge, destroying all the wooden structures on it – there were over 60 shops there – and killing crowds of people in both directions. These included both those fleeing the blaze, which was whipped up by strong winds from the south, and those coming from the north to help or merely gawp at the flames. Others died by diving into the swirling waters of the Thames in an effort to escape.

Had the authorities applied at the time the lessons that would be learned from the 1666 blaze, as they could have done, such as banning wooden homes in favour of stone and bricks the the 1666 fire need never have happened. Instead they continued to build in wood and to use buckets of water to dowse flames rather than more sophisticated devices.

For hundreds of years the 1212 inferno was known by everyone as "the Great Fire of London" but that sobriquet passed to the 1666 fire thereafter. This is understandable in view of the huge damage done, but cynics might say that in the end property was considered more important than lives.

The figure of 3,000 deaths comes from John Stow, writing much later in 1603, and is disputed by some modern historians, though no-one really knows.

Fires were commonplace in medieval London, with its wood and pitch buildings, and most had much higher death tolls than that of 1666. Boudica razed the city to the ground in 60 AD and there were fires in 675 and 989. St Paul's Cathedral was burnt to the ground during another one in 1087. In 1135 the London Bridge of that time was destroyed by flames.

164: BRIDEWELL PALACE

Two things Henry VIII was not short of were wives and palaces, but his palaces were more numerous. Among the most famous of the dozens of candidates are Westminster, Whitehall, St James's, Eltham, the Tower of London, Richmond, Hampton Court and, the most sumptuous of them all, Nonsuch, which Fate did not allow him to live long enough to see completed.

The location of one of the least well known is passed by thousands of Londoners and others every day as they emerge from the western exit of Blackfriars Underground station, though hardly any realise it. The whole of that side of New Bridge Street, from the end of the Unilever building along the banks of the Fleet river (now underground) to Fleet Street, was taken up by Bridewell Palace, with a watergate to the Thames being the main entrance. All visible traces of it have now gone, though some remains of it, including brick arches, are buried underneath and a reconstruction of part of the facade can still be seen.

Bridewell Palace was built by Cardinal Wolsey in around 1510 with what came to be known as Tudor brick, not the traditional stone. He once described it as "my poor house at Bridewell". It was taken over by Henry in 1515 after his palace at Westminster was destroyed and he lived there on and off for eight years.

It later morphed from palace to poor house when Bishop Ridley successfully pleaded with Edward VI in 1553 to give some of his empty palaces over to the city to house homeless women and children. The City of London took over the buildings 1556 and turned them into a prison, hospital and work rooms, which became known as Bridewell prison. The name Bridewell soon became the generic one for any large jail.

The atrocious conditions there can be gleaned in Ned Ward's famous book The London Spy. He said that men and women were whipped on their naked backs before the court of governors. The president apparently sat with his hammer in his hand, and the punishment ended when the president banged the table rather like an auctioneer.

The place was not without humour. During Charles II's reign one of the most infamous inmates was brothel keeper Elizabeth Cresswell, who left £10 in her will for a sermon to be read that said nothing ill of her. The young clergyman found to grant this wish apparently said: "By the will of the deceased it is expected that I should mention her and say nothing but what was well of her. All I shall say of her, therefore, is this — she was born well, lived well, and died well; for she was born with the name of Cresswell, lived at Clerkenwell, and died in Bridewell."

The prison was finally closed in 1855 and the buildings demolished in 1863-4 to make way for the De Keyser's Royal Hotel, which was later sold to Lever Brothers who demolished it. Unilever House has stood there since 1931. The only memory of the palace is a gatehouse in the style of the original at 14 New Bridge Street, including a relief portrait of Edward VI.

165: NICHOLAS BARBON AND THE BRICK-THROWING LAWYERS OF RED LION SQUARE

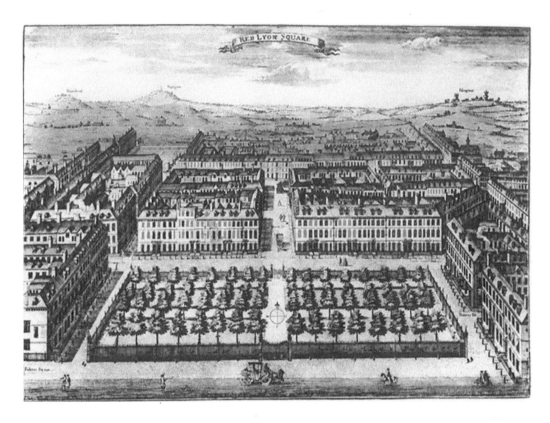

Holborn's Red Lion Square – one of London's oldest – harbours more celebrities in its history than most. They include Dante Gabriel Rosseti, Edward Burne-Jones, his room mate William Morris (who set up shop there), John Wilkes and John Harrison, the globally recognised inventor of the marine chronometer, which changed perceptions of longitude.

John Milton lived for a time nearby and the dead body of Oliver Cromwell, extracted from its grave in Westminster Abbey, spent the night at the Red Lion pub before continuing its journey to be ritualistically hanged at Tyburn the following day. Some say he is actually buried under the square. A bust of Bertrand Russell was erected there in 1980. But the most fascinating person connected to the square was the man who built it – the little-known but extraordinary Nicholas Barbon.

Barbon's life was never going to be normal. The son of the infamous Fifth Monarchist Praise-God Barebone (hence

"Barbon"), he was apparently christened "Unless-Jesus-Christ-Had-Died-For-Thee-Thou-Hadst-Been-Damned".

Such hellfire talk did not limit Barbon. He escaped from his childhood environment and became a polymath. He studied medicine in Holland, qualifying as a doctor, and later wrote treatises on economics that, nearly 300 years later, found favour with John Maynard Keynes and Joseph Schumpeter. Then he found his true vocation: property speculation, which he practised on a scale seldom seen since.

Barbon pulled down several palaces on the Strand, including the Earl of Essex's estate. In June 1684, he seized the opportunity to buy 17 acres of fields on what was then the very edge of London to build Red Lion Square. This incurred the wrath of lawyers at Grays Inn, who were based an open field away from the development, which they feared would destroy their "wholesome air".

When they took their case to court and lost – because the land had been legally purchased – they refused to give in, and on 10 June a fierce battle broke out between upwards of 100 lawyers armed with bricks and the workmen, led by the indomitable Barbon himself. He emerged victorious, notwithstanding many casualties. Maybe the circumstances of its birth explain why it was built with a watchtower at each corner – shown in the c.1725 engraving of the square by Sutton Nicholls – which could be used as prisons.

In recent years, Red Lion Square has been associated with the Conway Hall radical meeting place. it is less well known that in 1818 it saw the foundation of the London Mendicity Society – the Society for the Suppression of Mendicity, to give it its full name – whose curious aim was to stop people begging by bribing them to leave the area immediately, with prosecution threatened if they didn't.

The Society attracted so many donations that in 1824 the Times questioned how much of the money was being given to beggars compared with the bonus received by its Honourable Secretary. The controversy eventually faded and in 1860 Queen Victoria became patron. The Society closed down in 1960 on the grounds that it was no longer needed because of the success of the welfare state. If only.

166: THE WORLD-LEADING ANCHOR BREWERY

The Anchor brewery started life immediately next door to the Globe Theatre on Bankside in 1616 when Shakespeare was still alive. It went on to expand globally and become, by 1809, the biggest brewery in the world.

It is an amazing coincidence that neighbours on this once very insalubrious London road should become global icons for such contrasting activities. Shakespeare is still a worldwide success story while the brewery – all nine acres of it – has disappeared from sight. But it was not always so. After 1833, when the brewery was re-built following a fire, it became an international tourist venue, attracting celebrity visitors such as Napoleon, Bismarck and the Italian revolutionary Garibaldi during

his triumphal visit to London, when he attracted huge crowds wherever he went. Dr Johnson too had a close association with the brewery, even having his own room there for a while.

It is unlikely Shakespeare ever visited it, but it is bound up with his memory to this day. In 1834, nearly two centuries after the Globe was pulled down, the Anchor's owners constructed Anchor Terrace on part of the Globe site in Southwark Bridge Road, with houses to accommodate its senior executives.

This was long before it was realised

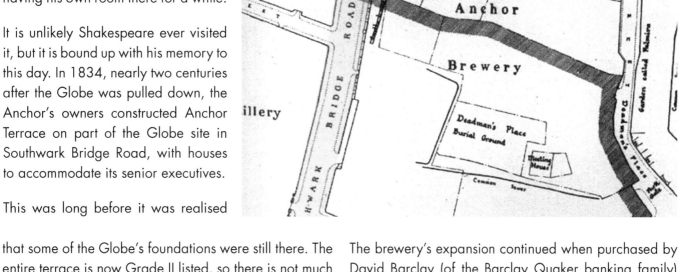

that some of the Globe's foundations were still there. The entire terrace is now Grade II listed, so there is not much that can be done about further excavations. But some of the rather sparse foundations of the Globe can still be seen below Anchor Terrace in Park Street. This is beside the river, a couple of roads from that highly successful recreation of the Globe, known as Shakespeare's Globe

There is another slightly odd connection between the Anchor and Shakespeare. The brewery was originally built by James Monger in Dead Man's Place on a site leased to him by Sir John Bodley, whose son Sir Thomas Bodley founded the revered Bodleian Library in Oxford and, famously, would not accept plays by the likes of Shakespeare as he believed it would be a scandal to the library if such "riff raff" were allowed in.

The brewery's expansion continued when purchased by David Barclay (of the Barclay Quaker banking family) who brought in his nephew Robert Barclay from America who, in the 1780s, teamed up with a senior employee, John Perkins, under the trading name Barclay Perkins. By 1809 they were producing a world-leading 260,000 barrels a year. In 1955, Barclay Perkins merged with a rival London brewer, Courage. Brewing continued there until the early 1970s. The buildings were demolished in 1981.

All that remains of the brewery now is a small plaque, but the memory is kept alive by the nearby Anchor Tavern, which dates back to the early 1770s.

167: PAXTON'S UNBUILT PARADISE

In June 1855, Sir Joseph Paxton, fresh from his triumphal construction of the Crystal Palace in Hyde Park for the Great Exhibition, presented to Parliament a plan for the most ambitious project to rebuild London since that of Christopher Wren. It amounted to constructing a continuous version of the Palace running for ten miles around Central London, foreshadowing the route of today's Circle Line but extending south of the river as well.

Inside the glass-domed creation, known as the Great Victorian Way, would be dwellings, shops, roads and no less than eight railway lines, utilising, so Paxton hoped, the then recently-invented smokeless pneumatic railway technology. It was to be a Paradise in glass, liberating the Victorian capital from its cold, damp, smoke-filled climate.

The scheme would have been dismissed as a pipe dream along with similar ones circulating at the time, except for that fact that the Crystal Palace had been sensationally successful. Its glass and ribbed iron construction had a huge influence on the development of hi-tech architecture: Norman Foster says it marked "the birth of modern architecture, of pre-fabrication, of soaring spans of transparency". It was made big profits, some of them invested in funds which support good causes to this day.

Unsurprisingly, a Commons select committee warmed to Paxton's plan it and it was also endorsed by Prince Albert, the force behind the Great Exhibition. Paxton, who was an MP as well as an architect, was an impressive witness.

But although Parliament authorised the creation of Paxton's scheme in principle, the project soon ran into an unsurpassable obstruction – The Great Stink of 1858. The unbearable odours of London's growing pollution stopped Parliament from operating. Something had to be done, and that something was the go-ahead instead for Joseph Bazalgette's mind-bending proposal to build modern sewers under Central London for conveying its detritus down to east London instead of polluting the Thames upstream.

All Londoners should be eternally grateful for that decision, even though it meant abandoning Paxton's glass circle plan. But even if it could have been built, it would never have survived the exponential growth of the world's biggest city. It was, as one critic observed, "architecture by aspiration".

168: THE GAS LIGHT AND COKE COMPANY AT HORSEFERRY ROAD

Coral is a well-known bookmaker with a branch in the unusually named Horseferry Road in Victoria. Its clients bet a lot on horses, but that is not how the street got its name. Rather, it is because, centuries ago, it was the road to a ferry that bore many horses across the Thames, where Lambeth Bridge now stands.

Horseferry Road wallows in history, not least the site where the bookmaker now resides. In 1812, it was occupied by the Gas Light and Coke Company, which was the first in the world to supply gas for public use. It had two large gasometers and several small ones at the rear of its premises, which stretched an entire block from the corner with Monck Street, where the Coral shop now stands, all the way to Great Peter Street.

History was made there. British Gas can trace its ancestry back to this company, which was founded by Frederick Albert Winsor, formerly known as Friedrich Albrecht Winzer. He was an immigrant from Brunswick, who used disputed French patents to set up his business. It installed the country's first gas-lit street lights, in Pall Mall. They soon spread out to the surrounding area.

There are still hundreds of gas lights in central London – not

The company's HQ in Horseferry Road

least in St James's Park – which can trace their origin back to the redoubtable Mr Winsor, although he was a visionary rather than an executive. The expansion of the firm was masterminded by Samuel Clegg, one of whose early decisions was to establish its headquarters at the Victoria site, rather than at Canon Row, close to today's Westminster Underground station, where the company already had an office and a wharf. Whether gasometers would have been installed there, so close to Parliament, can only be guessed at.

The Gas Light and Coke Company company went on to take over a large number of smaller ones. By the time it was nationalised in 1948 it was the dominant force in the North Thames Gas Board, which became a big part of British Gas. It wasn't the only world leader in Horseferry Road at the time of its foundation. Immediately opposite was the Broadwood piano factory, feted by Beethoven and others, the largest piano manufacturing works in the world. To have two global leaders across the same street from each other is, to say the least, unusual.

Frederick Winsor died in Paris, where he also worked, and was buried in the Père Lachaise Cemetery. But his London legacy is recognised by Winsor Terrace, a street near Beckton Gas Works in East Ham.

169: THE WESTMINSTER ABBEY ANCHORAGE

The photo shows the entrance to one of the least known hideaways in Westminster Abbey. And hideaway it certainly was, in the best possible sense of the word. It was through the doorway on the right of the photo that the Abbey's anchorite would pass, seldom to see the light of day again. He – or very occasionally she – would retire for a life of prayer and contemplation except for food deliveries and unusual occasions.

One such moment was when Henry V, mourning the death in 1413 of his father (which took place in Westminster Abbey as it happens), went to the anchorite with the purpose of, as Shakespeare put it, "laying bare to him the secret sins of his whole life".

Previously, during the Peasants' Revolt against the poll tax in 1381, Richard II left the Tower of London to escape the violence and visit the shrine of Edward the Confessor at the Abbey, where he had his confession heard by the anchorite, a word that comes from the Greek word "to withdraw". (One of the most unusual anchorites was St. Simeon Stylites who apparently spent three years in a hut before establishing his dwelling on top of a 60 foot column).

The anchorage at Westminster is close to Poet's Corner on the right hand side of the chapel of St Benedict, founder of the Benedictine order, which ran the monastery at Westminster until Henry VIII's dissolution in the 1530s. It had four stone walls with a window on to St Benedict's Chapel so the occupant could partake in services. He would be served with food by an attendant, who would also deal with matters of personal hygiene.

Anchorites have largely disappeared from religious life. It could be argued, though, that they have reappeared, involuntarily, in secular form as a consequence of the Covid-19 epidemic, which has led to lots of people, particularly older ones, being isolated in small rooms, often left to themselves throughout the day and night alleviated only by carers or relatives bringing food. Anchorites, of course, did this as a conscious choice to achieve spiritual fulfilment, whereas with modern day anchorites it often leads to depression.

The doorway to the anchorage, which has a bust of a monk above it – presumably St Benedict – was only rediscovered in 1878 during cleaning work, when a stone tablet was removed. The location of the cell had remained a mystery since being demolished at the dissolution of the monasteries. Even today you get an eerie feeling looking at this door to eternity.

170: THE COAL EXCHANGE

The Romans were the first to exploit coal in Britain on a large scale, so they would probably be unsurprised that the Victorians built a monument to it, the Coal Exchange, in the middle of the Roman-built City of London. Intended to facilitate the buying and selling of coal, it was even constructed, albeit unwittingly, above a Roman bath house.

You have probably guessed the rest: the Coal Exchange was pulled down after approaching 200 years of activity. But the foundations of the bath house, dating back to the second century AD, survive and can be visited by the public.

The industrial revolution couldn't have happened without coal. Britain was by far the biggest producer of it in the world, and the Coal Exchange enabled a monopoly of City merchants to organise their trade, buying and selling coal across the world, in a building opposite the original Billingsgate fish market.

The original Coal Exchange building was opened in 1770. A second one, dating from 1805 was replaced by the most recent one (pictured) which was opened by – who else? – Prince Albert on 30 October, 1849. It was unusual in being built from cast iron, several years before the Great Exhibition of 1851 – also opened by Prince Albert – made iron and glass structures world famous.

It was in 1848, during excavations for that version of the Coal Exchange that the remains of the Roman bath house were found, 13 feet beneath the surface. It was the home of a wealthy late fourth century Roman, who may have made a hasty exit judging by the coins scattered across the floor. Heat for the bath was produced in a furnace fired by wood – sadly not by coal, which would have made the serendipity complete – and drawn into chambers beneath the floor. It was called a hypocaust – a form of central heating that circulates hot air below the floor and up the walls.

The final Coal Exchange building was demolished in 1962, amid a huge conservationist controversy led by the Victorian Society and others, to allow widening of what is now Lower Thames Street.

In Country Life, Mark Girouard summed up the opposition with typical British understatement: "It seems a pity to destroy one of the City's most remarkable buildings, and a unique pioneer work of cast-iron construction, in order to gain three feet of road and save the back of the Custom House". Architecture critic Nicholas Pevsner said its destruction would be "unforgivable".

All this will seem strange to the new generation, because deep mined coal, once an industry so large it employed well over a million people, has completely disappeared. The disappearance of the Coal Exchange building has left in its place an ancient Roman monument open to visitors as part of the events industry. This has provided – at least until Covid – a few jobs for some of those displaced by the serial decline of manufacturing industry, once fuelled by the all-conquering power of coal. Some exchange.

171: THE LITERARY LEGACY OF HARLEY STREET

The name Harley Street immediately conjures up a network of private medical clinics and consultancies out of the reach or desire of ordinary folk. But the man whose family names adorn this and surrounding streets was an extraordinary person to whom the nation is still in debt. He blew the family's fortunes on books which we can still read today.

Edward Harley was the only son of Robert Harley, Queen Anne's chief minister, who had grabbed the title Earl of Oxford soon after the old line (which included an Earl of Oxford who may, or may not, have written the works of Shakespeare) had died out.

Edward married Lady Henrietta Cavendish Holles in 1713, a match that had been planned by Holles' father

the Duke of Newcastle. It brought with it the rich lands of the Manor of Tyburn (pictured above), including much of today's Marylebone, which the Duke had purchased at a bargain price shortly before he died. But what to do with all that money?

The couple started off by building fashionable houses among the fields north of Oxford Street. Cavendish Square (echoing one of Lady Harley's names) was at the centre, and most of the surrounding streets took their names from family connections, including Harley Street, Oxford Street, Wigmore and Wimpole (after their ancestral homes), Margaret, Henrietta and Holles and Portland Place.

The site of
TYBURN MANOR HOUSE
c. 1250 ~ 1791
USED BY HENRY VIII
AND ELIZABETH I
AS A HUNTING LODGE
Erected by HOWARD DE WALDEN ESTATES LIMITED 2002

Unlike his father, who ended up being imprisoned in the Tower of London, Edward Harley took little interest in public affairs, but managed to lose the family's wealth in a spectacular way – not on wild living or debauchery or drugs, but on books and other treasures.

He was first and foremost a bibliophile – like his father in that respect, but on an industrial scale. Either personally or through agents – who scoured Europe for old manuscripts and books – he built up a vast collection, which brought him to bankruptcy in 1740 but provided one of the three key founding endowments of the British Library. The others were by Sir Hans Sloane and Robert Cotton's family.

Ann Saunders, writing in the (sadly defunct) Westminster History Review gave us a glimpse of the scale of his addiction: "The manuscript collection stood at 7,618 volumes; there were 50,000 printed books, 350,000 pamphlets, 13,000 charters and some 41,000 prints and engravings besides an astonishing mass of printed ephemera, coins, medals, curiosa and literary memorabilia." After his bankruptcy, Harley turned seriously to drink. But readers at the British Library should say thank you to him every time they visit.

172: THE ROYAL PANOPTICON (AND AN OMINOUS ANTECEDENT)

The Royal Panopticon of Science and Art on the eastern side of Leicester Square – where the Odeon cinema now is – was a dramatic, self-confident building in the Moorish style (picture right). It was born of the Victorian ideal of "recreational learning" and completed in 1854, shortly after the Great Exhibition of 1851 in Hyde Park, and named after Argus Panoptes, an all-seeing multi-eyed giant in Greek mythology. There, for the price of a shilling, visitors could enjoy scientific exhibitions, lectures, fountains, demonstrations of electricity, a vast panorama and a host of other delights.

Alas, although it attracted over a thousand visitors a day, the Royal Panopticon only lasted two years before being auctioned off. It fared better than an earlier and more notorious building based on similar design principles, which never got off the ground. It did, though, have ominous repercussions which are still with us today.

A panopticon is an expression of a concept of human discipline. When utilitarian philosopher Jeremy Bentham drew up plans for a new National Penitentiary at Millbank beside the Thames in Westminster, his idea – or, more precisely, his brother Samuel's – was to build it as a panopticon. The lay out was intended to enable a single guard at the centre to supervise every convict in their cell without the convicts knowing what was going on. Bentham described it as a "new mode of obtaining power of mind over mind, in quantity hitherto without example".

As critics have not been slow to point out, the concept

has been adopted both in fiction (George Orwell's 1984) and in real life, as with the Chinese authorities' policy of surveying the lives of citizens remotely in real time, using digital technology. We experience some of the effects in Britain, where networks of CCTV security cameras enable one person to monitor what's going on all around a building or a network of streets or stations.

A Millbank Penitentiary, which looked a bit like a Panopticon from above, was eventually constructed (image left). It went through many phases – including being a staging post for prisoners being exiled to the colonies – but as an experiment in prison reform it was a failure. It was eventually demolished, but the bricks found a good home as part of the admirable Millbank housing estate behind it. And the site itself found an even better future when the Tate Gallery – now Tate Britain – was built in its place. Maybe we should view it as a Panopticon of British Art.

173: THE SIDELINED STATUE OF EDWARD JENNER, VACCINATION PIONEER

If there is one person of whom it can be said that they saved more lives than anyone else in history, then surely it would have to be the truly amazing Edward Jenner.

In 1796, Jenner, a doctor in the village of Berkeley in Gloucestershire, vaccinated a local child, James Phipps, with cowpox. It made him immune to smallpox. Jenner was not only a pioneer of vaccination he also invented its name. "Vacca" is the Latin word for cow. Louis Pasteur later made it the generic term for all immunisations.

In those days, smallpox was responsible for the deaths of over 10% of the entire population. In words that have resonance with today's hopes for a successful Covid-19 vaccine, Jenner predicted that smallpox could be eradicated as a disease. He was proved right.

Jenner's innovation was soon taken up in other countries, including Germany and France. He was festooned with international medals, and when a statue to his memory was eventually planned it was partly financed by international subscriptions.

And there's the rub. The statue, carved in bronze by William Calder Marshall, has become, well, a little lost. It stands, or rather, sits, admittedly in a rather magnificent position, on the edge of the Italian Gardens in Kensington Gardens (picture right), where it is seen by comparatively few people.

It was never meant to be there. It started life as a bust, one of the cultural exhibits in the phenomenally successful Great Exhibition of 1851. In 1853, a public fund was inaugurated, with many subscriptions from abroad, to establish a permanent memorial in Trafalgar Square. But as soon as it was installed there, it became controversial.

The statue had the backing of Prince Albert, consort of Queen Victoria, but was opposed by a formidable lobby of anti-vaccinationists, parliamentarians, the Times newspaper and, above all, by military grandees, who apparently not only objected to the fact that Jenner was not military, but also that he was sitting down rather than standing up like the square's military heroes.

This is a bit ironic, because Trafalgar Square was never intended to be a military shrine. The middle of it was designed by its architect Charles Barry to house the Royal Academy, to complement the National Gallery, until a parliamentary committee overruled him when it was trying to find a location for Nelson.

The military eventually got their way, and, barely two months after the death of its protector Prince Albert in December, 1861, Jenner's statue was moved. In the following year the British Medical Journal noted of Jenner that the military statues stayed in the square because "they killed their fellow creatures, whereas he only saved them".

Today, changed attitudes to Britain's colonial role in India make the Trafalgar Square statues of Charles James Napier and Henry Havelock – both national heroes their day – problematic. Who knows, Edward Jenner may yet find his way back there.

27

174: THE FESTIVAL OF BRITAIN

In all the annals of Lost London is there anything more tragic than the 1951 Festival of Britain? It was not the numbers: the Festival attracted almost 8.5 million visitors in six months, far more than the Millennium event of 2000 (barely six million) and even the hugely successful 1851 Great Exhibition in Hyde Park.

It was not the content: that provided a glimpse of Eden after the travails of post war austerity. I know, I was there, and can understand why the author Michael Frayn was bowled over. "I only intended to look in for half an hour, but I stayed all day. It was absolutely ravishing."

It was the consequences that were tragic. The Festival got mixed up in politics. The incoming Conservative government, led by Winston Churchill after his party's October 1951 win, regarded it as a waste of public money by spendthrift socialists and ordered its demolition.

Unlike the superstructures of the 1851 Exhibition and the Millennium Dome, all traces of the iconic features of the 1951 event were quickly dismantled except the Royal Festival Hall. Can you believe it? They were sold as scrap. What a tragedy.

And what features! The Dome of Discovery – the biggest dome in the world at the time, pictured left – and the Skylon – a huge cigar-shaped sculpture that appeared like a rocket suspended in mid take-off, pictured above – were icons then and would have been in the vanguard of modernism today. And in the background, the very tall Shot Tower, which made shot pellets out of falling molten lead, was a living example of the industry that once dominated the Lambeth side of the Thames.

It is a salutary reminder that, however impressive they were at the time, such exhibitions are usually remembered by posterity because of their infrastructure rather than for their inevitably forgotten content. The destruction of the Skylon and the Dome have rightly been singled out as major acts of cultural vandalism. Think of that when next you step across Jubilee Gardens near the London Eye, which occupies the footprint of the lost Dome.

175: THE LEGACY OF SIR PETER WARREN

Sir Peter Warren probably wouldn't spring immediately to mind if you were asked to name former MPs for Westminster. Yet, as my photograph shows, he is buried in a quite dramatic tomb in Westminster Abbey with a highly unusual sculpture to commemorate him, accompanied by an epitaph by Dr Johnson, no less.

The sculpture represents Hercules placing a bust of Sir Peter – made by the distinguished French sculptor Louis-François Roubiliac – on a pedestal, watched by a female figure representing Navigation. The model for Hercules, believe it or not, was a bare knuckle fighter, Jack Broughton, who, rather surprisingly, is also buried in the Abbey. There is a plaque on the floor of the East Cloister to commemorate him.

Peter Warren was born in Ireland, and in 1716, when only 13 years-old, joined the navy in Dublin as an ordinary seaman. To cut a long story short, he had a distinguished naval career, ending up as Admiral of the Fleet, patrolling American waters to keep the French out. Among the achievements of the team he led were the capture of 24 ships in four months in 1744 and supporting the forces of Massachusetts in taking Louisbourg from the French after a 47-day siege in 1745.

This expedition not only earned Warren a knighthood and promotion to rear-Admiral, but a small fortune as well. In those days, officers were allowed to keep much of the booty won and this, together with gifts and a bit of land speculation, enabled Warren to acquire thousands of acres in America, including 300 acres in what we today call Greenwich Village, where he built a mansion for himself and his American wife Susannah Delancey.

A New York website completes the story: "It was in 1747 that our hero was summoned to London to enter Parliament (1747-1752) and from that time on was a bright, particular star in English society. Known as 'the richest man in England', he was a truly magnificent figure in a magnificent day. Lady Warren, who was still a beauty and a wit, was a great favourite at court, and writers of the day declared her to be the cleverest woman in all England."

The towns of Warren, Rhode Island and Warren, New Hampshire are named after Warren, as are streets in Charleston, South Carolina, Louisbourg and New York City. In London, Warren Street, mainly famous for its Tube station, commemorates his wife.

Little known fact: George Bernard Shaw said that a scandal in this street inspired the name of the leading character in his play Mrs Warren's Profession.

Sacred to the Memory
of Sir PETER WARREN
Knight of the Bath,
Vice Admiral of the Red Squadron
of the British Fleet
and Member of Parliament
for the City and Liberty of Westminster

31

176: LONGDITCH AND AMELIA LANIER

Storey's Gate – named after Edward Storey, Charles II's bird keeper – runs from Tothill Street by Parliament Square to St James's Park (pictured right). It used to be called Longditch because it ran alongside a branch of the Tyburn river, which wound its way from Tothill Street to Whitehall where it flowed under a bridge into the Thames. It is also the scene of one of the world's ongoing literary mysteries. Here lived Amelia Lanier (1569-1645), thought by many to have been the "Dark Lady" of Shakespeare sonnets and, by some, even to have been the actual author of his works.

Lanier – whose forename is sometimes spelled Emelia or Aemilia, and surname Lanyer – was born in Spitalfields of a highly musical Italian-Jewish family from near Venice, who were prominent court musicians to Elizabeth I. She had purchased a house with the proceeds of a payoff from Henry Carey, Lord Hunsdon, whose mistress she had been since she was 18 years old (he was over 40 years older than her) and whose baby she was carrying. According to the diary of Simon Forman, her astrologer, she was "maintained in great pomp" with an allowance of 20 pounds a year.

Hunsdon was the son of Anne Boleyn's sister Mary, who was Henry VIII's long-time mistress before he fell for Anne, so he was quite likely Henry's illegitimate son. But, more particularly, he was the patron of the Lord Chamberlain's Men, Shakespeare's acting troupe. So, with her links to Hunsdon and her geographic closeness to Whitehall and to her musical family, which participated in lots of royal plays and masques, it would be surprising if Lanier was not at least acquainted with Shakespeare.

But Lanier doesn't any longer need an association with Shakespeare, whether literary or romantic, to ensure her place in history. She is now recognised as a formidable figure in her own right, being one of the very first women to publish a book of poetry and also a pioneer of proto-feminism through her emphasis on social and religious equality for women. She even dared to suggest in her verse that it may not have been Eve who tempted Adam in the Garden of Eden, but the other way round.

Did she write Shakespeare's works? Several books claim she did, including a recent one by John Hudson ("Shakespeare's Dark Lady") which argues, among numerous other things, that there is so much hidden Jewish imagery in the plays that they must have been written by a Jewish person. I was quite impressed with the evidence and would have been even more impressed had I not read another book shortly before which chronicles the amazing amount of Catholic imagery hidden in the text and purports to prove that Shakespeare was a Catholic. The Shakespeare authorship question is already the world's longest literary who-dun-it and shows no signs of flagging.

One of Shakespeare's Dark Lady sonnets includes lines which have been linked to Nicholas Hiliard's miniature of Lanier (see inset photo opposite):

> "My mistress' eyes are nothing like the sun;
>   Coral is far more red, than her lips red:
> If snow be white, why then her breasts are dun;
> If hairs be wires, black wires grow on her head."

There is a surprising amount of information about the inhabitants of Longditch going back to the 12th century, but sadly not enough about one of its most enigmatic inhabitants. The who-dun-it rolls on.

177: THE GORDON RIOTS

A rather plain reconstructed Roman Catholic church in Warwick Street, behind Golden Square, provides almost the only physical memory of an event that nearly became London's equivalent of the French revolution.

The Gordon Riots of 1780 were by far the worst disturbances London had seen since at least since the Peasants' Revolt of 1381. Their origins were a religious movement led by the eccentric Lord George Gordon against proposed, and quite minor, relaxations of the strict rules stopping Roman Catholics from taking part in public life. Gordon feared that if Catholics could join the army they would commit treason. In fact, Catholics had already been joining the army without problems and were much needed at a time when the British army was over-stretched fighting the American War of

Independence against French and Spanish forces.

After a large gathering in St George's Fields on 2 June, a crowd of up to 60,000, many with identifying blue cockades, marched to Parliament to present a petition. While Gordon entered the Commons the crowd outside grew increasingly agitated, with the carriages of some peers being vandalised, a situation not helped by the government's failure to mobilise local constables until a detachment of soldiers arrived.

The petition was overwhelmingly defeated, but hopes that the insurrection would fade were dashed that same night by the ransacking of what was then the (Catholic) Bavarian embassy chapel – now that reconstructed church (photo below) – and the Sardinian Embassy

chapel in Lincoln's Inn Fields, as well as the homes of rich Catholics.

The riots remained anti-Catholic, but soon fanned out into widespread protests about economic and social ills. London had seen nothing like it. The near-revolutionary unrest lasted for seven days. Eight debtors' prisons were attacked and the Bank of England was besieged, as was Lambeth Palace, the home of the Archbishop of Canterbury, amid cries of "No Popery". It was only saved by the timely arrival of troops after the Archbishop and his family had escaped by river.

Ignatius Sancho, a black African who had escaped a background of slavery to become a distinguished man of letters, lived near Parliament in King Charles Street. He provided a blow-by-blow account of what happened, referring to the "maddest people that the maddest times were ever plagued with". He added:

"Government is sunk in lethargic stupor—anarchy reigns . . . the Fleet prison, the Marshalsea,

King's-Bench, both Compeers [small debtors' prisons], Clerkenwell and Tothill Fields, with Newgate are all flung open and 300 felons from thence only let loose upon the world. Lord Mansfield's house [he was the Lord Chief Justice] in town suffered martyrdom; and his sweet box at Caen Wood [Kenwood, in Hampstead] escaped almost miraculously, for the mob had just arrived, and were beginning with it, when a strong detachment from the guards and light-horse came most critically to its rescue."

The library, and, what is of more consequence, papers and deeds of vast value, were all cruelly consumed in the flames. Lord North's house was attacked; but they had previous notice, and were ready for them. The Bank, the Treasury, and thirty of the chief noblemen's [houses], are doomed to suffer by the insurgent. There were six

of the rioters killed at Lord Mansfield's, and, what is remarkable, a daring chap, escaped from Newgate and condemned to die this day, was the most active in mischief at Lord Mansfield's, and was the first person shot by the soldiers: so he found death a few hours sooner than if he had not been released."

The upsurge moved to a conclusion when the army was at last called out on 7 June with orders to fire upon groups of more than four refusing to disperse. At least 285 people were shot dead and 200 more wounded. Around 450 rioters were arrested, of whom nearly 30 were tried and executed. Gordon was charged with high treason but found not guilty. The Lord Mayor was convicted of criminal negligence for not reading out the Riot Act and was fined £1,000. Thus ended riots that could easily have become England's revolution.

178: CARTWRIGHT, 'FATHER OF REFORM'

The statue in the photo does not commemorate Edmund Cartwright, inventor of the power loom. Edmund is remembered by the Cartwright Memorial Hall, a civic art gallery in Bradford, West Yorkshire. Nor does it commemorate his brother George, the explorer of Newfoundland and Labrador. George is remembered over there by the Cartwright settlement at the entrance to Sandwich Bay.

No, this statue, and Cartwright Gardens in Bloomsbury where it resides, commemorate a third remarkable Cartwright brother – John Cartwright (1740 – 1824), who is rightly known as "The Father of Reform" for his pioneering political initiatives.

John Cartwright was a naval officer and army major – not a normal background for radicals – and one of the very first people to call for universal suffrage (though in those days "universal" only meant men). He also campaigned for votes by ballot and for equal representation from constituencies to replace the absurd situation whereby Manchester had no MPs while "rotten boroughs" such as Old Sarum had several despite having few, if any, inhabitants.

As the monument on his gravestone in Finchley (reproduced in the gardens) reminds us, he was also the first English writer who openly supported the independence of the United States of America. He refused to fight in the war of independence against the rebels, whom he felt had right on their side.

In 1819, Cartwright was invited to speak at a reformist meeting in Manchester along with Henry "Orator" Hunt, but the elderly Cartwright could not attend what became known as the Peterloo Massacre. Later that year he was arrested for urging parliamentary reform at a meeting in Birmingham, indicted for conspiracy and fined £100.

Cartwright sent a copy of his book The English Constitution to Thomas Jefferson, the Founding Father and third President of the United States, who replied in 1824, saying he was very keen to meet him. "Your age of eighty-four, and mine of eighty-one years, ensure us of a speedy meeting. We may then commune at leisure, and more fully, on the good and evil, which in the course of our long lives, we have both witnessed; and in the meantime, I pray you to accept assurances of my high veneration and esteem for your person and character." Sadly, Cartwright died shortly after receiving Jefferson's letter.

John Cartwright now has a handsome memorial in Cartwright Gardens, and it should be seen in the context of what his two remarkable brothers also achieved. For three siblings to be memorialised in such contrasting ways is deserving of a separate memorial in its own right.

179: MRS MONTAGU'S BLUE STOCKINGS

These days the title "Queen of the Blues" brings to mind the great jazz singer Bessie Smith, but in 18th century London there was only one candidate for it – Elizabeth Montagu of Montagu House, Portman Square, Bloomsbury.

Montagu was dubbed "Queen of the Blues" by none other than Samuel Johnson. He was one of the male attendees of the Blue Stocking Club of mainly gentrified women, of which Elizabeth and her seriously rich friend Margaret Cavendish Bentinck, Duchess of Portland, were prominent members. Other men who attended her parties included Sir Joshua Reynolds, Edmund Burke and Horace Walpole.

In those days, the term "blue stocking" did not have today's dismissive meaning and, curiously, was not inspired by a woman but applied to a man who wore blue worsted stockings, usually associated with the peasantry, to a meeting rather than fashionable white silk ones.

The club began in the 1750s as a meeting place for gentry with time on their hands to talk about literature and engage in other intellectual activities. Although it was undoubtedly posh and exclusive, it also did its social bit. Members of the club were associated with the development of the Foundling Hospital for abandoned children, set up by the great Thomas Coram.

Mrs Montagu herself would hold regular meetings for chimney sweeps every May Day in her palatial London house and was, by all accounts, also popular with colliers in the north of England, despite the riches that her family had extracted from their extensive ownership of coal mines.

In the late 1760s she achieved literary fame in her own right when she published – initially anonymously – an "Essay on the Writings and Genius of Shakespeare" which successfully attacked Voltaire's dismissal of Shakespeare's importance. In 1776 she attended one of Voltaire's attacks on Shakespeare at the French Academy in Paris, where her essay had been well received. This helped fan Elizabeth's reputation as "the first woman for literary knowledge in England". Following her husband's death in 1775, Montagu proved herself to have a formidable business talent in managing the fortune and large estates which were left in her control.

Meanwhile, her good friend Margaret Cavendish Bentinck, Duchess of Portland, perhaps the richest woman in Britain, was steadily building up an amazing collection of artefacts of natural history and fine arts, which were housed in her Portland Museum in Whitehall. After Cavendish died, the contents were sold at her request. In 1786, an auction in 4,000 lots took place in the private garden of her house in Whitehall. It lasted from 24 April until 5 June.

In the words of the catalogue, it had been her intention "to have had every unknown species in the three kingdoms of nature described and published to the world". Other items included artefacts from Captain Cook's voyages and eighteen portraits by Rubens and Vandyke, not to mention the historic Portland Vase, which merits having a book written about it.

180: DOING THE LAMBETH WALK

In the age of rap you don't often hear the strains of The Lambeth Walk, a song and dance of Cockney nostalgia that once swept the world. Dozens and dozens of cover versions have been made, by everyone from Duke Ellington and Gracie Fields to the cast of Eastenders. A spoof version by British intelligence featuring German soldiers marching backwards and forwards to its rhythms became part of the war effort when an enraged Joseph Goebbels apparently stormed out of the viewing room kicking chairs as he went.

The original version was made famous by Lupino Lane, himself a Cockney, in the show Me and My Girl, which opened close to Lambeth at the Victoria Palace theatre on December 16, 1937. Its wistful lyrics and evocation of Cockney camaraderie glossed over the deprivation that made Lambeth Walk the slum it was at the time.

"Any time you're Lambeth way,
Any evening, any day,
You'll find us all
Doin' the Lambeth Walk. Oi!"

Lambeth Walk wasn't even the street's proper name. It was formerly known as Three Coney Walk. A coney (or cony) is an old word for "rabbit", reflecting the rural idyll that part of Lambeth once was.

While Lupino Lane was singing, residents were barely eking a living from 160 market stalls stretching over 200 yards selling goods and food purchased cheaply by costermongers or barrow boys from the surplus requirements of "authorised" markets elsewhere. Lambeth Walk was so poor it had three pawnbrokers offering loans to desperate residents in exchange for blankets or clothing or whatever to tide them over until payday.

Today, visitors find an ordinary street that seems to have shaken off its history. As you walk from the junction with Lambeth Road you pass a doctor's surgery, King's College maths school, an open air pulpit, a hostel and an array of shops. Not a single barrow or market stall in sight. When you come to Lollard Street (picture left) you are close to the road where the iconic picture of a few locals re-enacting the Lambeth Walk (above) took place. Apart from a few old houses that remain, urban renewal has swept history away.

181: HOW MILLWALL GOT ITS NAME (AND OTHER TALES OF WIND AND WATER)

Not many people outside the area know why Millwall is so called. It is because there once was a wall on the banks of the Thames which supported seven mills (see map below). They stood along the same stretch of water where the biggest ship in the world, the Great Eastern, was built in 1858 by Isambard Kingdom Brunel.

In those days, London was awash with windmills. For over 700 years they were its primary source of power and added elegance to its skylines. Along with mills powered by water, they were a major source of industrial power until the steam engine came along. Almost any place tagged "mill" probably has some association with an actual mill and, unlike coal mines and oil wells, they beautified their surroundings in an almost romantic way. Wikipedia has an exhaustive list of London mills past and present.

Millwall is only four miles from Sir Joseph Bazalgette's unusually attractive sewage treatment works at Abbey Mills – so called because it was built on the site of mills owned by the monks of Langthorne Abbey. Lambeth had five mills, including one just south of Waterloo Bridge and another south of Hungerford Bridge. A little further west along the Thames there was a mill at, surprise surprise, Millbank, run by the monks of Westminster Abbey, hence the road of that name. Constable painted a windmill that stood on Hampstead Heath on what looks like a very stormy day.

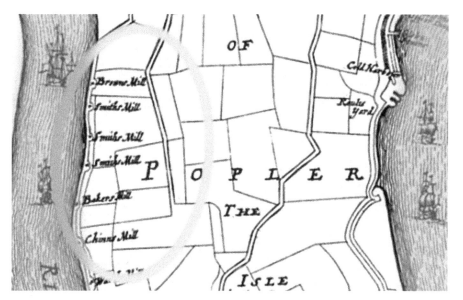

One of the most intriguing London mills can be seen on old prints of Newgate prison (such as below), where what must have been one of the earliest air-conditioning systems was employed in order to rid the prison of a pestilence which had killed many prisoners in close proximity with each other, as well as several judges. Sound familiar? When fresh air from the mill entered the prison, deaths fell dramatically.

There are still a very few mills open to the public, including the spectacular

Abraham's Mill in Upminster – which is open on summer weekends – and Shirley Windmill in Croydon, not forgetting the mill on Wimbledon Common, which is now a museum. Yet, sadly, there are no windmills left from bygone centuries in working order.

Except for one. A warm welcome to Brixton Windmill, a constant reminder of Lost London. Built in 1816, it is still going strong, even though these days it is powered by electricity not wind and so is technically not a wind-mill anymore. At the time of writing, it was being used as a community testing centre for Covid-19, but its volunteers were continuing to produce flour, made from locally sourced organic wheat, which, subject to social distancing, is being delivered to over a dozen local shops and food banks.

It would be nice to think that in this new age of wind power – thanks to the surge of wind-powered turbines on and offshore – that new technologies could restore the local London windmill in some form or other. The task is made difficult by the prevalence of high-rise buildings interrupting the flow of wind, but who knows what the future has in store. Wind is once again fashionable.

182: WHAT BECAME OF THE GENERAL POST OFFICE?

THE NEW POST OFFICE, ST MARTINS LE-GRAND.
TO SIR FRANCIS FREELING, BART SECRETARY THIS PLATE IS RESPECTFULLY INSCRIBED.
Published Aug. 30, 1828 by Jones & Co. 3 Acton Place, Kingsland Road, London.

At first glance this building could be mistaken for the British Museum. That would not be surprising. It was designed by the same architect – Sir Robert Smirke, the Greek revivalist – and built at around the same time as the BM in the 1820s. A contemporary description said it was "a post office concealed behind a front fit for a palace". The only difference is that the British Museum is still standing proud in Bloomsbury while the General Post Office near St Paul's has completely disappeared. It was pulled down in 1912 in what would today be described as an act of cultural vandalism.

Britain's postal service can be traced back to a 1635 decision of Charles I (1625-1649) to allow the Royal Mail to be used for private correspondence. Eight years later, the first general post office opened on Cloak Lane off Dowgate Hill in the City. That building and others lasted a long time, and when rapid expansion became inevitable at the start of the 19th century the GPO started buying up slum property on the east side of St. Martin's Le Grand. This cleared the way for the construction of Smirke's 120 metre long tour de force, which was built between 1825 and 1829 and illuminated at night by a thousand gas burners.

Postal history in the 19th century is mainly remembered for a stroke of genius by Rowland Hill and a major innovation by the novelist Anthony Trollope, both of whom were employees of the Post Office. Hill successfully argued for a uniform rate for postage linked to weight rather than, as was the case then, being based on distance travelled and the number of pages within the envelope. Postage – bizarrely – was paid by the recipient rather than the sender. This gave rise to all sorts of fiddles as people sometimes put short coded messages on the envelope so the recipient could both read the message and refuse to accept delivery.

Hill's proposals were supported by another genius, Charles Babbage, the "father of the computer", who argued that the critical cost of the postal system was not transport but the complex handling procedures at both ends, which pre-paid stamps could hugely reduce. But his plan did not receive universal approval. The Postmaster, Lord Lichfield, denounced his "wild and visionary schemes." while William Leader Maberly, Secretary to the Post Office, said: "This plan appears to be a preposterous one, utterly unsupported by facts and resting entirely on assumption." But successful it was, and soon led to the introduction of the world's first adhesive stamp, the Penny Black.

In the mid-1860s, Trollope, who had reached a moderately senior position within the Post Office despite differences with Hill, was credited with introducing the soon-to-be ubiquitous pillar-box.

Both of these innovations have been threatened by something neither Hill, Trollope or anyone else could have foreseen – that primary communications would need no stamps at all. The invention of emails has changed all that. It is quite possible in future that our only memory of the historic postal service will be the iconic post boxes – unless they too are lost in a fresh outburst of cultural vandalism.

183: HATCHARDS, FORTNUMS & THE RHS

Hatchards in Piccadilly is the oldest bookshop in the UK and one of the oldest in the world. It was founded in 1797 by John Hatchard, a former pupil of the local Greycoat Hospital school, which was founded even earlier in 1698 and is still going strong today as an academy.

Hatchards is situated immediately next door to another British institution founded in Piccadilly, 90 years earlier: Fortnum and Mason, grocer to royalty. The two have stuck together ever since Hatchards appeared, even though both are now subsidiaries of bigger companies (Hatchards is owned by Waterstones and Fortnums by the Garfield Weston Foundation). They even have adjacent shops at St Pancras International station. It seems to be a symbiotic relationship.

And there's a further long-running strand to the Hatchards story. If you look above its Piccadilly shop front, you will see a faded plaque (pictured below) which is almost impossible to read yet points to another flourishing British institution with its roots on this very spot.

On 7 March 1804, seven men met at Hatchard's bookshop to discuss the possibility of establishing a horticultural society in the UK. They included John Wedgwood, (son of Josiah), Sir Joseph Banks, President of the Royal Society, and William Forsyth, after whom the shrub forsythia is named. He was head gardener at the Chelsea Physic Garden and also a royal gardener.

From this curious beginning the amazingly successful Royal Horticultural Society was born. It now has well over 500,000 paying members and runs the world famous Chelsea Flower Show as well as a string of other garden showpieces around the country.

It is remarkable that these three institutions spawned within a few yards of each other still exist and are doing much the same things as when they began. Most of the companies that were operating at about that time have disappeared without trace. Maybe it is time for a reunion – in Hatchards, of course, with hampers supplied from next door and flowers by you-know-who.

184: JOHN NASH'S CAR PARK

I don't suppose many people have lost sleep over what a car park would look like if it had been built by John Nash, the great Georgian architect. One of the problems is that cars had not been invented then, so it would have been difficult for Nash to have designed one. Except that he did. Or, at least, there is a car park in London, the structure of which was designed by Nash. And it is a bit of a scandal too.

Practically everyone who passes it does not even realise what it is. It stretches for over 100 yards along the north side of The Mall on the western side of the Duke of Yorks steps. The Institute of Contemporary Arts (ICA) is on the other side of them. There is nothing to suggest it is a car park. There is no obvious entrance, and the windows are too high and blurred to look through. If you want to see the entrance, you will have to climb the steps and turn left, when you will see it at the top of a steep slope to the car park itself.

Even before the Covid-19 lockdown there were not many cars inside. It appears to have been used by people in the building above, such as the Royal Society, plus corporate contractors. What a waste of space to be providing a daytime shelter for cars that shouldn't be driven into the centre of London anyway.

It would be a good place for some other prestigious project, such as a learning centre for the proposed Holocaust Memorial (which, at the time of writing, is going to disfigure the green space in Victoria Tower Gardens) or a home for the government's own art collection, which will now be housed on the opposite side of The Mall.

The ground on which the car park is built used to be part of the gardens of Carlton House, the extravagant home – or, rather, palace – of the Prince Regent who, when he became George the IV, decided that he wanted to spend even more money enhancing Buckingham Palace. It was left to Nash to rebuild the whole area, right up to the aptly named Regent Street.

A lot of people assume that the Duke of York's column and statue was part of Nash's plan. Not at all. He wanted to build a huge domed fountain in the space between his two terraces in the Mall. Instead, he had to live with a huge monument to the Duke. What he would have said if he knew that part of his terrace would become a car park can only be imagined.

John Nash's car park

185: GERMANY-ON-THAMES

In 1989, archaeologists digging next to Cannon Street station by the passage of the River Walbrook found the remains of a building nearly 60 feet long. It turned out to be the Guildhall of the Merchants of Cologne and dated back to 1175. Known as the Steelyard (scene below on Wenceslaus Hollar's largely correct map as "the Stiliard"), it later became the enclosed London centre of a German-dominated international trading block known as the Hanseatic League. Yes, it was Germany-on-Thames.

The building was occupied by young, upwardly mobile German merchants who stayed for a few years in what have been described as near monastic conditions –

sometimes honoured in the breach – before going home to resume their careers. They ate in hall together and were discouraged from marrying or even being out late.

The Hanseatic League was lauded as a free trade area by those who were a part of it, but as a monopoly by those outside. It occasionally descended into warfare across Europe as Hanseatic cities supported each other against intruders. At its peak of power, the League could count on the support of nearly 200 towns across northern Europe.

As early as 1157, Henry II (1133 -1189) granted traders exemption from all tolls in London and some

Stiliard

taxes, allowing them to trade at fairs throughout the land. If all this sounds a bit like the free ports the government is planning for the UK, one can only say "watch this space".

By 1475, the site had been purchased by the Hanseatic League itself, and its descendants retained ownership of the Steelyard long after the League itself had disbanded. The remnants were not finally sold off until 1852, when the station was

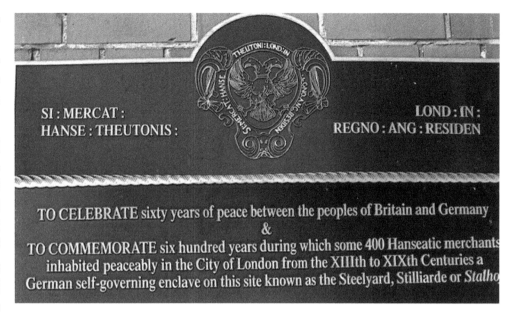

SI : MERCAT :
HANSE : THEUTONIS :

LOND : IN :
REGNO : ANG : RESIDEN

TO CELEBRATE sixty years of peace between the peoples of Britain and Germany
&
TO COMMEMORATE six hundred years during which some 400 Hanseatic merchants
inhabited peaceably in the City of London from the XIIIth to XIXth Centuries a
German self-governing enclave on this site known as the Steelyard, Stilliarde or *Stalho*

built by the South Eastern Railway company. Some of the remains of the trading house found in 1989 may still be buried underneath. It appears that the Steelyard had several rows of warehouses, with chambers above and vaults and cellars below.

Nothing of the trading post remains above ground but there are still plenty of memorials, such as: Hanseatic Walk behind the station on the Thames Walk; Steelyard Passage, which runs under it (and is as near as you will get to the original site); the Pelt Trader pub (recalling trade in skins) under a railway arch; and a plaque celebrating "600 years during which time some 400 Hanseatic merchants inhabited peacefully in the City of London".

Dowgate Hill, which runs into Cousin Lane to the west of the station, has had the same name since the early days, while the former Church Lane on the east side has become All Hallows Lane, a reference to the church the leaguers attended

It is still debatable why the League's London base came to be known as the Steelyard. The most likely explanation is the metal seals that were used to certify the origin of different cloths brought here for export.

While London was never officially one of the Hanseatic cities, it was nevertheless a major trading post intimately linked to them. According to Jens Tholstrup, an economist, the League probably had a 15% market share of English imports and exports. Not bad for a small Thames-side enclave.

And don't write the League off yet. In 2006, King's Lynn (one of the original English Leaguers) became the first English member of a new Hanseatic League formed in Zwolle in the Netherlands in 1980. It was joined by Hull in 2012 and Boston in 2016. It remains to be seen what becomes of that initiative in these straitened times.

186: JOHN MILTON'S STREET OF TRUTH & JUSTICE

The location of the "pretty garden house" where John Milton lived when he wrote much of Paradise Lost has more than enough in its past to make psychogeographers quake.

Themes of truth and liberty run indelibly through the history and inhabitants of Petty France, or York Street as it was renamed for a time. Milton moved there in 1651. Judging by old maps, his house would have been where the engraving of it is superimposed on the photo below.

Today, Sir Basil Spence's brutalist office building stands on the site. Completed in 1976, it is currently the home of the Ministry of Justice. Justice is a subject which, along with censorship, Milton spent a long time worrying about. Today, he would have been even more worried. Consider his most famous assertion:

"Though all winds of doctrine were let loose to play upon the earth, so truth be in the field, we do injuriously by licensing and prohibiting to misdoubt her strength."

It is often quoted as a precursor to the 1st Amendment of the US Constitution, but has been tested almost to destruction in Trump's America and to actual destruction in China and Russia.

Milton's House above and below

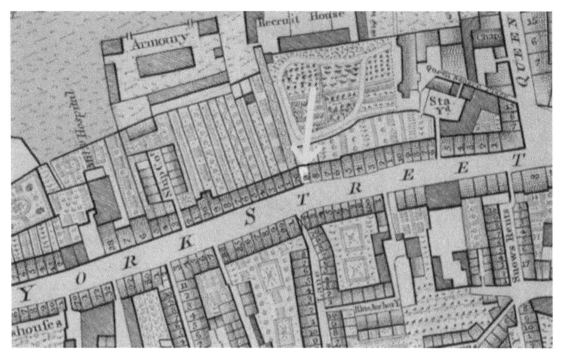

Justice also took a hit in the form of the building which previously stood on this spot. In 1877, a dodgy City banker erected Queen Anne's Mansions to a then unprecedented 12 storeys, more than twice as high as the law allowed, without obtaining planning permission. He got away with it.

This would have offended the principles of a subsequent owner of Milton's house, Jeremy Bentham, whose guiding principle – the greatest happiness of the greatest number – was in direct opposition to the ethos of Queen Anne's Mansions. Bentham erected a small plaque with the words "Sacred to Milton" at the top of what was at that time 19 York Street. You might be able to see it in the engraving if your eyesight or magnifying glass are good enough.

Bentham's utilitarianism was later attacked by John Stuart Mill, who believe it or not, was another resident of 19 York Street. So too was his father James Mill, a student and collaborator of Bentham. The younger Mill thought Bentham "to have done and to be doing very serious evil", not least for failing to see conscience as a driving force.

The same house was later occupied by the great essayist William Hazlitt, another great proponent of liberty and the rights of man, though this didn't always extend to the rights of his dinner guests. On one occasion Hazlitt turned up very late to a christening party at number 19 for his own son. His guests were appalled by the food – almost uneatable stodgy potatoes followed by overcooked beef. Sometimes, the greatest happiness of the greatest number took a holiday at this house. It was demolished in 1873.

PS: The location of Milton's house as stated here is nearly 100 yards from a plaque honouring Bentham in Queen Anne's Gate. Little known fact: Milton was no "mean performer on the organ".

187: SOUTHWARK FAIR

The picture is by William Hogarth of the seedy medieval Southwark Fair, commonly known as "an occasion fir revekry and debsuchery" which accompanied his series The Rake's Progress. Like the more famous Gin Lane it is really a novel in a single picture. So much is happening. Every part tells a tale, including the collapsing stage on the left bringing Shakespearean characters Pistol, Falstaff and Justice Shallow and others to the ground. A grim horseman enters right, challenging everyone, and a fashionable lady with a large drum marches in the middle accompanied by a black bugle boy.

Southwark Fair and its more famous near-neighbour Bartholomew Fair are often dismissed as low life interludes of little cultural significance. But as Tiffany Stern pointed out in a fascinating recent lecture to London Historians, there was a symbiotic relationship between the London playhouses on Bankside and the fairs. Theatres were forced to close down when the fairs were on, as they couldn't really stand the competition. The empty playhouses were often used as medieval Airbnbs for performers at the fairs. The fairs were supposed to last only a few days, but expanded to almost two weeks.

The rivals started feeding off each other. The fairs would stage mini-plays – like Julius Caesar or Tamburlaine the Great – often through Punch and Judy shows. They had the advantage of not needing to be pre-approved by the authorities, because they were improvised by "interpreters" and so had no written-down text. This practice came in handy when the playhouses were later shut under the rule of Oliver Cromwell's Puritans during the interregnum.

Playwrights in turn introduced fairground references to hold the attention of the audience as well as classical ones, such as Virgil. This is not surprising, as the same range of people came to both forms of entertainment. The impression given is that the clientele from the playhouses, including the upper classes, groundlings, hucksters and prostitutes, all moved eastward to Southwark or northwards to Bartholomew at Smithfield when the fairs were on.

Southwark Fair has been set in aspic by Hogarth. He never painted Bartholomew Fair, which was left to a playwright, Ben Jonson, to immortalise. Both give us an unrivalled insight into England at play in that period. It was not always a pretty sight. Southwark Fair was abolished in 1762 because of increasing vice and disturbances.

188: THE CURIOUS COUNTESS OF TART HALL

Alethea Talbot, Countess of Arundel (1585-1654), though hardly known outside academia, has a good claim to be one of the first woman pioneers of scientific method. She has faded from history almost as fast as her favoured London home, Tart Hall, which has accomplished one of the least-known disappearing tricks from British architecture's past.

Inelegantly named yet palatial, Tart Hall was situated immediately next door to Buckingham House (now Buckingham Palace), looking on to St James's Park. There is nothing of it left and the only inkling we have of what it might have looked like comes from a glimpse of part of it peeping out from behind the Countess's skirt (see image opposite) in an etching done by the great Wenceslaus Hollar, who was employed by the family.

Horace Walpole described the building as "very large and has a very venerable appearance". It was Alethea's plaything but also as a laboratory modelled on an Italian "casino" or pleasure dome. Tart Hall wasn't her main home. As well as being rich in her own right – her father was the Earl of Shrewsbury – she was married to the Earl of Arundel, whose family home Arundel House, between the Strand and the Thames, was one of the huge aristocratic mansions of its time. There was also a country estate at Albury and, of course, the family's historic seat at Arundel Castle

In 1616, the Countess inherited a third of the Shrewsbury estate, which helped finance not only her scientific experiments but many of her husband's acquisitions. When he died, Alethea inherited 600 paintings and drawings by Rembrandt, Rubens, Holbein, Titian, Brueghel and a host of others.

But Tart House was her pride and joy. It combined entertainment and art with a particular emphasis on her so-called Pranketing Room, which contained her precious collection of porcelain and was the scene of experiments employing empirical research in the tradition of Francis Bacon.

The Countess began collecting medical and culinary recipes – prescriptions might be a better word – from 1606. They were published in 1655, after her death in Amsterdam where, as a Catholic, she had moved to escape the wrath of Cromwell's Puritans, who had ravaged Arundel House. The Book, Natura Exenterata (or "Nature Unbowelled") contained

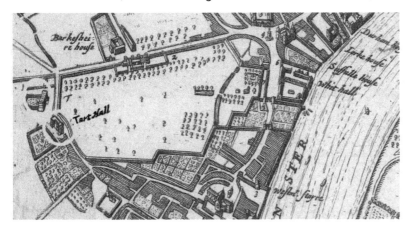

1,720 "secrets digested into Receipts fitted for the Cure of all sorts of Infirmities".

The author was named as Philiatros – "friend of medicine" – with an engraving of her on the front, a clear reference to the Countess as author, even though it is not known for certain how much she wrote and how much she supervised.

If you have a swelling in the throat, it advises:

"Taka good handfull of Vervine or two, cut it small and put it in a Morter, then take ounces of Comminseeds and pound them very fine, and lay them upon a very fine linnen cloath, and apply it to the swelling, and use it till it be whole".

For a windy Stomach:

"Boyl a little Camomile, wild Tyme, and wild Parsley which is called Saxifrage in posset-drink made with milk and White-wine, drink a good draught thereof fasting, and to bed⬚ward warm."

There were also outlandish ones such as "viper wine" for which you would have needed "eight gallons of sack (wine) and at least thirty vipers". Let's just say they were of their time.

On Alethea's death, Tart Hall was inherited by her second son William, Viscount Stafford. He was one of the

The most Illustrious & most excellent Lady the Lady Alathea Talbot &c. Countesse of Arundel, Surry & the first Countesse of England

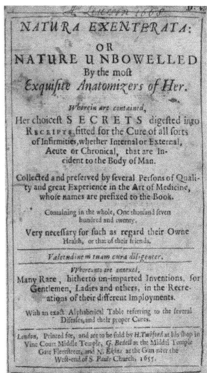

NATURA EXENTERATA:
OR
NATURE UNBOWELLED
By the most
Exquisite Anatomizers of Her.

Wherein are contained,
Her choicest SECRETS digested into Receipts, fitted for the Cure of all sorts of Infirmities, whether Internal or External, Acute or Chronical, that are Incident to the Body of Man.

Collected and preserved by several Persons of Quality and great Experience in the Art of Medicine, whose names are prefixed to the Book.

Containing in the whole, One thousand seven hundred and twenty.

Very necessary for such as regard their Owne Health, or that of their friends.

Valetudinem tuam cura diligenter.

Whereunto are annexed,
Many Rare, hitherto un-imparted Inventions, for Gentlemen, Ladies and others, in the Recreations of their different Imployments.

With an exact Alphabetical Table referring to the several Diseases, and their proper Cures.

London, Printed for, and are to be sold by H. Twiford at his shop in Vine Court Middle Temple, G. Bedell at the Middle Temple Gate Fleetstreet, and N. Ekins at the Gun neer the West-end of S. Pauls Church. 1655.

innocent victims of the infamous plot dreamed up by the Protestant priest Titus Oates in 1680 alleging a Jesuit-led plan to kill King Charles II. It led to over 15 innocent people being executed, including Stafford, after conviction by the notorious Judge Jeffreys.

The gateway to Tart Hall was kept closed after Stafford's last exit until it was demolished. He is remembered today by Stafford Place, a site that once formed the grounds of Tart Hall and is its only abiding memory.

189: SHAKESPEARE, FALSTAFF AND FAKE NEWS

During excavations in the early 1990s around Hays Wharf in Tooley Street, archaeologists unearthed extensive remains of the 16th century moated Fastolf Place, including evidence of a water mill. Over 200 metal objects were recovered from the site.

They were from the London abode of a distinguished man who ducks in and out of history in Shakespeare's plays. His name was Sir John Fastolf. If you think that is a mis-spelling of Sir John Falstaff, the anti-hero of Shakespeare's Henry IV (and resurrected in the Merry Wives of Windsor), hang on a bit.

Sir John Fastolf was a real warrior who distinguished himself – barring one or two controversial events – during the Hundred Years War under Henry V. Shakespeare's imaginative depiction of the heroic claims made by his near namesake seem clearly to have been inspired by Fastolf's real life exploits.

Shakespeare conjured up the name Falstaff for the man who corrupted the young Henry V because his original choice for the character, Sir John Oldcastle, ran into trouble with the authorities. Oldcastle was a real person who had been a friend of Henry V but fell out with him when he led the rebellious Lollards religious rebellion, which resulted in him being put to death. Shakespeare must have thought he was on safe ground using the name of someone who had died nearly a hundred years earlier, but it was not to be.

One of Oldcastle's descendants was William Brooke, Lord Cobham, who in 1596 became Lord Chamberlain, which meant he was in charge of plays. He withdrew the official protection Shakespeare's troupe had enjoyed under their previous patron, Lord Hunsdon. Brooke objected to his ancestral name Oldcastle being abused and had it withdrawn. Shakespeare may have got a bit of his own back when he introduced a character called Brook in satirical mode in the Merry Wives.

Fastolf was not only a real person but, curiously, he had already appeared under his own name in Shakespeare's

Henry VI, which was actually written before the Henry IV series. In early folios, the name was spelled "Falstaffe". He owned several London properties, which he left to Magdalene College, Oxford of which he was a major benefactor. They included the Boar's Head in Southwark where Shakespeare lived and worked for part of his life. It is very likely that he visited the inn, though that would have been long after Fastolf had died.

ITEM: During the Hundred Years, when Joan of Arc heard that the "Bastard of Orleans" (the illegitimate son of The Duke of Orleans) was planning to abandon his city because of the imminent arrival of Fastolf she responded: "Bastard, Bastard, in the name of God I command you that as soon as you hear of Fastolf's coming, you will let me know. For if he gets through without my knowing it, I swear to you that I will have your head cut off."

Fastolf lost that skirmish, but the episode shows that he was feared. He won other battles in France and his valour was not in doubt. Such is the power of Shakespeare's pen that his depiction of Falstaff cast a shadow over the reputation of Fastolf for centuries. The brave, bold buccaneer was everything that Falstaff was not. The remains of Fastolf Place have not been memorialised with a plaque, but their remains below ground are today an invisible reminder of how easy it is for fake news to triumph over truth.

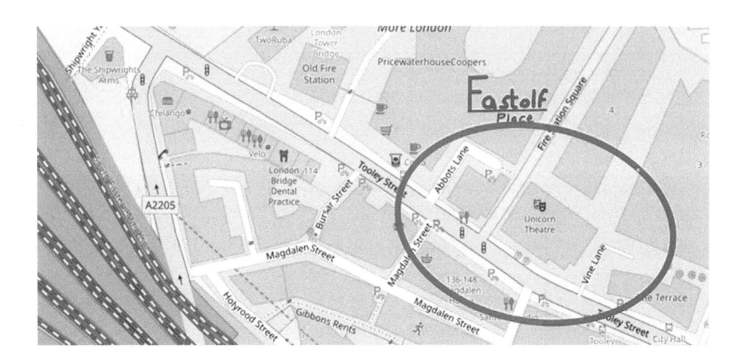

190: THE GIGANTIC WHEEL OF EARLS COURT

In 1889, George Washington built the first Ferris Wheel for the 1893 World's Columbian Exposition in Chicago. It was a pioneering move by Washington – or to give him his full name George Washington Gale Ferris Jr – which spun a chain of imitators around the world in what might be called urban icon wars. The project was partly a response to the construction of the much taller Eiffel Tower on the Champ de Mars in Paris. It generated huge publicity for the city, which Chicago eyed enviously.

The Chicago wheel had hardly been finished before London started thinking of an even bigger one. The resulting Gigantic Wheel was eventually built in Earls Court and rose to the amazing height of 308 feet – comfortably taller than the 264 feet of the Chicago wheel. A result!

The Gigantic Wheel was able to carry an impressive 1,200 passengers in its 40 carriages and by the time it stopped turning in 1906 it had been ridden by over 2.5 million people. It was constructed by engineers who went on to build similar wheels around the world. The Earls Court giant has now passed out of the city's memory – who needs it when we have the London Eye! – and so, sadly, has the extraordinary event of which it was a part.

The wheel was a feature of the Empire of India Exhibition, which opened in Earls Court in 1895. This was the brainchild of Imre Kiralfy, a brilliant Hungarian entrepreneur who converted the 24-acre site into a Mughal style extravaganza, in which Indian scenery was reproduced, reflecting the country's past and present history. Its overall theme, that "modern India was the product of British patience and genius" ,would not ring many bells in today's counter-imperialist age. But it had the support of the Indian government, which gave £10,000 to it, plus four Maharajas and Rajas as patrons.

During the 164 days the exhibition was open it attracted almost 5.6 million visitors. This compares with 6.5 million for the Millennium Dome in 2000, which was open for a full year at a time when London's population was over double what it had been in the 1880s.

As part of the exhibition complex, Kiralfy also built the huge Empress Theatre (or Empress Hall as it was later known by) as a tribute to Queen Victoria, the Empress of India. It was a unique theatre in that it could hold over 5,000 people all seated on the same level, giving an uninterrupted view of the stage from any angle.

Imre Kiralfy became a British citizen in 1901. He died on 27 April 27, 1919 aged 74 in Brighton. He is buried in the family mausoleum in Green-Wood Cemetery, New York, but there is also a family mausoleum at Kensal Green Cemetery.

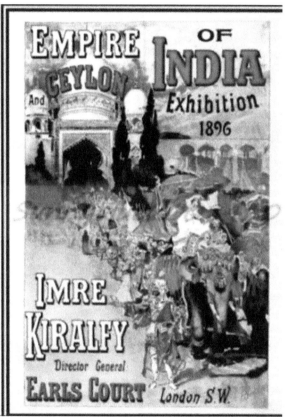

191: HOW WELLINGTON NEARLY MET HIS WATERLOO IN BATTERSEA

Early in the morning of 21 March, 1829 a horse and carriage carrying the then Prime Minister, the Duke of Wellington, drove through The Green Park and along the King's Road before crossing Battersea Bridge to the south of the Thames.

Turning left, they stopped somewhere near the southern end of where Chelsea Bridge would later be built, close to the notorious Red House inn. The PM returned to Downing Street at around 8 a.m. to continue with matters of state, including a visit to Windsor Castle to report to George IV.

Such mundane matters would not need to be mentioned except for one thing. The reason the Duke went to Battersea was to fight a duel with the Earl of Winchilsea. The Earl, a staunch Protestant, was fiercely opposed to Wellington's change of mind to supporting the Catholic Relief Bill, which he had initially opposed.

The Bill proposed giving limited freedom to Catholics to hold public office, including becoming MPs. Winchilsea had accused Wellington, himself a Protestant, of "an insidious design" that would allow "popery into every department of the State". The Duke's honour was impinged. Honour and masculinity were at stake. Winchilsea would not apologise. There was only one way out. And so it was.

Whether the hero of Waterloo fired deliberately to miss or simply aimed badly is still a moot point among some historians. One version, not corroborated, says Wellington's shot went through his adversary's hat. Winchilsea responded by shooting his bullet into the air. Reparations were deemed to have been made as Winchilsea had "stood his adversary's fire".

It turned out to be the last time a British Prime Minister was involved in a duel. The previous occasion was when William Pitt faced the MP for Southwark, George Tierney, on Putney Heath in 1798.

It may also have helped to hasten the decline of duelling in England, where it faded long before it did in the continent (where swords rather than pistols were employed).

The area around the disreputable Red House – now occupied by new Berkeley houses on the site of Battersea Power Station – was the most likely place for a duel, being among other things the place where crack shots assembled to shoot pigeons.

Thomas Kirk, former City missionary in Battersea, described the Red House thus: "If ever there was a place out of hell that surpassed Sodom and Gomorrah in ungodliness and abomination, this was it. Here the worst men and the vilest of the human race seemed to try to outvie each other in wicked deeds".

We know exactly where the Red House was thanks to excavations by archaeologists from the Museum of London in 2001 on a site at the southern side of Chelsea Bridge. The excavations revealed the walls of the Red House, which can be seen in the photo above right.

Whether there is any relevance of all this to today is arguable. But if ministers had to resort to duels to resolve transgressions we soon might not have any at all.

192: ST JAMES'S THEATRE

Stand on King Street, SW1 and weep a theatrical tear. Just off that road, between Crown Passage and Angel Court, once stood the St James's Theatre, a fascinating Greek revival building constructed in 1835 and demolished in 1957.

It was on the site of Nerot's Hotel, a favourite of Edmund Burke and Lord Nelson – who met his wife there on his return from the Battle of the Nile in 1800. It became lost after being unexpectedly sold to a property developer during a record-breaking run of Terence Rattigan's Separate Tables despite a nation-wide campaign to save it, led by Vivien Leigh and Lawrence Olivier.

One fond memory is a review in the Times newspaper in September 1836 of a play written by someone under a pseudonym. The reviewer, in a mildly sympathetic tone, said "plot there was none that would require to be told".

The anonymous playwright turned out to have a lot of plots that required to be told. His name was Charles Dickens and, in what was clearly a good career move, he turned to writing novels.

Dickens later appeared at St James's in the cast of an amateur performance of Ben Jonson's Every Man in his Humour and his luck with it took a further turn for the better when a production of Oliver Twist was performed there in 1838.

A similarly wise career move was made by Henry James, who had written a play, Guy Domville, about someone who renounced the priesthood to save his family by producing an heir. It had already been turned down by one London theatre but St James's accepted it. On 5 January 1895, we are told, it was "received politely by those in the more expensive parts of the house and

St James's Theatre, London

impolitely by those in the cheaper seats".

Such vignettes do not do justice to the long and distinguished history of St James's. In the 1890s it staged the first performance of The Importance of Being Earnest and also Lady Windermere's Fan and became Oscar Wilde's favourite theatre. Olivier featured in Anthony and Cleopatra and Caesar and Cleopatra, not to mention Separate Tables, also starring Margaret Leighton and Eric Portman, which ran for 726 performances, the longest in the theatre's history.

This sadly marked its end, as it was

 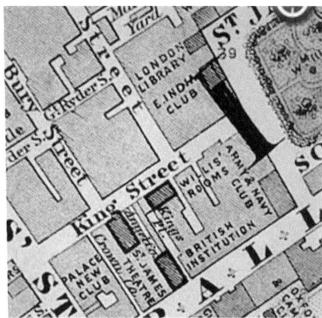

closed soon after planning permission had been granted for the building that would replace it. Then began a series of events that could have been the plot of a play. The London County Council soon regretted giving consent to the developer, but couldn't meet the compensation that would have to be paid to rescue St James's.

There were street demonstrations to try to save it and the House of Lords defied the government by voting against the demolition. One noble lord accused the administration of having a "murder on your conscience". Lord Mancroft, the government spokesman in the Lords, made no secret of the fact that he was against the destruction of an institution he had visited 24 times, or that the government too was opposed but felt it too couldn't justify finding the £50,000 price of stopping it going ahead.

Lord Silkin summed the situation up: "We have the extraordinary paradox that a theatre which everybody would recognise is required and should remain in existence is being demolished, and that a block of offices, which everyone would recognise is not essential in that area at the present time, is to take its place".

As it turned out, the office block which replaced the theatre didn't last long either. It had to be replaced by another and, after that, yet another. All that now remains of St James's is a plaque on a wall and an arrow pointing to a "theatre bar" upstairs. However, if you walk down Angel Court you will see some fading sculptures (above left) with one face looking remarkably like Wilde's.

They are all that is left after the curtain came down on a special piece of London's theatrical history.

193: HIGHBURY AND ISLINGTON STATION

It is not a palazzo in Venice. It is not an English country mansion gone walkabout. It is Highbury and Islington station. Not today's version but the former one from 1872, an era when stations were designed to be admired and not just passed through.

Its spectacular Gothic revival style – with Venetian touches – was described by the Illustrated London News as being "of a distinctive design not repeated elsewhere on the railways in England".

What a contrast with today's banal (though happily pedestrianised) station frontage, though there is a link with the past. The tall column of brickwork – to which the arrow is pointing in the photograph opposite – is part of the original building.

The old station's architect was 29-year-old Edwin Henry Horne from Regent's Park, whose drawings for the station were exhibited in the Royal Academy Summer Exhibition of 1873 (see image below). On the left of the building is the Cock Tavern, which dates back to 1780 and is still there, a mecca for Arsenal fans. In the centre was the actual station, with its vast booking emporium and billiards hall with a row of shops to the right.

John Betjeman, the patron saint of Victoriana and saviour of St Pancras, loved these stations and was angry at the way British Rail was stripping the North London Line of its glorious architectural heritage – but to no avail. Later on, in 2015, a petition to Parliament calling for the reconstruction of the facade of the original 1872 station,

which had suffered severe damage from bombs during the Second World War, failed to get enough votes to proceed. It attracted only 157 signatures.

It was one of six stations Horne was commissioned to build by the imaginative North London Railway Company to replace and enhance six earlier wooden ones at Bow, Barnsbury, Canonbury, Camden Town, Highbury and Hackney. In 1870, The Engineer journal said of the one at Bow (which had a 1,000 seater concert hall on top): "The building, is, in our opinion, as good an example of what a railway station should be as any we have ever seen".

Almost all of those stations have disappeared, apart from a renamed Camden Road and Hackney Central, which has been turned into a music venue next to the new station.

It was not only the buildings that disappeared. So did the architect. There is no record of Horne between 1880, when he was living in Old Broad Street, and 1891 when he re-appeared in lodgings in Dover using a number of different names. Whatever happened to him during those lost years is a mystery yet to be solved. It could have involved a lot of interesting buildings that were never built.

194: PETTY WALES

People walking along this street adjoining the Tower of London – these days dominated by Pret a Manger and Wagamama – are unlikely to notice its unusual name. It is called "Petty Wales" and is in exactly the same place as it was over 400 years ago, as can be seen from the Agas map insert below.

Most Londoners know that Petty France, where the Passport Office used to be, is so called because of the number of French people – mainly Huguenots – who settled there. But how many know about Petty Wales (a curious Franglais word), and what on earth is it doing next to the Tower of London?

There are a number of roads called Petty France in the UK (including two in London), but it appears there is only one Petty Wales anywhere and it is in danger of being lost in the mists of time.

Fortunately, some of the mists were lifted a long time ago by the meticulous historian John Stow. His famous Survey of London referred to the remains of a large stone building in Little Wales, which was also known as Galley Row because of the considerable number of ships that used to unload there from the shores of the Thames, including galleys from Italy discharging cargoes of wine and other merchandise.

Stow didn't believe local stories that it had been built by Julius Caesar, possibly as his London home. He thought it much more likely that it acquired the name because it had become the London abode of successive Princes of Wales, in much the same way that the ancient parcel of land called "Scotland" or Scotland Yard at the Charing Cross end of Whitehall was the London retreat of the Kings of Scotland. The heir to the throne in England has been given the title Prince of Wales since the early 14th century – most famously when Edward III bestowed it on his ill-fated son, Edward the Black Prince.

Why the Princes of Wales chose to live at the edge of the City walls – a long way from where they would have entered London from Wales – rather than near the Palace of Westminster as Scottish kings did is a moot point. Maybe they wanted to be in the City where the money was or just felt safer being so close to the Tower of London, where kings and queens often dwelled for short periods. Maybe they didn't visit Wales that often anyway.

The prevalence of merchants and seamen in such a busy trading area inevitably led to the construction of stone houses for the gentry and taverns for the seamen. One such inn, Stow says, was run by a lady called Mother Mampudding. According to the Drinkingcup website, England's earliest recorded spirits bar was the aptly named Aqua Vitae ("Water of Life") House, established in 1572. This "drinking den", it says, was located between two ale houses named the Ram's Head and Mother Mampudding's in Petty Wales. That may not be the reason the Princes of Wales came to live here, but it is another boost for the long forgotten history of this fascinating street.

69

195: KING'S CROSS-DRESSERS

Why Stella and Fanny, the two ladies pictured, needed an escort of five policemen would have needed some explanation for readers of The Illustrated Police News, in which the image appeared in 1870. The incident shown also attracted the attention of the Times, which observed: "Whatever the results of the investigation, there is much in this matter which is very strange, and, indeed, almost unintelligible."

What was unintelligible to the Times was the fact that Stella and Fanny were not women, but men who liked to dress up in women's clothes. Ernest Boulton and Frederick Park were the most famous cross-dressers of Victorian times. They were arrested after leaving a London theatre and charged with conspiracy to commit sodomy, a crime with a maximum sentence of life with hard labour.

It took a year for the case to come to court and the couple, who had maintained that they just liked to don drag in theatrical way, were acquitted on the main charge of sodomy. The prosecution produced an array of doctors, whose examinations proved that carnal relations had taken place, but the defence produced even more experts who, after similar physical examinations, declared that intercourse had not. Sounds like a lawyer's paradise.

Boulton and Park were, however, found guilty of a lesser charge of dressing up as women, for which they received a suspended sentence. According to the Illustrated Police News, the defence argued that theatre and its "ontological status" as unmoored from truth or authenticity could explain away all the "dark features" of the case. So now you know. But the couple were bound over for two years for admitting to appearing in public dressed as women, which was deemed "an offence against public morals and common decency".

The trial was more complicated than that, as two other defendants faced similar charges of conspiracy and incitement, including the United States consul in Leith, Edinburgh. Three others absconded. Another, Lord Arthur Clinton, whose love letters to Boulton had been uncovered during the investigation, died. It was reported at the time that natural causes were responsible, but some suspected suicide.

Such a case could not easily happen in today's more enlightened times. It marks a milestone in gay history, which is commemorated by a small plaque on a wall in Wakefield Street, off Regent Square in Kings Cross, where Boulton and Park lived for a time.

196: THE UMPTEENTH MANOR HOUSE OF HENRY VIII

It is easy to pass by 18 to 26 Cheyne Walk in Chelsea without noticing a small but concise plaque on the wall of an adjoining alley. It states that this was the exact position of a manor house built by Henry VIII. You might wonder why the almost impossibly acquisitive Henry – who had dozens and dozens of palaces, manor houses and hunting lodges up and down the country – needed yet another one. You would, of course, be absolutely right to. But this one was at least different.

Thomas Faulkner, in his classic study of Chelsea in 1810, said it was "one of the most interesting and historical spots in London". That was partly because of its looks but also because of its association with queens of England and the curious fact that it nearly became the site of the British Museum.

The manor house itself is long gone – but then again it isn't. Some fragments, insignificant perhaps, but nonetheless real, are incorporated into the houses on the site. The old brickwork of the garden walls has not altogether disappeared. The tall wall to the west of number 26 is largely Tudor and archaeologists point out that the bottom courses of the front walls, which can still be seen, are of two-inch Tudor bricks from the original foundations.

In the basement of number 24 – beneath the alleyway of Cheyne Mews – are the remains of seven chambers vaulted in brickwork dating back to the original mansion. The gardens at the back, protected by high walls, have apparently retained strong features of the original palatial gardens, including, it is claimed by some, an original Tudor mulberry tree. If only…

It was here that Henry built his new manor house soon after the execution of his erstwhile friend Thomas More, who had lived nearby. It was here in Chelsea (according to a contemporary report) that Henry secretly married his third wife Jane Seymour in advance of the official ceremony in Whitehall, having been betrothed to her, bizarrely, the day after the execution of Anne Boleyn. It was here too that Henry's fourth wife Anne of Cleves – their marriage in 1540 lasted a mere six months – eventually died in 1557, having outlived Henry and all his other wives.

In 1543 Henry married his sixth wife, Catherine Parr, to whom he assigned the manor house in which the future Queen Elizabeth was nurtured under Catherine's care. This was not the end of the link with English queens, because Lady Jane Grey, who reigned for nine days in 1553, also lived here for part of her life.

The seventeenth century was not without incident for Henry's Chelsea manor house either, not least because of its sequestration by Oliver Cromwell's parliament during the civil war. But of more consequence was its purchase by Sir Hans Sloane in 1712. This could have led to it becoming the British Museum.

Sir Hans's hitherto untarnished memory is being re-appraised these days because of his wife's shares in slave owning companies and his own first-hand knowledge of

the West Indies. But he was a major philanthropist, and you only have to make a short journey from Cheyne Walk to see evidence of this in the Chelsea Physic Garden, which he endowed to the nation.

Sloane purchased Henry's Manor House in 1712 (pictures above superimosed on today's street), and in 1742 started moving his enormous collection of books and curiosities to Chelsea, where his earnest desire was that the building and its contents would be bought at a bargain price by the government to start a national collection. This didn't happen. However, the collection

was purchased and moved to Bloomsbury where, along with the Cotton collection and the Earl of Oxford's treasures, it became a launching pad for the British Museum.

The manor house was pulled down shortly afterwards to make way for new houses. Sad to say, this may have been the right decision. Cheyne Walk was too inaccessible and the building too small to house the eventual contents of the BM. But it is still possible to walk along the posh houses of today's street and imagine what might have been.

197: GRIMALDI, THE CLOWN'S CLOWN

Not many clowns have parks named after them or have their lives written up by famous authors. Joseph Grimaldi, a master of his craft, had both. Charles Dickens edited his biography and Grimaldi himself is buried in Joseph Grimaldi Park, a former churchyard, not far from King's Cross station (see photo).

Grimaldi was a clown's clown. The most popular entertainer of the Regency era, he was reckoned to be the "funniest and best loved" man in the theatre. He knew riches but, like so many of his kind, there was unhappiness behind the mask. He died a pauper, depressed and alcoholic.

Grimaldi spawned thousands of imitators, who adopted his pioneering antics. As with all comedians he had a catchphrase, "Here we are!", which became nationally famous. Dickens apparently shouted it as he bounded into the foyer of the Tremont hotel in New York on one of his literary tours.

Clowns have been around in one form or another since Egyptian and Greek times. They appeared in England with medieval minstrels or as jesters in the court, in Italy as Harlequins, and in France as Pierrots. Shakespeare used the comic actors William Kempe and Robert Armin as clowns, who often improvised.

Some trace British clowns back to the buffoons of the medieval mystery plays planting the seeds for the likes of Grimaldi, who was the template of the modern circus clown with his whitewashed face, red nose and slapstick comedy, even though he didn't actually do circuses. His lasting influence has been recognised for decades through a memorial service held each year at the Holy Trinity church in Hackney, which attracts hundreds of costumed clowns from around the world.

Sadly, Grimaldi's life echoed the joy and sadness of a typical clown's routine. He was born in 1778 in Clare Market, a very poor area of London, where the London School of Economics campus now stands. His father was an entertainer and a serial philanderer with at least ten children from various mistresses. He brought young Joseph into his shows at an early stage until he became a star in his own right, notably at the Theatre Royal, Drury Lane and the Sadler's Wells and Covent Garden theatres.

Grimaldi had his failures – Puss in Boots was booed off the stage in 1818 and closed after one night – but in general he was so extraordinarily successful that clowns became known as "Joeys". His most successful show was the highly profitable Mother Goose in 1806, which made a record £20,000 in profit in the currency of the day and ran for 111 performances over two years at the Covent Garden Theatre. Grimaldi himself was dissatisfied

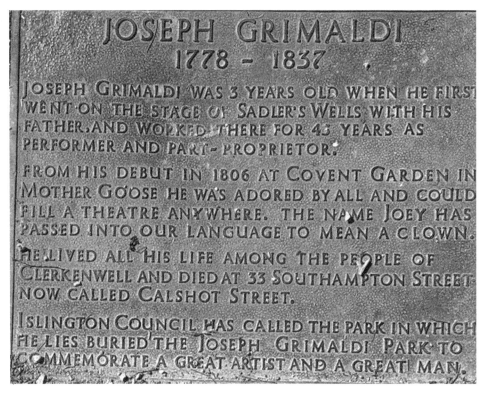

with his performance. Others thought it a work of genius.

He eagerly took up provincial gigs as they paid better. He played Scaramouche in a revival of Don Juan in Cheltenham based on Byron's original poem, after which he met the famous poet in nearby Gloucester. Instead of Grimaldi being impressed by Lord Byron it was the other way round. Byron said he felt "great and unbounded satisfaction in becoming acquainted with a man of such rare and profound talents".

But Grimaldi's steadily declined later in his life. From 1828 until 1836 he had to rely on charity payments. He was almost crippled and his wife Mary suffered a stroke shortly before the death of their son. He could still make light of his condition: "I make you laugh at night but am Grim-all-day" he quipped, but the end was near. The pair made a suicide pact but the poisons only produced stomach aches and the plan was abandoned. After Mary died in 1834, Grimaldi moved to 33 Southampton Street, Islington (now Calshot Street) where he ended his years.

On May 31 1837, despite feeling chest pains, he had his final night at his local pub, The Marquis of Cornwallis (now defunct), where he apparently spent a convivial evening entertaining fellow customers and drinking to excess. He was found dead in bed by his housekeeper the following morning. The coroner concluded that he had "died by the visitation of God" which probably wouldn't have surprised the Prince of Clowns.

He was buried on 5 June 5 1837 in St. James's Churchyard, Pentonville, which was later renamed in his honour.

198: THE SUPREME COURT'S CRIMINAL PAST

The Supreme Court building in Parliament Square is on the exact spot where long stood Westminster's medieval Bell Tower, whose bells rang for over 300 years until about 1750. The tower was the main building of the Abbey's sanctuary, an area roughly where Parliament Square is today, where criminals and others could legally evade the authorities as long as they confessed to their wrongdoings. Not even the King or his retainers were allowed in under pain of excommunication.

If that sanctuary existed today, you could be sure that immigrants in fear of being deported would seek refuge there. Not even the Supreme Court could have done anything about it.

Most abbeys had sanctuaries. The one at Westminster was instituted by Edward the Confessor and lasted until James I abolished it. However, the local culture of criminality lasted for long after, which was why the nearby area behind today's Victoria Street was so ridden with crime and prostitution that it became known as "The Devil's Acre", a phrase popularised by Charles Dickens.

The Bell Tower, or Clocktower as it was also called, naturally had bells – three of them to begin with. There was a belfry with bells in the cloisters of nearby St Stephen's Chapel dating from even earlier times. There were also bells in the Abbey itself and presumably also in the adjacent St Margaret's Church. Bells everywhere. When the three great bells of the clocktower were rung for special occasions, such as funerals and memorials, it was said that their ringing "soured all the

NEW PALACE YARD, WESTMINSTER HALL &c. AS THEY APPEAR'D IN THE YEAR 1647.

drink in the town".

The privilege of sanctuary did not offer exemption from market forces. This helps to explain why the houses in the sanctuary, which on old engravings look like shanty towns, commanded high rents – a straight case of demand exceeding supply.

The bell tower was about 75 feet square and about 60 feet high and would have been accessed through the High Gate into the Abbey precinct from King Street (today's Whitehall), where the statue of Winston Churchill is today.

It had only one door and one window on the ground floor, but two chapels on different floors where refugees could hear mass and hopefully put themselves on the road to redemption. Its history is preserved in today's street names such as The Sanctuary and Little Sanctuary, which meanders around the west side of the Supreme Court. An old picture of its remains is shown below.

The most famous refugee was Elizabeth Woodville, wife of Edward IV, who twice fled to the sanctuary, though she was accommodated in the Abbot's Cheynegates apartments rather than with "the common sort".

During her second stay, she was conned by the Duke of Buckingham and the Archbishop of York into surrendering her younger son so he could "safely" join his brother in the Tower of London, where they were both almost certainly murdered at the behest of Richard III. The pair are now known as the Princes in the Tower.

It is interesting that not even the ruthless Richard, who didn't flinch from murder, didn't dare kidnap the prince from the sanctuary. He had to resort to false promises that his young namesake would be safe in the Tower and a claim that the sanctuary was for criminals, not children. The Bell Tower building was later converted into Three Tuns Tavern, not far from another tavern, curiously called The Quaker, in Great Sanctuary, where Samuel Pepys dined in 1660.

Today, the Supreme Court stands on the remains of two previous Guildhall buildings dating to the early and late 19th centuries. In 1912, foundations of the medieval structure and earlier Saxon remains were uncovered by archaeologists.

The Supreme Court building can almost be viewed as a work of conceptual art. As mentioned in the first of my Lost London dispatches, if you go to the back of the Supreme Court in Little Sanctuary you will see a stone-framed doorway which used to be the entrance to the medieval Tothill Fields prison. This was situated where today's Greencoat pub is in Greencoat Place at the other end of Victoria Street. No-one seems to know how it got there.

Thus the pinnacle of English justice is built on the site of a sanctuary where you could have escaped justice with the entrance to a prison tacked on to it. You couldn't make it up.

199: WHY ROBERT RAIKES DESERVES HIS STATUE

Whenever I pass the larger than life statue of Robert Raikes (picture right) in Victoria Embankment Gardens I feel I owe it an apology. For years, I thought it a prime case for relocation under any sensible "rotation of statues" policy, because Sunday schools, which Raikes pioneered, were surely an anachronism in today's largely secular society with universal state education.

But while that may be the case now, in the late 18th century education was a privilege of the rich. Although a prime motive was to provide religious education, Sunday schools also taught reading, writing and arithmetic at a time of widespread illiteracy among poorer people. A few Sunday schools existed before, but it was Raikes, helped by publicity in the Gloucester Journal, which he edited, who took hold of the idea and ran with it.

He started off in July 1780 by gathering some street boys into a room in Sooty Alley, Gloucester. Soon, there were as many as 100 attending. By the time Raikes died in 1811 there were an estimated 400,000 children in the Sunday-schools of Great Britain – a formidable achievement – and it is reckoned that by 1831 the figure had risen to 1,250,000. Although this was only 25 per cent of the eligible population it provided a vital stopgap until the 1870 Education Act provided universal elementary education.

None other than Adam Smith endorsed them with the words: "No plan has promised to effect a change of manners with equal ease and simplicity since the days of the Apostles."

Raikes's Sunday school movement began in Gloucester,

but London soon joined in thanks to the Reverend Rowland Hill who, in 1784, founded one at the fascinating Surrey Chapel in Blackfriars Road south of the Thames, not far from where the statue of Raikes stands.

The Reverend Hill – not to be confused with the Rowland Hill who revolutionised the postal service or the Rowland Hill who served with distinction under Wellington at Waterloo – was a star in his own right. This Hill was a strong advocate of vaccination, and the Surrey Chapel became one of the most effective vaccination boards in London. The building (pictured above) was circular, which Hill claimed stopped the Devil from hiding in the corners. Hill was buried, at his own request, below the pulpit, but

was later re-buried below the Lincoln Memorial Tower of the successor chapel, Christ Church in Kennington Road.

Surrey Chapel, though owned and managed by independent trustees primarily as a Nonconformist chapel, was also operated as a venue for music, singing, and for the meetings of charities, associations and societies, several of which became closely associated with it. For a time, the composer and arranger Benjamin Jacob was the organist there, attracting thousands. His was a practical response to Hill's well known concern about chapel music of the time: 'Why should the Devil have all the good tunes?'

200: THE LAWLESS SANCTUARY OF ALSATIA

For much of the 17th century, Britain was engaged in making her writ obeyed across the globe from India to America. But, curiously, kings and queens failed to get their laws obeyed in key parts of London. One of the most notorious of these "liberties", where people could take refuge from legal authority, was Alsatia, which took up much of the land between Fleet Street and the Thames.

Alsatia's curious name was derived from Alsace, a disputed land both France and Germany laid claim to which was well known for its lawlessness. Alsatia was the most famous of the dozen or so legal safe havens in London. It was occupied by the Whitefriars monks until Henry VIII's dissolution of the monasteries. Residents enjoyed immunity from arrest, claiming ecclesiastical privileges dating back to the time of Edward the Confessor. The Whitefriars monastery has long been pulled down, but parts of it can still be observed.

The connection between Alsatia's monastic origins and its state of lawlessness was but one example of the tradition of areas around monasteries not being subject to cannon law or ordinary civil law – one that continued after the dissolution. When Henry was divvying out the confiscated monasteries to his cronies, he gave the Alsatian lands to his physician Dr William Butts, under whose neglect they degenerated into a self-governing slum.

Filled with criminals and bankrupts, Alsatia became a no-go area for police and provided the location for one of Walter Scott's Waverley novels – The Fortunes of Nigel – and appeared in other literary works, such as Thomas Shadwell's 1688 play The Square of Alsatia. Shadwell observed that England had conquered Ireland, subdued Wales and united Scotland, yet "there are some few spots of ground in London, just in the face of the Government, unconquer'd yet, that hold in Rebellion still". He thought it strange that "places so near the Kings Palace should be no parts of his Dominions".

Among those who took refuge in Alsatia was Daniel Defoe, author of Robinson Crusoe, who apparently escaped to it in 1692 after being pursued by the authorities for writing seditious material.

In 1608, King James I had actually confirmed the privileges of the liberties in a formal charter, and those rights remained until 1697, when they were abolished by an Act of Parliament. Even so, like other liberties, Alsatia maintained its disreputable character for long afterwards.

One of the extraordinary things about Alsatia was that some of the shops along Fleet Street had back doors which, when unlocked, opened into it – an alternative world of lawlessness whose shelter rogues being pursued by creditors could escape into. That is probably what is happening in Hogarth's print (right). It is believed to be set just off Fleet Street in Hanging Sword Alley.

In 1581, a widow called Pandley was accused of having "a backdoor into the white fryers, and for receiving of lewd persons, both men and women, to eate and drink in her cellar…" The famous Mitre tavern in Fleet Street (later part of the site of Hoare's Bank) had a door which led into Ram Alley (or Hare Court as it was later called) "by means whereof such persons as do frequent the house upon search made after them are conveyed out of the way."

It sounds more like a virtual reality game than real life. But that was Fleet Street in the heady days of Alsatia.

201: HORSE RACING IN NOTTING HILL

If you want to go to a racecourse from Central London today you will have to travel at least 15 miles. It was not always so. There used to be one a little west of Kensington Gardens in what today is known as Notting Hill.

And it was not just any old racecourse. Although The Times decried it on its opening in 1837 as "disgusting", a reporter for the Sporting Magazine was rather enthusiastic: "Entering, I was by no means prepared for what opened upon me. Here, without figure of speech, was the most perfect racecourse that I had ever seen…Here was, almost at our doors, a racing emporium more extensive and attractive than Ascot or Epsom, with ten times the accommodation of either, and where carriages are charged for admission at three fourths less."

Welcome to the Bayswater Hippodrome or any of the other names the course was given during its short life, including the Notting Hill Hippodrome, the Kensington Hippodrome and Victoria Park.

It could be argued that it reached its zenith on day one – Saturday, 3 June, 1837 – when up to 30,000 people converged on it, "including a large representation from the nobility" and several thousand on horseback, which delayed the start by an hour. One of the key races was the "Hippodrome 50 Sovereigns Plate", run over two miles. It was won by a horse called Lottery, which was later entered for the first ever Grand National at Aintree. Lottery started as favourite and won in what was described as a "hack canter".

The racecourse had no such luck, not least because the entrepreneur who had built it, John Whyte, enclosed the 140 acres he had leased from the Ladbroke Estate with a seven foot high fence. This shut off a valued right of way, to the consternation of local residents who appealed to Parliament. This was not successful, but Whyte had to give way eventually.

But the biggest problem lay beneath the ground, where the proprietors had overlooked the fact that the subsoil was of strong clay. This was perfect for the neighbouring brick and pottery industry (hence today's Pottery Lane nearby) but not good for horse racing, as it meant the course was waterlogged for much of the year while at other times the ground was so hard jockeys declined to take part.

This defect proved terminal. The last public meeting at the course was held in June 1841, barely four years after it started. Parts of it continued to be used for riding, particularly by women, but racing stopped and then building began on this choice land conveniently near the centre of the capital. Horse racing's loss was Notting Hill's gain. The rest is history.

THE HIPPODROME

BAYSWATER.

202: ST ANDREW'S – THE CHURCH THAT MOVED

This is a tale of two remarkable churches. They were once cosy High Anglican neighbours barely 50 yards apart, almost Siamese twins, built within a few years of each other around 1850. Now, they are separated by 10 miles after the first of them, St Andrews, in Wells Street (north of Oxford Street) was dismantled brick by brick almost 90 years ago and reassembled at Kingsbury.

In its time, St Andrews was a very fashionable church with first class music and lovely statues whose attendees included William Gladstone. So why was it moved from London? Maybe it just couldn't stand the competition, because its new neighbour was, and is, a church even agnostics drool over.

William Butterfield's Grade 1-listed All Saints in Margaret Street is a Gothic masterpiece. The architecture critic Ian Nairn said it can only be understood in terms of overwhelming passion: "Here is the force of Wuthering Heights translated into dusky red and black bricks, put down in a mundane Marylebone street to rivet you, pluck you into the courtyard with its harsh welcoming wings and quivering steeple". Walking inside, you could be forgiven for thinking that there hadn't been a Reformation. The walls have been painted with zealous enthusiasm and there are statues of the Virgin Mary and even a bijou confessional.

It is still a bit of a puzzle why two High Anglican churches were built so close together in the first place. The end came not from divine intervention but from mundane market forces. Numbers of congregants dropped as the area lost its houses and became more commercialised. Sadly, 50 yards was too close to accommodate both churches and the doors of St Andrews closed on Easter Sunday, 1931.

It would have been completely destroyed but for a public outcry against the demolition of a beautiful church. This led to it being pulled down in 1933-34 with each brick meticulously labelled and moved to the expanding commuter town near Wembley in what was dubbed "the biggest jig-saw puzzle in the world".

The relocation of the church was judged a big success, not least because, freed from the constraining buildings next door in Wells Street, more light came in to illuminate some of the treasures within, which had been built up to compete with All Saints. They initially included an altar and window by Pugin, a wall monument by William Burgess, fittings by G E Street and even a lectern by All Saints architect Butterfield. If ever there was a case for two churches to be "'twinned" this is it.

203: SHAKESPEARE AT THE MERMAID TAVERN

If Doctor Who offered you a trip in his Tardis to a lost London tavern of your choice, it would be easy to draw up a shortlist of two but difficult to choose between them. Would it be the Mitre in Fleet Street or the Mermaid in Bread Street, off Cheapside? Both are saturated with literary associations, but the critical question is: in which one would you be more likely to meet William Shakespeare in full throttle?

The Mitre will forever be associated with another literary giant, Dr Johnson who, after superstitiously touching every street post on his way there from his nearby Fleet Street lodgings, would hold forth to everyone at the Mitre with his faithful biographer James Boswell, occasionally downing a whole bottle of port wine. It was there that they planned their Tour to the Hebrides. The Mitre was at 39 Fleet Street on part of the site now occupied by the banking house of Hoare, where there is a plaque.

The earliest recorded mention of the Mitre is in the register of St Dunstan's Church in 1613, though the tavern existed before that. Shakespeare died in 1616, and although he spent much of his last years at Stratford-upon-Avon he could have visited the Mitre. Of course, the words "could have" are used often about Shakespeare, who left tantalisingly few clues to his whereabouts. A book of poems by Richard Jackson published in the late 1620s contains one entitled "Shakespeare's Rime which he made at ye Myter' in Flete strete," though without any authentication it is not taken seriously by scholars.

But who needs authentication about the Mermaid when we can dream that there really was a club set up by Sir Walter Raleigh at which Shakespeare, Francis Beaumont,

Ben Jonson, John Donne and others pitted their wits against each other in what has been described as a combination of "more talent and genius than ever met together before or since". As Beaumont put it to Jonson:

"With the best gamesters. What things have we seen
Done at the 'Mermaid?' Heard words that have been
So nimble, and so full of subtle flame,
As if that every one from whence they came
Had meant to put his whole wit in a jest".

Or John Keats much later:

"Souls of Poets dead and gone,
What Elysium have ye known,
Happy field or mossy cavern,
Choicer than the Mermaid Tavern?"

Sadly, there is no evidence that Raleigh was involved. Could Shakespeare have been there? There are no documented facts, but there is strong circumstantial evidence.

Not only was the creator of Falstaff a friend of the habitués of the Mermaid, he was also a close friend of William Johnson, the Mermaid's landlord. Johnson was named as a trustee in the document recording Shakespeare's purchase of the Gatehouse in Blackfriars, the only property in London he is known to have bought. This makes it difficult to believe that Shakespeare would not have visited this iconic inn. The rest can only be left to our imaginations.

204: ENGLAND'S EIFFEL TOWER

When the old Wembley Stadium was being demolished, builders came across an unusual structure underneath the Twin Towers. It was part of London's answer to the Eiffel Tower, a near-replica of the Paris original planned and partially built in the late 19th century by the great railway entrepreneur Sir Edward Watkin MP.

Watkin had actually tried to get Gustave Eiffel, architect of the Paris tower – completed and unveiled in 1889 – to build it, but the canny Frenchman rightly thought that to create an even taller version for the British might tarnish his credentials as a true Frenchman.

The Watkin project nevertheless went ahead. The design, the winning entry in a competition which received 68 submissions, was for a tower 46 metres higher than the Eiffel and featuring a cornucopia of attractions, with two observation decks holding a hotel, restaurants, theatres, exhibitions, an observatory and Turkish baths. Many of the unsuccessful submissions were more amazing still, including one with a spiral railway to the top. No kidding.

The Great Tower of London, as it was billed, reached a height of 47 metres – with a lift for visitors installed – before lack of money and structural problems scuppered the project. Part of the problem was that the original design was scaled back from being supported by eight legs on the rather marshy ground to only four.

The tower was to have been the centrepiece of an otherwise successful grand pleasure park with ornamental gardens hosting football and cricket pitches – all connected to the centre of London by the Metropolitan Line, whose company chairman Watkin was. Had the Grand Tower been completed it would have been stunning and it is likely that the first Wembley Stadium would have been built somewhere else.

Of course, the biggest objection to Watkin's tower was that it was derivative. Unlike London's pleasure gardens of old – Vauxhall, Ranelagh, Cremorne and so on – which were imitated around the world, the one in Wembley would have been playing catch-up with France. Yet in many ways Watkin was a man way ahead of his time.

Born in Salford, he planned a railway line from the north of England into London and then to Paris and onwards. This, of course, would have needed a Channel Tunnel. Watkin not only knew this but actually started to build one in cooperation with the French. At the UK end, boring reached nearly two miles out to sea before the government, fearful of a theoretical French invasion, put a stop to it. The remains are still there, off the coast of Kent, suitably boarded up.

Another of the numerous ideas of this amazing man was to transform the economy of Ireland by building a tunnel to it from Scotland. Don't tell you-know-who.

WEMBLEY TOWER

89

205: THE MORAL DESCENT OF CREMORNE GARDENS

The decline and fall of London's pleasure gardens, once imitated around the world, reached its nadir with what became the seediest of them all – Cremorne Gardens

This 19th century pleasuredome stretched from the King's Road to the Thames, where the World's End multi-storey housing estate now stands. Unlike its two major rivals, Vauxhall Gardens and Ranelagh Gardens, whose landscapes you can still walk around, Cremorne Gardens have disappeared except for a small and altered remnant by the river at the start of Lots Road where their restored original gateway can be seen.

This has been moved from its original position on the King's Road near the junction with Edith Grove, so I have produced an image of where it first stood in the composite photograph opposite. The re-located gateway has been given back its former splendour, complete with golden pineapples, a symbol of hospitality, at the top. It is the only significant artefact that remains (almost) in situ as a memorial to the golden age of pleasure gardens, but if you walk around the World's End estate it is possible to imagine that some of its lovely green gardens are part of the old Cremorne land.

The Earl of Cremorne's former estate had various dodgy owners from the early 1830s until it was acquired around 1846 by Thomas Bartlett Simpson, the former head waiter of a pub off Drury Lane. He somehow found £5,000 to enlarge and upgrade the gardens with a banqueting hall, a theatre and "delightful lavender bowers" so that the anticipated 1,500 guests could do whatever one does in lavender bowers.

Cremorne had full panoply of entertainments, including a circus and numerous side shows. It maintained the tradition of balloon ascents pioneered by earlier gardens, but pushed them to new and eventually tragic heights. According to a contemporary report, in 1853 a French balloonist called Bouthellier rose on a trapeze attached to the base of the balloon's basket and, after twisting himself "almost in a knot", unravelled his body to hang by his neck and then his heels to the consternation of the watching crowds. That same year, a Madame Poitevin went too far. She ascended on a heifer attached to her balloon, resulting in she and the Gardens being fined for cruelty to animals.

The aerial experiments ended in tragedy when a 50 year-old man, Henri Latour, went up lashed to a parachute attached to a balloon, which failed to detach itself as intended. The balloon was blown to the marshes of Tottenham and where landed with fatal consequences for Monsieur Latour.

Attempts to move the gardens "upmarket" failed, most notably on 9 July, 1858, when an Aristocratic Fête arranged by "a committee of gentlemen" and assisted by lady patronesses turned out to be on one of the wettest days of the year, thrusting the aristocratic ambitions of Cremorne into reverse.

For much of its existence activities there were fairly respectable but, as with other pleasure gardens, it became vulnerable to pleasures of a baser kind. In 1857, the Chelsea Vestry submitted the first of a series of petitions against the renewal of the Gardens' licence, quoting the inconvenience caused by its late hours, the immoral character of its female frequenters (not, curiously, the male ones) and the bad effect on the morals of the neighbourhood. The downward effect on property prices was also a factor. As time went on, wantonness grew and eventually brought about Cremorne's demise.

Its series of unusual proprietors included Edward Tyrell Smith, whose CV said he had been a policeman, run pubs and

theatres (including Drury Lane, the Lyceum and Her Majesty's), managed Astley's circus by Westminster Bridge, and founded the Alhambra in Leicester Square. He also appeared to have been proprietor of the Sunday Times. At Cremorne he introduced a female answer to the tightrope walker Charles Blondin. In his final year (1869) he exhibited a balloon which could hold 30 people and provide an aerial voyage across London at 2,000 feet.

The Gardens' last proprietor, John Baum, arrived in 1870. One his innovations featured a flying machine in which a Monsieur de Groof attempted to fly using 37-foot long wings, inspired by the flight of a bat. The wind carried the attached balloon to Brandon in Essex, where de Groof emerged unhurt after a dangerous landing. He later died after a similar flight elsewhere.

By this time, Cremorne itself was in descent, resulting from dozens and dozens of cases reaching the police courts, often related to tanked-up young men returning from the races. Complaints about immorality continued to be led by the Vestry. The end came after Baum was sued for the goings-on in the garden. He won the case, but was left with a farthing in damages and hefty costs. He withdrew his application for a licence and thus, in 1878, ended the last of London's great pleasure gardens.

206: LA BELLE SAUVAGE

In 1873, a building on Ludgate Hill was demolished in order to erect a railway viaduct which obscured a historic view of St Paul's Cathedral. It was described by Historical Eye as "one of the most serious disfigurements in the City of London". Walter Thornbury, in his Old and New London, was even less flattering: "Of all the eyesores of modern London, surely the most hideous is the Ludgate Hill Viaduct – that enormous flat iron that lies across the chest of Ludgate Hill like a bar of metal on the breast of a wretch in a torture-chamber".

The building that was destroyed was La Belle Sauvage (main picture), one of the most iconic of London's medieval inns, which had served the capital's changing tastes since the 14th century. The main business of the inn, which has also been known as the Bell Savage and various other similar names, was serving the coach travel trade, providing 40 rooms and facilities for 100 horses. But it was also one of four taverns licensed by the City of London, including during Shakespeare's time, as a venue for plays. Love's Labour Lost was once performed there and Queen Elizabeth I's players, with their famed ad-lib clown Richard Tarlton, had a residency.

The other licensed inns at that time were the Bull, which, like La Belle Sauvage, staged its plays outside in its courtyard, while the Cross Keys and the Bell were indoor venues. All were closed in 1594 by the Privy Council, urged on by the Lord Mayor, paving the way for the later success of more famous theatres – such as the Globe and the Rose – in Southwark, outside the constraints of the Puritan-run City.

The theatres were not just for watching plays, as a contemporary account by Stephen Gosson notes: "In the playhouses at London, it is the fashion of youths to go first into the yard, and to carry their eye through every gallery, then like ravens…thither they fly, and press as near to the fairest as they can…and either bring them home to their houses on small acquaintance, or slip into taverns when the plays are done." We get the message.

The inn hosted other activities too. It was in La Belle Sauvage around 1672 that Britain's greatest wood sculptor Grinling Gibbons had his workshop. Apparently, a sculpted vase of wooden flowers there was so delicate that passing carriages caused it to flutter in the wind. And it was there that Pocahontas, the American Indian princess brought to England by the Virginia Company of London, stayed during her triumphant visit in 1616-1617.

It was also at La Belle Sauvage that a revolt led by Sir Thomas Wyatt to oust the Catholic Queen Mary in 1554 came to a grinding halt when the entrance to the City at nearby Ludgate was closed to him and his rebel army, leaving him, according to one account, to "rest awhile upon a stall over against La Bell Savage gate". Soon after, he surrendered at Temple Bar and was later executed.

From 1851, the then-expanding publishing company of John Cassell had office space there. A descendant of that firm, Cassell & Company Ltd, would later be based at Red Lion Square, where it erected a statue of Pocahontas as a reminder of the connection to La Belle Sauvage. It has been argued that the inn was named after her, but it is probably linked to an early proprietor called William Savage or his wife Iso(bel) Savage.

La Belle Sauvage was near the foot of Ludgate Hill, which was not ideal as it backed on to the notorious Fleet prison in Fleet Street from which debtors begged for food and money through openings in the walls. Ludgate was a principal entrance gate to London, and the main road from the City of London to the administrative centre, Westminster, went through it.

The gate itself was demolished in 1760 in order to widen the road and has been lost without trace, but statues of King

Lud and his sons, which used to grace the gate, have longevity on their side. They were removed from Ludgate when it was dismantled, along with a statue of Queen Elizabeth. All can be viewed to this day outside the church of St Dunstan-in-the-West in Fleet Street. The statue of Elizabeth is the only contemporary one currently on public display in London.

That "hideous" viaduct (pictured right) which caused the destruction of La Belle Sauvage is itself long gone and the railway has been re-routed underground. The statues are all that remain of the lost gateway to Ludgate Hill. We should be thankful for small memories.

207: THOMAS MORE'S LITTLE PLACE IN CHELSEA

Sir Thomas More was an ascetic who often wore a hair shirt and submitted to execution rather than admit that his former friend Henry VIII was head of the Catholic Church in England and not the Pope. When younger, he contemplated becoming a monk. But as he ascended in public life to become Lord Chancellor, he built a mansion – Beaufort House in Chelsea – which was bigger than most monasteries.

British History Online says of it: "It yielded to no other house in importance, not to King Henry VIII's manor house in Cheyne Walk, nor to the Earl of Shrewsbury's mansion, nor to the old manor house with which it shared the dignity of a proprietary chapel in the old Church."

More's mansion stretched all the way from Cheyne Walk beside the river up to the King's Road to the north (so called because for much of its early existence it was the King's private carriageway). The top of the gardens and the adjoining kitchen garden

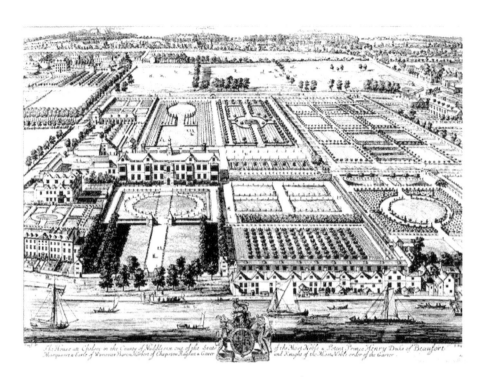

ran along King's Road roughly from Milman's Street to opposite the Bluebird Restaurant.

At the river end, the property stretched from the bottom of the same Milman's Street to Church Street, a substantial length either side of Battersea Bridge. If you walk down Beaufort Street towards the bridge today, you are walking on top of part of More's considerable garden, leading to the landing stage where he would have taken a boat to the Palace Of Westminster.

If you stop by the spacious Moravian Garden, where King's Road and Milman's Street meet, you are where his stables used to be. It is now a burial ground for the Moravian Church, with four pollarded fig trees in the centre. They were not around in More's time, but the walls on the eastern and southern sides were (photo above, right). When you are there it is easy to imagine yourself in a Tudor time warp.

The largest remains, however, are on the other side of Beaufort Street, where the original wall runs for almost its entire length from the river to the King's Road. It is mainly hidden behind mansion blocks with historic names like Beaufort and Burleigh House. Much of it has been whitewashed, but it is definitely there and must be a strong candidate for the longest Tudor remains in London (photo below).

The size and calm of the garden must have looked to outsiders like a glimpse of the perfect world described in More's literary masterpiece Utopia, which is still a global seller 500 years after its publication – in Latin – at Leuven in Holland. Utopia was way ahead of its time in envisaging a world of universal adult voting, a six hour working day, a sort of national health service, religious freedom, state education and the ordination of women.

The catch was that the ideal society was to be implemented in a severely authoritarian way, with ale houses and other pleasures forbidden and free discussion of public policy ultimately punishable by death to discourage "subversion" of the constitution. This helps to explain one of the enigmas of More's life. He died with heroic dignity as a true martyr, yet as Lord Chancellor he appears to have presided over the burning of "heretics". So much for religious toleration.

208: A VERY SPECIAL CRICKET MATCH IN WALWORTH

On 16 August, 1796, one of the most remarkable games of cricket ever played took place before "an immense concourse of people" in what was called Aram's New Ground in Montpelier Gardens, off the Walworth Road near Elephant and Castle.

It lasted for two days and was played between the Chelsea Hospital Pensioners and the Greenwich Pensioners. What made it unusual was that all eleven members of the Greenwich team had only one leg and those of the Chelsea team, one arm.

The famous match started at about 10.00 am. The Greenwich team was first to bat and scored an astonishing 93 runs. Play was interrupted in the afternoon, when the Chelsea team was batting, after the gates to the ground were forced open by the enormous number of people trying to gain admittance. Parts of the fencing broke and a shed collapsed under the weight of people sitting on top of it.

According to a report in the Hampshire Chronicle, the game was resumed at 6.00 pm and the Chelsea team completed its innings with a score of got 42. The Grrenwich team then "commenced their second innings, and six were bowled out after they got 60, so that left off 111 more than those with one arm". The match was supposed to last for one day but, partly because of the disruptions, spilled into 17 August.

The event was a wonderful early example of people with disabilities engaging in sporting activities, though one report said that five wooden legs were broken during the

The Cricket Match between The Greenwich & Chelsea Hospital Pensioners
HENRY ALKEN

game, which was apparently played for a purse of a thousand guineas – a lot of money in those days.

Aram's New Ground (named after a George Aram) was created in the same year as the match took place and the Montpelier Cricket Club, which was based there, was founded at around the same time. The ground hosted major Montpelier matches for the next ten years, including one against the Marylebone Cricket Club – a rare example of the MCC playing the MCC.

The entance to Montpelier Gardens (arrowed in map below) and its cricket pitch would have been close to the junction of Walworth Road and today's Fielding Street (then called Olney Street) after the railway bridge – roughly where the bend in Fielding Street meets Langdale Close and Olney Road today.

Cricket was also played in fields to the north of Montpelier Gardens, which were the grounds of the Bee Hive pub at the end of Carter Place (formerly Carter Street), also off the Walworth Road. To complicate matters further Montpelier was often known as the "Bee Hive Ground" because it was so near the actual one. The Bee Hive pub is still there, though closed at the time of writing.

The Montpelier club went on to make a big contribution to the future of cricket in England. The full story is a little misty, but it is clear that in around 1845 its members were prime movers in the formation of Surrey County Cricket Club.

William Houghton, one of Montpelier's presidents, found a suitable venue for the proposed new club on a market garden in Vauxhall, which we know today as The Oval. Houghton negotiated a 31-year lease from the Duchy of Cornwall, and soon set about building a cricket ground on the land with the help of 10,000 turfs extracted from Tooting Common.

The Surrey County Cricket Club came into exisistence on 22 August, 1845, at the Horns Tavern in south London, when around 100 cricket clubs represented there agreed "that a Surrey club be now formed". It has never looked back, even though some nostalgics might wish it was called the Montpelier Cricket Club so that the MCC could, at least in theory, still play the MCC.

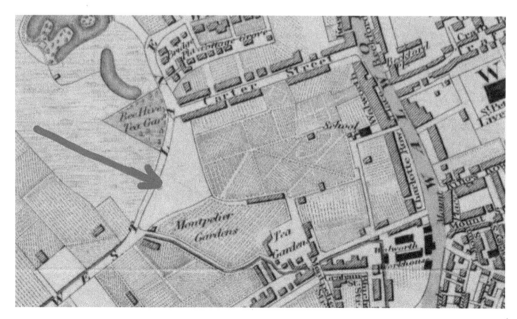

209: BUILDINGS OF THE BRAZEN BARBARA VILLIERS

As mistresses go, Barbara Villiers, Duchess of Cleveland and Countess Castlemaine, was surely Queen Bee. Baptised in 1640 at St Margaret's church, next to Westminster Abbey, she rose and rose to become the most notorious of Charles II's numerous mistresses. Often known as the "Uncrowned Queen", she exerted power out of all proportion to her position, not least over the actual Queen, Catherine of Braganza.

Nell Gwyn may have been the more vivacious of Charles's mistresses but Barbara was the real deal, exerting influence long after having to move from the royal palace in Whitehall to her own palatial mansion, purchased by the King, on the edge of the Green Park. She even had a hold over the King when he moved on to other mistresses.

Samuel Pepys, the great diarist, was captivated by her beauty but worried about the increasing influence she had over the King, and at one stage confided: "I know well enough she is a whore". And so she was, faithful neither to her husband nor to the King himself (not that he was one to set an example). She bore him six children, five of which he acknowledged, including their eldest son Charles Fitzroy who, can you believe it, was born at Hampton Court Palace while the King was actually on his honeymoon with Catherine. And the King's reaction? He made Barbara Lady of the Bedchamber to his wife. You couldn't make it up.

Charles gave Barbara Berkshire House adjoining the Green Park for services rendered. After being made Duchess of Cleveland in 1670, she renamed the

dwelling Cleveland House (main image) and extended it by buying surrounding properties, enabling an eastern and western wing to be built and an ice house, which was excavated in 1956 (picture below). The site of the excavation was behind a recently constructed building also named after her – Castlemaine House – in Little St James's Place. Cleveland House covered much of the footprint of today's Bridgewater House, a beautiful building which backs on to Green Park. Its garden can be seen on the left as you walk along the alleyway from the Park.

But the Duchess will long be remembered not for what she built but for what she destroyed. She was a serial gambler, who ran up enormous debts and had to be bailed out on several occasions by the King.

Also in 1670, she was given Nonsuch Palace near Cheam and created Baroness Nonsuch to go with it. This was no ordinary palace. It was called Nonsuch because Henry VIII, whose project it originally was, intended it to exceed every other European palace in magnificence, including the dozens of mansions and palaces he already owned. There was to be nothing like it.

It beggars belief that the Duchess had the palace demolished as it was a drain on her finances at a time when she was burdened with gambling debts. This removed what would have been an international tourist attraction today. The stones, bricks and other materials were sold off, with many of them incorporated into other great houses. Some ended up in the British Museum.

There is nothing left of Nonsuch Palace (pictured left) today. The only reminder of the incredible Barbara Villiers, apart from Cleveland Row which runs from Green Park to St James's Palace, is the ghostly outline of part of the foundations of Cleveland House said to appear in the garden of Bridgewater House.

210: THE LONDON HORSE DEPOSITORY

The story of what remains of 277 Gray's Inn Road begins 3,500 years ago. The site is presently called Hand Axe Yard. Why? Because in 1679 the remarkable discovery of a 3,500 year old axe was made nearby by archaeologists. The axe was acquired by Sir Hans Sloane and given to the British Museum as part of its founding collection. It is still on display, providing an unusual glimpse into early human history.

The address also offers a rather different glimpse into a more recent past. These days, we are trying to find ways of keeping cars off the roads, but in Victorian times the big challenge was reducing the number of horses on them. It is reckoned that by the 1850s there were around 25,000 horses moving around London on a typical day, providing the main means of transport for individuals and companies before the railways arrived.

The horses needed water – hence the troughs still scattered around the capital – and the authorities needed ways of dealing with the growing problem of, er, discharges. In 1894, the Times predicted that 50 years hence every street in London would be buried under nine feet of horse manure. The period would later be dubbed "The Great Horse Manure Crisis of 1894".

Of course, the horses also needed places to stay, and where better than 277 Gray's Inn Road, which started

its modern life around 1827 as the rather unromantically named North London Horse Depository? It was rather a grand building (main image) for its purpose, though one patronising critic dismissed it as a "large courtyard, treated in stucco with some architectural pretension". It occupied a large area between Gray's Inn Road and today's Birkenhead Street. The only bit of the architectural pretension still there are the remains of the entrance, which are Grade II listed.

In 1829, a man named William Bromley relaunched the building as the Royal London Bazaar, an exhibition space for novelty attractions, including what has been described as a "panoramic picture in needlework of 1200 square feet". In 1834-35, the first permanent exhibition of Madame Tussauds waxworks was based there. But by then, starting in 1832, the building had also become a base for the pioneering socialist Robert Owen and his Equitable Labour Exchange.

Owen was an extraordinary man. He had not long returned from America, where, in 1824, he had, with is son William, founded a utopian village called New Harmony. It was based on 180 buildings he had purchased from an existing community called Harmony, run by a George Rapp.

In 1825, Owen addressed Congress and the House of Representatives about his vision for New Harmony. Among those present were three former presidents – John Adams, Thomas Jefferson, and James Madison – as well as the outgoing US president James Monroe, not to mention the president-elect, John Quincy Adams. Not many people since could claim such an audience.

However, nothing seemed to last very long at 277 Gray's Inn Road. By the 1850s it was being used as a depository for goods rather than horses, and by 1872 it was a bottling store for the brewers Whitbread. Even so, it is easy to imagine what might have been. Immediately to its north was the ill-fated Panharmonium leisure park and to its south of it was Bagnigge Wells, a successful spa and tea garden. Put together, these attractions could have formed an entertainment complex to rival the pleasure gardens to the south either side of the Thames, rather than a Bermuda Triangle of missed opportunities.

Today, 277 Gray's Inn Road is marked only as 277A above the entrance to an award-winning residential development (photo below). But at least it's name 'Hand Axe Yard' recalls the beginning of the story.

211: NICHOLAS BARBON

Buckingham Street has got to be the most fascinating cul-de-sac in the whole of London. It is built on a small part of the site of York House, Cardinal Wolsey's vast palace one of a chain of aristocratic palaces along the Strand fronting the Thames.

All that remains of that Tudor extravagance is the building which peeps up at the end of the cul-de-sac. This was the watergate in Embankment Gardens, from which the Earl of Essex was taken to the Tower of London to be executed for his part in a rebellion against the government of Elizabeth I. In those days, before the Embankment was built, the Thames flowed right up to the gates of York House.

The two Grade-1 listed houses on the right at the end of the street were once occupied by the great diarist, Samuel Pepys. He moved to number 12 in 1667 and lived there for nine years before moving to number 14.

After Pepys left 14, it was occupied by Robert Harley, Earl of Oxford and one time Chancellor of the Exchequer, whose son sold the family's vast collection of books to the British Museum at a bargain price as one of the three founding donors. Number 12 later became the Salt Office from where the short-lived and much hated salt tax

was administered.

But the most interesting thing about Buckingham Street is not the celebrities who lived there – of which there were an amazing number – but the man who masterminded it. He is hardly known, but was one of the most extraordinary people of his time.

Meet Nicholas Barbon – or to give him his full name "Nicholas If-Jesus-Christ-had-not-Died-For-Thee-Thou-Hadst-Been-Damned Barbon". He had a difficult childhood as the son of the fanatical dissenter Praise-God Barebones (or Barbon), a member of the ill-fated Barebones Parliament during Cromwell's Protectorate.

Barbon junior was also fanatical, but in a different way.

He became one of the most spectacularly successful and ruthless property speculators that London has ever seen. Barbon changed the face of London as much as Christopher Wren or John Nash, though not on the same aesthetic level.

It was Barbon who purchased the whole of York House from its owner by that time, George Villiers, first Duke of Buckingham, and proceeded to dismantle it and build houses, or more likely sell leases for the land, as he thought dealing with bricks was for little people. We would call it commoditisation today.

As part of the deal, Barbon had to agree to make sure that Buckingham's legacy was reflected in the new street names – hence Duke Street, Buckingham Street Villiers Street and George Street.

Barbon also purchased Essex House at the other end of the chain of palaces along the Strand and had it rebuilt. There was opposition from the lawyers at the adjacent Middle Temple, but they were appeased with the construction of Fountain Court and the Devereux pub nearby (originally the Grecian Coffee House where members of the Royal Society met – photo above). Both can still be seen within the wonderful time-warp of the Middle Temple, which is a

must to walk through if you are near.

It would need a book to do justice to Barbon, whose work changed St James's Square, Covent Garden, the northern side of the Strand (the Exeter Exchange site where the Strand Palace Hotel is today) and Bloomsbury, including Lambs Conduit Street and much of Great Ormond Street, where there is an unusual alley called Barbon Close dedicated to him (photo left). At the start of the Close lies No 49 Great Ormond Street, a Barbon house about which its owner Alec Forshaw has written a lovely book called An Address in Bloomsbury". At the end of the alley you can see the children's hospital.

Most spectacularly of all, Barbon purchased 17 acres to build Red Lion Square and its surrounding streets without planning permission after hand-to-hand fighting with Nimbyish lawyers from nearby Grays Inn, who worried that their view would be spoiled.

Even more surprisingly, Barbon, who had qualified as a doctor (though he never practised), also built up a reputation as an economist and financier. Long before Keynes dismissed the gold standard as a "barbarous relic" Barbon had said you might as well use iron, and that the currency should be linked to an economy based on credit-led expansion (sound familiar?).

Karl Marx quotes him approvingly in the opening chapter of Das Kapital: "Or, as old Barbon says: 'One sort of wares are as good as another, if the value be equal. There is no difference or distinction in things of equal value'." Barbon also invented fire insurance as a means of profiting from the Great Fire of London.

One could go on, but best to go back to Buckingham Street. Barbon had built up a reputation for a ruthless pursuit of profit and for what today we would call jerry building. Buckingham Street was an exception. Although, like so many of Barbon's buildings, it has been much altered by individual builders, it has stood the test of time.

The renowned Survey of London observes that all the original houses were actually erected before 1680, describing this as "especially surprising when it is considered that for well over a century, and in some cases for nearly two centuries, the premises have been used for commercial purposes". Number 12 is the only one of Samuel Pepys's London homes to survive. Barbon built that one better.

212: FINDING LUNDENWIC

How many people gripped by a performance at the Royal Opera House in Covent Garden realise they are sitting above the remains of a once thriving Saxon settlement? The discovery of Saxon London – it stretched along the Thames from Trafalgar Square to the start of Fleet Street – is the capital's biggest postwar archaeological discovery.

Lundenwic, as it was called, meaning "London Trading Town", was an international trading post described by the historian Bede in 731 as "an emporium for many nations who come to it by land and sea". Yet archeologists from the Museum of London Archaeology (MOLA), who have published a hugely detailed report of their excavations, admit Lundenwic was a bit of an enigma. It was only as recently as the 1980s that they realised it had existed on such a large scale.

Before then, it was thought that historic London was divided between the seat of governance at Westminster on Thorney Island (formed by the convergence of the Thames with the River Tyburn, where Parliament is today) and

the Roman city of Londinium in the east. Most rich people would have travelled between the two centres by water. It seemed not a lot had happened in between, until, more recently, a chain of aristocratic mansions was built between the Strand and the Thames.

The most likely founder of Lundenwic, according to MOLA, was the Mercian king Wulfhere. Saxon occupation reached its height during the second and third quarters of the 8th century, when the population probably reached about 8,000 people. The purpose of a "wic", such as Lundenwic, was to raise money from tolls for the government or the church. There were several around the coast of Britain, including a flourishing one at Ipswich, some remains of which survive. Its pottery, known as "Ipswich ware", had wide distribution, from Yorkshire to Kent.

Roman Londinium had been abandoned in the late 5th century, before the Saxons arrived, although the London Wall that defined its boundaries remained intact, and multiple traces of it can still be found. After the Saxons left and Viking invaders had been repelled, Londinium, by then called Lundenburg, was re-established. We call it the City of London.

It is now known that Saxon London was a hive of activity, not least in the area around the Royal Opera House (pictured above), where 63 buildings, including a couple of blacksmiths and possibly a tanner, were uncovered as well as the usual rubbish pits. It is reckoned that activity in the area reached its zenith in the second and third quarters of the 8th century. The time may be ripe to write something serious about it. An opera perhaps?

213: HOW HORSEFERRY ROAD GOT ITS NAME

Even local residents might be surprised to learn why one of the busiest streets in Victoria is called Horseferry Road. Today, it leads cars and pedestrians to Lambeth Bridge, but in days gone by it led, as its name suggests, to a ferry that carried horses. It was the only way that they, the main means of transport in London in those days, could cross the Thames unless the sole other option was taken, the narrow, congested and expensive London Bridge.

It still beggars belief that for over 500 years the great capital city had only one bridge across its central river. The reason for that is simple: powerful vested interests wanted it that way. It was the result of an unholy alliance between three groups – the Archbishop of Canterbury at Lambeth Palace, who collected lucrative charges for the horse ferry, the thousands of wherrymen, who ferried people across the Thames in small boats, and the City of London, which ran London Bridge.

The profits from London Bridge were so huge that the trust established by the City in 1282 to maintain the bridge, Bridge House Estates, is still making money from them, and supporting good causes through its charitable arm. The City and the Archbishop thus stood to lose huge sums of money from any change, and the wherrymen rightly feared for their jobs. Thus did self-interest create the strongest monopoly this country has ever known.

A serious proposal for a second bridge was made in 1664, but was fiercely resisted by the vested interests. It ended with the City giving Charles II £100,000 – an enormous sum in those days – to scrap the whole idea. Doubtless at the time it would have been promoted as a charitable contribution. Today we would call it a bribe.

The absence of competition enabled the horseferry at Lambeth to continue with its charmed existence until the original Westminster Bridge was finally built in 1750. As with so many monopolies, there wasn't as much investment in infrastructure as there should have been, and the ferry frequently sank.

Among the celebrity sinkings, two stand out. The horses and servants of Archbishop Laud were sent to the bottom soon after his arrival at Lambeth Palace. Happily, no-one died but the incident was later regarded as an omen for the Archbishop's later

execution at Tyburn for his un-Puritanical beliefs. A decade later, a similar fate befell Oliver Cromwell's coach and horses. This too was seen as a bad sign, not least because the ferry itself had been confiscated by the Protectorate during the Civil War.

These accidents were only remembered because of the famous people involved. There must have been lots of others, as can be gleaned from the paintings of the time, which suggest an unstable journey. It is not even clear what the means of propulsion was. Some paintings make it look as if poles were used to punt the ferry across, which must have been very dodgy in rough weather.

The most famous event involving the ferry was in 1688, when Mary of Modena, James II's queen, escaped on it in stormy conditions with her baby son and two nurses. When she reached the other side, she had to crouch against the church wall of St Mary's church next to Lambeth Palace to wait – or so some accounts claim – for her connecting coach to arrive. The following day, James himself fled across the river in a wherry, casting his seal of office into the Thames en route (months later it was reportedly picked up accidentally in a fishing net).

The horseferry closed after the Westminster Bridge was built. The Archbishop of Canterbury received £3,000 in compensation, a very large sum at today's prices. It is an ill wind that blows nobody any good.

214: RAISING THE TONE OF KING'S CROSS

The structure pictured opposite was one of the most unusual monuments in Victorian London. It looks like a Hawksmoor steeple gone wrong. In fact, it is a 20-yard high tower with a police station at the bottom (later upgraded into a pub), a camera obscura somewhere high up, a clock and, at the very top, an 11-foot high statue of George IV, who didn't live to see its completion.

The column was built in 1830 in an attempt to raise the tone of the neighbourhood as part of a grand but short-lived entertainment complex called the Panharmonium. It graced the intersection where today's Euston, Pentonville and Grays Inn roads meet, but didn't last very long: the statue of George was pulled down in 1842 and the rest went a few years later to ease traffic flow. However, its name became firmly attached to the junction where it stood and to the wider area – King's Cross.

This was despite George not being a hit with the public and the King's Cross building being dismissed by author Walter Thornbury as "a ridiculous octagonal structure crowned by an absurd statue". Its name soon appeared on maps (see below), prevailing over the area's former one of "Battle Bridge", which derived from a crossing over the River Fleet, since covered in, where a battle was popularly believed to have taken place between the Romans and Britons under Queen Boudica (If only).

Recently, there have been moves to put the King back into King's Cross, so far to no avail. Billions of pounds have gone into the King's Cross redevelopment, and a revival of the statue of the monarch who gave it its name would have added only a small extra cost.

A simple solution may be at hand, though. There is a little noticed bronze statue of George IV on horseback at the north-east end of Trafalgar Square. It was originally intended to go on the top of the Marble Arch, at the time when the arch itself was going to be positioned outside Buckingham Palace. Instead, if you're still with me, the statue was plonked on its Trafalgar Square plinth as a temporary resting place and has been there ever since.

It makes sense for there to be a model of George IV at King's Cross, even though he wasn't a model king. George IV's reign saw some achievements, but few of them were down to George himself, who was profligate in his official and private lives. For example, he ejected his wife from his coronation at Westminster Abbey as he had by then become besotted with one of his numerous mistresses. Kings will be kings.

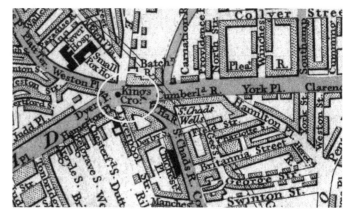

215: GREYFRIARS CHURCHES AND GARDEN

If you fancy a walk through one of London's hidden time warps, start at an alley off Giltspur Street next to the lovely Viaduct Tavern – still looking like the gin palace it used to be – which has cells beneath it which, or so it's claimed, were once linked to the long-demolished Newgate prison.

Walk to the other end of the alley and step back in time: you are now on land where the medieval Greyfriars Franciscan monastery once stood, established in 1225. Look through a window and get a glimpse of something much older – the remains of the old London Wall built by the Romans. It's just a section of much more extensive wall remains that are preserved within a building occupied by Bank of America and can be seen for free if you book a visit.

From there, step forward in time again by walking through the vestibule of the bank, a citadel of modern capitalism, only to emerge in a garden and a Grade I listed bomb site.

The garden is where the nave of Christ Church Greyfriars used to be, part of the monastery complex. The church was destroyed by the Great Fire of 1666, but by 1704 it had been rebuilt on a smaller scale by Christopher Wren. Then, in 1940, the body of Wren's church was destroyed by German bombs. Only its west tower still stands. The Christchurch Greyfriars Church Garden was established in 1989, reflecting the floor plan of the original medieval church (picture below).

If you look at the base of the Wren church's spire you will see some large stone pineapples. These were a personal motif the architect included in a number of his works,

including nearby St Paul's. They are a medieval symbol of hospitality. It is said that Wren even wanted to put one on top of the St Paul's dome.

Christ Church Greyfriars was the largest church in London after St Paul's and Westminster Abbey and one of an astonishing 126 churches within the boundaries of the City. In those days religion was literally all around you. Regular church attendance was compulsory and there were priests in every parish to say prayers for the dead.

It lasted as a place of worship until Henry VIII's dissolution of the monasteries in 1538. After being moved by a

sermon by Bishop Ridley urging him to do something about the poor, Henry bequeathed the monastery for that purpose. In the 1550s under Henry's successor Edward VI it became a school, Christ's Hospital (picture right), which sought to educate 400 poor youngsters out of poverty, though Edward provided nothing for its upkeep.

The school moved out to Horsham in 1902 because of bad sanitary conditions amid outbreaks of scarlet fever, but its memory is preserved in some delightful street sculptures of

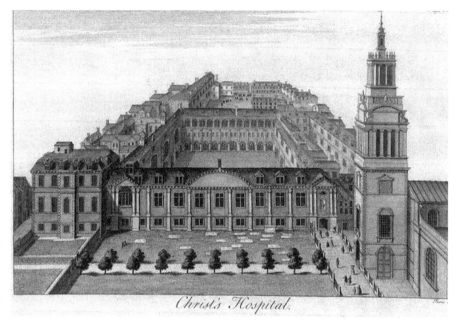

Christ's Hospital.

anonymous pupils at the side of the ruins of Wren's church (pictured left). Parts of the entrance to the original school were moved to Horsham brick by numbered brick and are still there.

It was decided in 1949 not to rebuild Wren's church but in 1950, instead of allowing the land to be redeveloped into yet more office blocks, its remains were designated Grade I listed. It is rather magical to look at the ruins within the present garden, its reconstructed steeple and, of course, those pineapples.

216: THE PANTHEON OF OXFORD STREET

If ever a structure was constructed out of superlatives it was this one. In 1774 Horace Walpole described it as "still the most beautiful edifice in England". His friend William Mason went further, claiming it was "the most astonishing and perfect piece of architecture that can possibly be conceived". Edward Gibbon, author of the Decline and Fall of the Roman Empire, declared that "in point of Ennui and Magnificence [it] is the wonder of the XVIII Century and the British Empire". The authoritative Survey of London observed that it was regarded "both by natives and foreigners, as the most elegant structure in Europe, if not on the globe".

One could go on but suffice to say that no building facing on to Oxford Street before or since has gathered such plaudits as James Wyatt's Pantheon. It was opened on 27 January 1772 on part of the site occupied today by Marks and Spencer. Why, you might ask, would anyone want to build a structure of such magnificence in of all places Oxford Street, which is more famous for the sound of money than the lure of beauty.

The answer may be found in Fanny Burney's (anonymously published) novel of 1778, Evelina. Its eponymous heroine thought the Pantheon was not as satisfying as the notorious Ranelagh Gardens in Chelsea, the erotic playground of the rich. And there's the clue. The Ranelagh was enormously popular – among those who could afford it – but it was only open in the summer. Patrons wanted a similar place of public entertainment to go to in the winter.

Soundings were taken among people of "rank or fortune" as to whether a Pantheon for winter entertainment to fill the social gap caused by the closure of Ranelagh would be appropriate. The answer was a resounding "yes" and after the usual complications attached to new buildings, not least sharply escalating costs, the Ranelagh of the West End was finally opened and attended by approaching 2,000 of the great and the good, including eight dukes and duchesses and a complete set of foreign ambassadors.

They were, by all accounts, impressed by the interior of the complex, not least by the dome which topped its central area, whose dimensions had been copied meticulously from the Pantheon in Rome. According to the antiquary John Timbs, the Pantheon contained 14 rooms, exclusive of the rotunda which had double colonnades "ornamented with Grecian reliefs; and in niches at the base of the dome were statues of the heathen deities".

After an opening like this what could possibly go wrong? After healthy profits in its first few years, things did. It was partly because the Pantheon had ideas above its station, especially in its early days, when admission required the "recommendation of a Peeress". It had to compete with Ranelagh Gardens during the summer seasons, when it struggled to attract enough people even after resorting to balloon demonstrations and scientific experiments.

The Pantheon enjoyed a brief revival when it became an opera house following a fire which destroyed the King's Theatre in Haymarket in June 1789, but that proved short-lived as the Pantheon itself was ravaged by fire in January, 1792. Thereafter various attempts were made to revive it, without success. In 1867 the Pantheon, by then a bazaar, closed and the building was purchased by Gilbey, the wine and spirit merchants, who sold it to Marks & Spencer in 1937. Attempts were made to

preserve the facade for erection elsewhere, but to no avail. The stones of the Pantheon will almost certainly have been incorporated into other buildings in London or, perish the thought, used as hardcore.

Meanwhile, the Pantheon in Rome built by Hadrian in 126 AD on the site of Agrippa's original, still stands proud in Rome. There is a moral there somewhere.

217: WHERE GANDHI STAYED IN WESTMINSTER

It is unlikely there has ever been a hotel in London more beautifully situated than the Westminster Palace Hotel. Opened in 1860 with 317 rooms, it peered out onto the pristine splendour of the Houses of Parliament and Big Ben with not a modern building in sight. The Royal Aquarium (on the right of the photo opposite) was not built until 16 years later. Westminster Abbey was so close you could almost touch it. The hotel was luxurious, complete with the country's first hydraulic lifts, though it boasted "a moderate tariff" and "no charge for attendance", whatever that meant.

The site of the hotel is better known for earlier uses. The Abbey's almonry, which distributed alms to the very poor – an activity not normally associated with luxury hotels – used to be there. William Caxton set up the country's first printing press in this location in 1476. In his Curiosities of London, published in 1868, John Timbs wrote that the position of Caxton's house was "immediately adjoining the spot now occupied by the principal entrance to the Westminster Palace Hotel".

An edition of The Canterbury Tales was produced there and Caxton's endeavours helped to shape modern English as a language because he had to choose among different dialects from up and down the land to find a version common to all. The hotel apparently had a statue of Caxton to remind itself of its heritage. No-one knows what happened to it. Westminster Council could do worse than commission a new one in honour of one of its most influential sons.

But although overshadowed by prior local history, the Westminster Palace Hotel made its own contribution. It lost much of its capacity in the very year it opened, when the government's newly created India Office leased 140 rooms at the rear of the building before moving into its permanent offices in Whitehall next to the Foreign Office seven years later. For that period, therefore, India was governed from the hotel.

This gave rise to a puzzle some years later when Mahatma Gandhi, the pacifist leader of the movement against British rule in India, stayed at the hotel. He occupied a room where Sir Richard Vivian, a former military commander in Madras who was a member of the governing Council of India, had stayed. It is not known whether Gandhi knew this at the time or indeed that his country had been ruled from the premises. During his stay, on 1 October 1909, Gandhi wrote a fascinating letter to Leo Tolstoy in which he outlined the fate of British Indians in South Africa and sought his permission to print 20,000 copies of a letter Tolstoy had written about the unrest.

Before that, in 1867, the hotel hosted the conference that created Canada as a country. It was the last of a series of such gatherings which brought the major regions of Canada into a single confederation. The tactical genius of the conference was Sir John Macdonald who went on to become Canada's first Prime Minister.

In 1908 the hotel was the setting for the launch of a domestic political movement: the Women's National Anti-Suffrage League was formed there with the aim of opposing women being granted the right to vote in

parliamentary elections. Yes, you read that correctly – a group of women wanted to prevent women being able to vote for MPs (though it didn't mind them voting in municipal elections). In 1910 the Women's National Anti-Suffrage League merged with the Men's National League for Opposing Women's Suffrage to form the National League of Opposing Women's Suffrage. It was not successful.

There are many stories yet to be told of the Westminster Palace Hotel's 317 rooms, though it wasn't in business for all that long. It closed in the 1920s and the building was used for offices instead before being demolished in 1974. A branch of Barclays bank – address, 2 Victoria Street – now occupies the space. It is hard to imagine a hotel on such a prime site being knocked down today.

218: WESTMINSTER CATHEDRAL'S MISSING MARBLES

Westminster Cathedral, with its skyscraping campanile, looks anything but lost as it flaunts its Byzantine brick magnificence across the pedestrianised piazza that links it to Victoria Street. You would never think it has lost its marbles. But it has – well, some of them.

The cathedral is rightly celebrated for its marble floors and columns imported from 25 countries, but there is also an unsolved mystery about them. How was it that some of the finest marble intended for the cathedral ended up in the Surrey House head office of the Aviva insurance company in the centre of Norwich?

One version of events – almost certainly untrue – is that marbles journey by sea from Europe was disrupted by a strike on board the ship. Another is that there was an accident en route which resulted in the cathedral making a successful insurance claim on the grounds that the cargo was lost, only for the marble to later be recovered, whereupon the Norwich Union insurance company – as Aviva used to be known – took possession of it. Much more likely is that the cathedral simply ran out of money or encountered what are politely called "logistical problems".

Whatever the reason, a lot of marble destined for the cathedral wasn't used there. The suppliers, Lambeth-based Farmer and Brindley, were able to offer the architect of the Norwich building, George Skipper, quantities of the highest quality coloured marble from around Europe at a discount. Skipper persuaded the directors to break their budget and accept the treasures. That is why being in the entrance hall of Surrey House (pictured below) is like entering a fairytale palace. Quite astonishing. It inspires a sense of awe that is normally reserved for, well, an abbey or cathedral.

Marble, however, is not the only thing lost in Westminster Cathedral's history. It is now a well established, highly successful Roman Catholic institution and a well-loved tourist attraction, but its story was nearly very different. It was originally to be a Gothic extravaganza inspired by Cologne Cathedral and designed by Henry Clutton, who was commissioned by Cardinal Manning, the Archbishop of Westminster – somewhat controversially as the two men were cousins.

Clutton spent six years years on various versions (example opposite), including one that would have been only slightly smaller than its Cologne model.

But after Manning died and Cardinal Vaughan took over it was accepted that the Clutton project was far too expensive, would have inviting unwelcome comparisons with Westminster Abbey and could have taken up to a century to complete. Instead, John Francis Bentley's stunning Byzantine alternative was built. It featured internal walls left empty that could be "ornamented at leisure" with mosaic, a process that is still far from finished.

One important thing was not lost in this saga. The cathedral was constructed on the site of Tothill Fields Bridewell prison, which

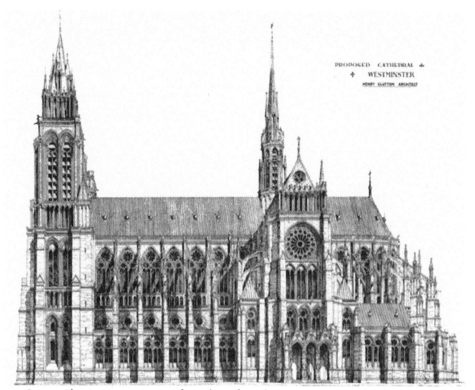

stretched from Victoria Street to Francis Street. The institution's nine foot deep foundations were so solid that most of them were retained and the cathedral built upon them.

You can't see the foundations from inside the building but in May 2014 when a trench was being dug in Thirleby Road, part of Ashley Gardens flats, it revealed some of their brickwork. This was seen by the London Historians group, which happened

to be meeting nearby in what was then called the Cardinal pub – after Cardinal Manning – and has since reverted to its original name, the Windsor Castle.

The Cathedral (left) is now a beautiful sight. But it was not always easy to see. Until 1975, if you were walking along Victoria Street, particularly on the south side, the view of it was obscured by a terrace of offices and shops. The opening of the piazza has been an unqualified success. A little bit of London that was lost to view is now unlost. It is not often we can say that.

219: ORIGINS THE LIFE-SAVING NEW RIVER

If you are walking past Sadler's Wells Theatre in Clerkenwell towards the centre of town you are unlikely to give the buildings next door to it a second glance. Yet they are the remains of an engineering project which, over 400 years ago, arguably did more to improve life in London than any other.

The HS2 railway project will cost around £80 billion to produce a comparatively modest reduction in journey times from London to Birmingham. By contrast, the New River Company's 28-mile long canal from Chadwell Springs in Hertfordshire to this location in the capital saved thousands of lives and reduced illnesses in London by bringing relatively fresh water to Londoners in place of that of the polluted Thames.

It wasn't the first scheme of its kind: during the 13th century clean water from the Tyburn river was carried from upstream to the City via a conduit. The difference is that the New River, which opened in 1613, still provides a significant amount of London's drinking water.

These days the canal stops at Stoke Newington – though some "heritage" parts can still be seen and walked

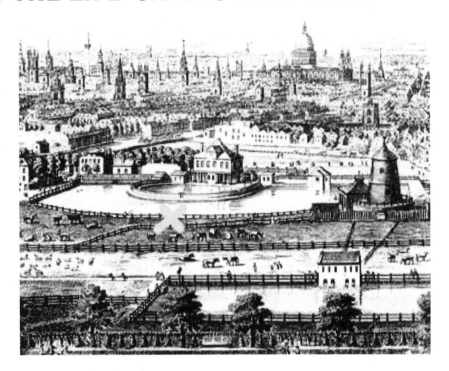

beside in Canonbury – but it used to terminate next to where the dance theatre now is at New River Head. There are plenty of reminders of this heritage there, not least one of the entrance shafts to the 50-mile long ring main water system, (photo opposite) which is visible from Amwell Street.

There is also the stub of a windmill, the engine house and the remains of reservoirs which were part of a site that once covered seven acres. A large building on Rosebery Avenue used to be the headquarters of the New River Company and later Thames Water has, like other former water company buildings around it, been converted into flats.

The New River project began in 1600 when Captain Edmund Colthurst had the bright idea of bringing water to London at a time of widespread pollution. He started the work at his own expense but ran out of money after completing three miles, at which point Sir Hugh Myddelton, a City grandee, took over until he too ran short of money.

The risk-averse City was reluctant to provide support, but the river was rescued by no less than King James I who, in 1611, agreed to meet half the cost in return for half of the profits. In its way this was a prototype of the private-public sector deals which have built so many schools and hospitals in recent years, though at considerable cost.

Unlike HS2, the artificial river was a low energy endeavour because gravity took the strain: the water flowed downhill into London through terrain that dropped by five inches every mile. The expense came from having to hire hundreds of labourers to dig the channel, which was ten feet wide by four deep, over a four-year period. There was also the usual opposition from Nimbyish landowners, who objected to the canal going through their land, to contend with.

The new waterway's completion was officially marked on Michaelmas Day 1614 when a gathering of the great and the good rode to the cistern in Islington to witness the flow of water accompanied by at least 60 labourers carrying spades and pickaxes, each wearing one of the ubiquitous green Monmouth caps that had swept the country.

When the speeches had finished the floodgates flew open and the new stream flowed into a reservoir built on the site of a ducking pond. Most of the vast infrastructure, including all the gravity-fed wooden pipes delivering the water to consumers all over London, has now gone.

The best way to absorb what the New River is all about is to walk behind Sadler's Wells to the end of Myddelton Passage – whose brick wall is the last surviving section of the site perimeter as it was in 1806 – where, as long as volunteers have opened the gate, there is a fascinating amount of information about the history of the project.

There is a viewing platform whose position is marked the yellow "x" is on the engraving shown opposite. From there one can get good glimpses of this extraordinary project. It does not, of course, compare with the grandeur of, say, the Great Pyramid or Stonehenge. But in terms of the social good it continues to do there is no comparison.

There is a pathway along the canal, the New River Walk, which can be followed all the way from Islington to Chadwell Springs or vice-versa.

220: JACK SHEPPARD'S CRIMINAL VAPOUR TRAIL

If you are going to write about London's most charismatic criminal of the early 18th century, where better to start than the Rummer Tavern and brothel shown in this William Hogarth engraving, just off Trafalgar Square. It was there, in 1722, that Jack Sheppard committed his first offence – stealing a couple of silver spoons a short distance from where he is buried at the nearby church of St Martin-in-the-Fields.

A criminal buried in a fashionable church? Yes. Sheppard was no ordinary villain. He was a small man – only 5 feet 4 inches tall – and also small-ish in terms of the crimes he committed. But for a fairly minor crook from Spitalfields, who died in 1724 at the age of 23, he left an enormous vapour trail.

Sheppard achieved widespread fame by escaping

from prison four times, including twice from Newgate, the most notorious high security penitentiary of them all. He became such a celebrity that Newgate gaolers charged high society visitors four shillings to see him, and the King's painter James Thornhill did a portrait of him.

It has been estimated that 200,000 onlookers filled the streets to watch the carriage that took Sheppard from Newgate along Holborn, stopping for the customary "one for the road" at a tavern on Oxford Street, to his execution at Tyburn. If that figure is correct it was something like a third of London's population at the time. Several prominent people had sent a petition to King George I begging for the death sentence to be reduced to transportation, but to no effect. Sheppard could have received a lesser sentence if he had grassed on associates, but refused to do so.

Daniel Defoe, author of Robinson Crusoe and himself a former Newgate inmate, is credited with ghosting Sheppard's autobiography. John Gay based his famous criminal MacHeath, a character in The Beggars Opera, on Sheppard. Later, in 1839 and 1840, Bentley's Miscellany serialised William Harrison Ainsworth's novel simply called Jack Sheppard. Profusely illustrated by George Cruikshank, it proved hugely popular.

Representations of Sheppard featured in many subsequent London plays, and in 1859 the Lord Chamberlain banned them all. William Thackeray, who didn't like Ainsworth's novel, reported an early example of what can only be described as merchandise branding. Vendors sold "Jack Sheppard bags", filled with burglary tools, in the lobbies of the theatres and, Thackeray wrote, "one or two young gentlemen have already confessed how much they were indebted to Jack Sheppard who gave them ideas of pocket-picking and thieving [which] they never would have had but for the play".

Given all this, it is a great shame that Hogarth's picture does not

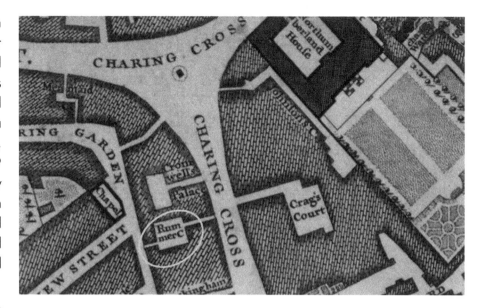

depict Sheppard, although it does include a prostitute spilling urine over an inebriated freemason, a character based on a real life head of lodge who was also a judge known for his severe sentencing. The mason is being seen home by his "tyler" or gatekeeper while rough sleepers crouch under the window of a barber surgeon viciously extracting teeth.

The location of the Rummer Tavern can easily be located from old maps and from the painting itself. In the background is a statue of Charles I, which was erected by his son Charles II. It still stands in the same spot in Trafalgar Square as it did then. Charles I and Sheppard had one thing in common – both received their death sentences after being tried in Westminster Hall, not far down the road from the Rummer.

There is a footnote. Sheppard's ultimate great escape was thwarted. Friends had planned to seize his body from the Tyburn gallows after it had hung for the required 15 minutes and take it to a doctor to be revived. They failed because of onlookers surging forward. His remains were buried in the churchyard of St Martin-in-the-Fields that same evening. So long Jack Sheppard.

221: MILE END'S PEOPLE'S PALACE

In 1887 Queen Victoria, in the first official engagement of her Jubilee year, opened a building in the East End of London. It was called The People's Palace and was designed to bring "intellectual improvement and rational recreation" to a deprived area of London.

The rich already had their entertainment outlets with such spectacular playgrounds as Vauxhall Gardens and, later, Ranelagh Gardens. These had pricing policies designed to keep out the working and lower middle classes. The People's Palace in the Mile End

Road was, like its counterpart Alexander Palace, intended to right this wrong.

Built on the site of Bancroft's School and Almshouses on land bought from the Draper's Company, one of the City of London's ancient livery companies, its central feature was the huge Queen's Hall (see above), a concert venue named in Victoria's honour. It could accommodate 4,000 people and was described by the Times as a "happy experiment in practical socialism".

The complex also contained an octagonal library of 250,000 books – inspired by the reading room of the British Museum – a glass-enclosed Winter Garden, a gym, gardens and baths. The Draper's Company also established two technical schools, known as the People's Palace Institute, adjacent to the Palace itself. These opened in October 1888 and provided much needed day and evening classes in technical and practical skills ranging from tailoring to carpentry and needlework.

It was built with the help of money from philanthropists such as businessman Sir Edmund Hay Currie, public donations and the unstinting generosity of the Draper's Company. But the idea for it came from a remarkable man and an unusual source – Walter Besant, who is barely known today except to enthusiastic historians of London.

Besant wrote a number of detailed books about different areas of London and was an important force behind the monumental Survey of London. He also wrote, or in some instances co-wrote, over 40 novels. Some at the time ranked only George Meredith and Thomas Hardy above Besant as contemporary novelists.

One of Besant's novels is regarded as the first of a new genre of "slum fiction". It was called All Sorts and Conditions of

Men and sold over 250,000 copies. In it, Besant imagined a "palace of delights" of education and entertainment for the working classes of the East End. This was the origin of the People's Palace.

It was intended to remedy a situation in which the two million or so working class east Londoners had, in Besant's words, "no institutions of their own to speak of, no public buildings of any importance, no municipality, no gentry, no carriages, no soldiers, no picture galleries, no theatres, no opera — they have nothing".

The Peoples' Palace proved enormously popular, receiving 26,000 visitors on a single bank holiday and 1.5 million in its first year. The two technical

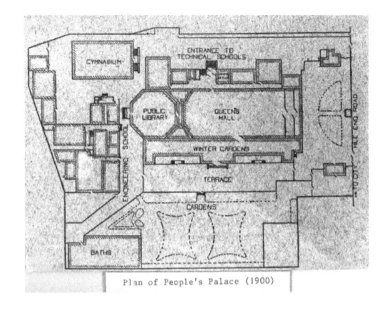

Plan of People's Palace (1900)

schools, where a range of subjects including engineering and physics were taught, became the East London Technical College, then East London College and then, in 1916, Queen Mary College, the queen being Mary of Teck, wife of King George V. These successes were, as the lawyer Sir Lynden Macassey wrote in the Times, a "striking refutation of all the early critics, who thought that university education was an unnecessary luxury for east London".

All went well with The Peoples' Palace until 1931 when the Queen's Hall burned down. This, bizarrely, echoed a similar fate that had caused extensive damage to Alexandra Palace – also known as a "People's Palace" – soon after it opened and the Crystal Palace after it had moved to Sydenham. All that was left was the frontage of the building.

However, the library survived and with the rest of the palace came under the sole use of the college, which in 1934 was given a royal charter and became Queen Mary University. The library is now the university's Octagon venue, available for banquets, conferences and receptions. A new hall, the Great Hall, though also known as a new Peoples' Palace, was built and opened by George VI in February 1937. It too still stands today.

Walter Besant was a bit of a university in his own right. In addition to his novels and voluminous works on London he wrote biographies of the philosopher Michel de Montaigne, Francois Rabelais and French humourists from the twelfth to the nineteenth century. In 1884 he founded the Society of Authors, the first serious organisation to campaign for the protection of literary rights for writers in the United Kingdom.

Besant's fame faded after his death, but Queen Mary University of London is his epitaph. A small seed planted by him grew and grew to become an international educational institution and a member of the prestigious Russell Group of universities while remaining rooted in the East End. And it all sprang from the pages of a novel, a fairy story come true.

222: BRUNEL IN DUKE STREET

For someone who died over 150 years ago, Isambard Kingdom Brunel has left an astonishing legacy of structures that are still intact. They include the SS Great Britain (on show at Bristol), the Great Western Railway, albeit on a changed gauge, the Clifton Suspension Bridge and, in London, the world's first underwater tunnel at Rotherhithe (now part of the London Overground) and key parts of Hungerford Bridge. And they are just some of the best known.

What we don't know so much about is the house where he lived for much of his

life and where he died or even what it looked like. It has long since been pulled down, and no paintings, engravings or photographs of it have been found.

I was mildly surprised when I first read that he resided at and often worked from 18 Duke Street, which is today's Horse Guards Road at the eastern end of St James's Park. Given that in 1848 he also purchased number 17 next door, he would have occupied a large portion of the buildings at the corner of King Charles Street running towards Birdcage Walk (see image above). He wouldn't have needed a garden as he had St James's Park at his front door.

The house, close to where the notorious Judge Jeffreys lived almost 200 years earlier, was pulled down at the end of the 19th century to build what became Her Majesty's Treasury. The nearest thing we have to knowing what the house looked like is a painting by Lady Carthy depicting his office (opposite) believed to have been done during the 1840s.

Through the window in the painting you can see what look like plane trees in St James's Park, which are similar to those in front of the Treasury today. It would have been in this room that Brunel designed much of the Great Eastern, launched in 1858. It was the biggest ship in the world at the time, and retained that status for 40 years.

It is less well known that Brunel was not only a formidable engineer but also a connoisseur of art. Over a period of several years he commissioned and oversaw a series of 10 paintings by leading artists such as Edwin Landseer, reflecting scenes from Shakespeare's plays. Nine of them were hung in his commodious dining room in Duke Street, which he used for entertaining. It came to be known as the Shakespeare Room, continuing a fascinating revival of Shakespeare paintings in that part of London.

At one stage it looked as though Brunel might leave these artistic works to the nation, but it was not to be. They were all sold. A few are still in Britain, including at the Leicester art gallery and the Royal Shakespeare Theatre in Stratford-upon-Avon, but, more's the pity, most of the others have gone abroad or come under the category "present whereabouts unknown".

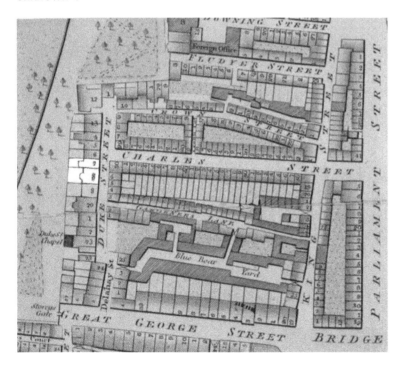

Numbers 7 and 8 Duke Street, highlighted in yellow in this map, were actually 17 and 18 in the notation of the time. Charles Street is today's King Charles Street, which has the controversial statue of Robert Clive at one end of it. The whole of the block south of Charles Street to Great George Street is now occupied by Treasury. St James's Park is on the left.

17 RECRUITING OFFICE
18 Brunel J K, civil engineer
26 York J O, engineer

223: CAXTON HALL

What do Roger Moore, Peter Sellers, Diana Dors, Elizabeth Taylor, Ringo Starr, Orson Welles, Joan Collins, Adam Faith, Ray Ellington, Cary Grant, Billy Butlin, Burl Ives, Barry Gibb, the 14th Duke of Bedford and Harry Pollitt, founder member of the Communist Party of Great Britain, got in common? Answer: they all took their lifetime marital vows at Caxton Hall in Westminster, some of them more than once.

Caxton Hall wears its history lightly. Built on the corner

of Caxton Street and Palmer Street as parochial offices and a public hall for several local parishes, it opened in 1883 under the name of Westminster Town Hall. The style of the building has been described as "undernourished Renaissance" but to me it looks ever more attractive as the recently built skyscrapers try to eclipse it.

It has now, surprise, surprise, been converted into apartments, but for decades until its closure in 1977 it was famous because famous people got married there. The phrase "a Caxton Hall wedding" became a cliché in newspaper headlines. But it wasn't only for celebrities, as it was the register office for all residents of Westminster. (Full disclosure: I too was married there).

There is more to Caxton Hall than meets the headlines. It is a history book in its own right, though nothing much to do with William Caxton, the pioneering printer whose works were located a few roads away in the precincts of Westminster Abbey and after whom the hall was named.

Caxton Hall was impressively liberal and non-denominational in terms of the meetings it hosted. They included the first Pan-African Congress (1900), the first meeting of the Suffragettes (1906: (there is a memorial in nearby

Christchurch Gardens), the Russell-Einstein anti-nuclear manifesto (1955), the first public meeting of the Homosexual Law Reform Society (1960), and also the formation of the National Front (1967). There is a plaque on the wall which says Winston Churchill "spoke here", though with no further details.

The most dramatic event at the hall took place in 1940 after a speech by Michael O'Dwyer, a former Lieutenant Governor of the Punjab, who was assassinated there by an Indian nationalist, Sardar Udnam Singh, in revenge for an act that had taken place over 20 years previously – O'Dwyer had ordered his troops to fire on villagers peacefully gathered to celebrate the Sikh festival of Baisakhi. Sardar walked towards O'Dwyer and after calling out his name shot him dead.

Caxton Hall's celebrity wedding days are long gone, but the individuals whose likenesses are embedded in terracotta across the front of the building above the windows on the first floor may still be celebrated. Who are they? The website London Remembers is fairly sure John Milton, Caxton and William Shakespeare are there, and speculates that a fourth may be John Fisher, Bishop of Rochester. Have a go yourself when you are passing by.

224: THE MANY QUIRKS OF ALL HALLOWS CHURCH

All Hallows-on-the-Wall is little noticed by cars speeding along London Wall, one of the busiest roads in the City. This is unsurprising as, from the outside, it looks like a warehouse with a tower attached when it is, of course, a working church which does a lot of charitable work. It rightly describes itself as being "on-the-wall" because it indeed stands above one – and no ordinary wall either but the original London Wall, built by the Romans.

It is a church of many quirks. Its predecessor on the site dated from the early 12th century and parts of the medieval structure are still visible along the approach to the entrance

to the current one, with what remains of the Roman wall deeper underground. It was rebuilt its present form by the 24-year-old George Dance the Younger in 1767. The north wall of the church rests on the wall's Roman foundations and its semicircular vestry rests on one of the wall's bastions, or external fortifications.

There was design in Dance's veins, as his father was George Dance the Elder, who built the Mansion House, but it was still a singular achievement for one so young that his first commission was to create a church on such a historic site.

As you enter the church, you move from its bland exterior to a blaze of whiteness with no columns to interrupt the pristine view. Your eye is immediately drawn to the quirkiest pulpit you have ever seen. It is stuck on the wall (to the left of the photo opposite) with no visible means of ascending to it. In order to reach the pulpit the preacher has to go outside the church and re-enter. As the London Wall once formed the perimeter of the capital, with open fields beyond, it would be said that preachers had to briefly leave the City of London before returning to deliver a sermon there.

Proving his versatility, Dance went on to build the notorious Newgate Prison. The two institutions had something curious in common, in that occupants of both were incarcerated there. The difference was that Newgate's were

jailed against their will, while All Hallows was famous in olden times for its anchorites – hermits locked voluntarily in cells attached to the church for love of God.

The most famous was Simon the Anchorite who is mentioned in the medieval account book of the church in 1512 as one of a succession of anchorites or "ankers" who quite likely dwelt on the Roman wall at the point where the vestry now is. Anchorites were known for their piety and were the recipients of considerable offerings, most of which were passed on to the church.

The prison, which was closed in 1902 and pulled down two years later, also included a Roman wall. The Old Bailey courthouse was later erected on the site, and part of the wall can still be seen in its bowels. But anchorites are there none.

225: BAGNIGGE WELLS

At some point in 1760 a place called Bagnigge House along what would be today's King's Cross Road (main picture) became suddenly famous. Important reserves were found under the ground. Not oil – it was a bit early for that. Not coal – it was too far south. What had been discovered was water.

It wasn't run of the mill water from the nearby River Fleet, which ran parallel to the road, but mineral water from two springs in the garden of the house. They contained traces of iron, which was claimed to be good for the eyes.

The Fleet near Bagnigge Wells

John Davis, described as the proprietor, was in no doubt. He paid for publicity in the July 1775 issue of the Daily Advertisement to inform the public that: "both the chalybeate and purging waters are in the greatest perfection ever known".

The poet W. Woty agreed. In Shrubs of Parnassus he wrote:

"Long have two springs in dull stagnation slept;
But taught at length by subtle art to flow,
They rise, forth from oblivion's bed they rise,
And manifest their virtues to mankind."

Not everyone accepted this – A Miss Edgeworth described a place of vulgar resort:

"The City to Bagnigge Wells repair,
To swallow dust, and call it air."

It didn't seem to matter. The area around Bagnigge was already a destination for countryside-seeking Londoners, and it took off after the discovery of the water. You don't have to believe the house had been the summer home of

Nell Gwyn, where she entertained Charles II in her inimitable way. But it is definitely true that Bagnigge Wells became an entertainment hotspot, attracting poets and peers as well as ordinary folk.

Hundreds of people came to drink the waters in the mornings and drink tea in the afternoons. There were several beautiful walks and a curious fountain representing Cupid bestriding a swan, which shot water to a great height, not to mention the willows and shrubs on the banks of the Fleet and the Bagnigge Wells Tavern.

It wasn't the only hotspot in the area. Nearby was Sadler's Wells, which was not at that time associated with music and ballet but the discovery of another mineral spring in 1683 for which health claims were made and around which Richard Sadler built an entertainment house.

These were tempting amenities for Londoners, who only had to leave Clerkenwell by way of today's Gray's Inn Road to be out of London. A map from 1746 actually shows a tiny community around "Black Mary's Hole", which the historian Cromwell says was named after a black woman named Woolaston who lived near one of the springs and sold the water. This is quite possible, as there were a lot more black people in London at that time than is generally known, though there have been other explanations for the name.

Like other pleasure gardens in London, Bagnigge went into decline and fall. Today, there is nothing of it left, though the period in which it flourished is acknowledged by a fascinating stone plaque behind a bus shelter which stands before numbers 61 and 63 King's Cross Road. Its inscription says:

This is Bagnigge House neare The Pindar a Wakefeild 1680.

The Pindar of Wakefield pub was almost next door to Bagnigge. The late London historian Peter Jackson claimed the plaque was London's oldest advert.

In 1863, the editor of The Builder magazine, George Godwin, welcomed the preservation of the plaque and later urged in an editorial that such tablets should mark the homes of famous inhabitants. Readers were enthusiastic and the Society of Arts – of which Godwin was a fellow – sponsored a scheme which eventually led to London's iconic blue plaques. Surely, this white plaque deserves a blue plaque of its own.

226: ESCOFFIER'S DREAM

Over 100 years ago a small group of luminaries from the hospitality sector, including Auguste Escoffier, the most famous chef of his era, and the hotelier Cesar Ritz, were worried about the lack of young people in London qualified to work in catering establishments.

Sound familiar? They decided to do something about it. With the help of money from heiress Baroness Angela Burdett-Coutts, who had a special interest in the field, they came together to develop a school for professional cookery. What would we give today to have an institution with such distinguished heritage?

Actually, we have. Escoffier's school still exists and although revered by those who know about it – not least for its associated restaurant – it remains one of London's hidden gems. It stands on the corner of Vincent Square and Rochester Row under the banner WK Westminster Kingsway College. It is a neighbour of St Stephen's church and a primary school, both of which were also built by Burdett-Coutts, who inherited a large fortune which, with advice from Charles Dickens, she devoted to philanthropy.

But first, a bit of background. The Vincent Square site was originally established by the Baroness in 1894 as an institute for teaching technical skills to local children, not least alumni of her primary school close by. At first, evening courses were provided for practical skills such as construction, plumbing, carriage-building and other trades before going on to offer a wider range of engineering courses.

In 1904 the technical institute merged with the flourishing Westminster School of Art, which moved to Vincent Square from Tufton Street near Westminster Abbey, where it had been part of the Royal Architectural Museum. The hospitality and catering section was launched in 1910 and blossomed into today's Westminster Catering College, the first institution of its kind in the country. It has to be said that its "brand" has become somewhat hidden behind that of its parent institution, the Westminster Kingsway College. But underneath it is a hive of culinary activity.

This is obvious as soon as you enter the building. On your right is a bar area leading to a large well-appointed brasserie in which students cook and serve delicious meals during term time. Ahead of you is – you've guessed – the Escoffier Room, where third year students will offer you a tasty menu considerably cheaper than elsewhere. And as you go in you can hardly fail to notice a sculpted plaque of the great man himself.

In this building you can learn to be anything from the front of house person to a chef, helped by an amazing number of kitchens behind the scenes including one devoted to chocolate making. Its alumni include celebrity chefs such as Jamie Oliver and Ainsley Harriott as well has a huge number in restaurants throughout the country. It is Escoffier's dream come true.

227: ALL HALLOWS – A HIDDEN CHURCH IN THE HEART OF THE CITY

The City of London prides itself on the peaceful co-existence of God and Mammon. Dozens of churches have survived in what became one of the most densely concentrated areas in the world dedicated to the worship of money. The most poignant example is at the junction of two of the City's most iconic roads. One is Gracechurch Street, whose name is derived from preceding ones including, according to A Survey of London (1603) "because the Grasse market went downe that way". The other is Lombard Street, named after Italian financiers from Lombardy who, in 1318, established goldsmith shops there, the forerunners of modern banks.

One of the most famous of those banks was Barclays, which for many years owned nearly all the properties where the two streets meet as its head office. This manifestation of Mammon well nigh smothered All Hallows church – not to be confused with the All Hallows of London Wall – which can trace its origins back to Christian worship on the site since 1053. But despite being obscured, it maintained its presence for centuries, being twice rebuilt and incorporating a stone porch taken from the priory of St John of Jerusalem in Clerkenwell after Henry VIII dissolved the monasteries in the 16th century.

It did not escape the Great Fire of 1966, which destroyed the church completely. But 20 years later a completely new one was built by Christopher Wren on the same spot (main image), even though it couldn't be seen from the street. In the 1830s, George Godwin, founder of that influential journal The Builder, commented that All Hallows was so hemmed in by other buildings, that "it is with difficulty discovered, even when looked for; it has in consequence been called 'the invisible church'."

It is now completely invisible on its original site in that it isn't there anymore. In 1939 it was pulled down, though Wren's tower and porch were preserved, dismantled and taken stone by stone to Twickenham to form part

of another brand new All Hallows, which stands close to the famous rugby stadium there (see above). It also contains the pews and the pulpit from the City site and a stunning altarpiece, which is quite possibly the work of the eminent carver Grinling Gibbons, or his studio.

All Hallows wasn't the only London church to be demolished and re-erected elsewhere. St Andrew's north of Oxford Street was moved 10 miles to Kingsbury, and St Mary, Aldermanbury, went all the way to Fulton, Missouri. Others, such as Christchurch Greyfriars and

the lovely St Dunstan in the East, have been preserved as iconic public spaces on land worth many millions at today's prices.

The wonder is that so many churches have survived during a period of soaring land prices. Most of them are still active, but you don't have to be religious to marvel at the architecture and the buried history in each and every one of them. The New Testament may be right that you can't serve God and Mammon, but the City of London appears to have found an acceptable compromise.

228: VICTORIA'S ARMY AND NAVY STORES

Anyone who has lived in Victoria for a long time remains nostalgic for the Army and Navy Stores on Victoria Street. Many still use the name when referring to the building where the flagship branch was most recently based, even though it was rebranded in 2005 as an outlet of House of Fraser, which took over the company in 1973.

Now the building itself is to be demolished and replaced by a 14-storey office block, so take a good look at the photo of it below. Built in 1977, it was never likely to win an architecture prize but it seems absolutely pointless to pull it down. And it serves as a reminder of the curious history of the piece of the street on which it stands.

The Army and Navy Stores (A&N) started life in 1871 as a cooperative venture, selling a variety of goods to officers and others in the army and navy at competitive prices and much loved by its customers, not least certain characters in Agatha Christie novels. It started off as a grocery shop before branching out into surplus clothing, drapery, fancy goods, pharmacy, wine and banking. It even had a guns department. Many of its goods were manufactured in local factories and workshops.

In 1878 A&N reduced its prices across the board due to the unexpectedly large profits it was making. As its clientele widened, competing retailers complained and successfully called for a House of Commons select

committee to examine allegations of unfair competition, but MPs concluded there was no evidence to merit its closure. A&N expanded at home and abroad, following the tracks of the Empire to ready-made base loads of military customers. It was one of the great success stories of its age.

Its image was established by the look of its original home on the same part of Victoria Street, the palatial premises shown below. As a longtime resident of the area, I was surprised to learn that the company didn't build its

iconic base itself. In fact, it simply leased part of what was actually the large distillery of Joseph and John Vickers & Co, though as A&N expanded it soon bought up the whole of it.

There is a deeper history too. The distillery was built in an unusual part of London known as Palmer's Village after local vicar and benefactor James Palmer, who donated the site to raise money for his almshouses. Palmer Street is named after him. The village, recreated Merrie England, complete with a wayside inn – the Prince of Orange – and a village green with a maypole.

It appears to have been an oasis of relative calm in an environment notorious for destitution and criminality, being barely a hundred yards from the start of what Charles Dickens popularised as the Devil's Acre. To the south and west were the swamps of Tothill Fields – remembered by Tothill Street nearby – where thieves and duellists hung out. Palmer's Village must have seemed like the last outpost of civilisation before south west London petered out.

229: THE MEDIEVAL ORIGINS OF WATNEY'S

Hundreds of years ago, the western side of Parliament Square, where the Supreme Court and the statue of Abraham Lincoln stand today, was known as Greene's Alley. That was because the Greene family, from which many offspring came, ran two pubs and a small brewery along the alley close to Westminster Abbey's own brewhouse in Dean's Yard. From these small beginnings can be traced the growth of what became the biggest brewery group in the country — the Watney Mann empire.

The Greenes had been in the industry since at least 1420 when Thomas Greene became Master of the Brewers' Company. But business growth began in earnest around 1607, when descendants of Thomas started to move their activities from the Abbey precincts and set up at what became known as the Stag Brewery in Pimlico.

The brewery belonged to the Greene family until 1787 and it didn't do badly — in 1722 it was described as being "the finest Brewhouse in Europe". Expansion gathered pace and in 1837 when James Watney, a miller, bought a quarter share and became a partner along with John Lettsom Elliot.

For a while the premises were known as those of the Elliot Watney and Company (see map opposite). The entrance was at the end of

Castle Lane, which used to be called Cabbage Lane and had two alleys running off it: Powder Beef Court and Mustard Alley, presumably to enhance the cabbage. The site, part of which is shown in the photo above, was opposite today's Victoria Palace theatre, where a branch of Marks and Spencer currently takes up part of the space.

By 1858 the brewery was under Watney's control, and he led a trend for gobbling up competition through mergers and takeovers. The fusion of Watney with Combe and Co of Long Acre and Reid's stout of Clerkenwell into Watney, Combe & Reid is reckoned to have been the first big merger in the history of British brewing. In 1958 came an even bigger union when Watney merged with Mann, Crossman & Paulin to form Watney Mann. The Stag brewery lasted until 1959, well within the memory of many local residents, but was deemed too small for the enlarged company's needs and closed down.

Watney achieved considerable success with its alliterative slogan "What we want is Watney's" but ran into trouble when the emerging Campaign for Real Ale went for it and other big brewers in a big way, with sustained criticism of its huge promotion of the Red Barrel keg beer.

Nothing remains of the brewery building, though its name became attached to a brewery in Mortlake. An old photo (below) shows the site of the Stag Tap pub in Castle Lane, which was used by brewery employees and Westminster Archives has produced photographic memories of what it was like to

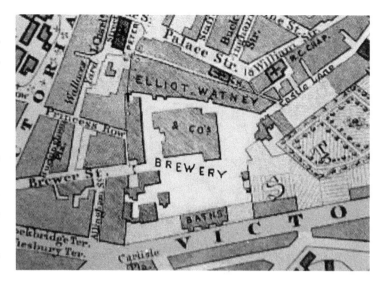

work there. The building behind the Stag Tap is the Westminster Chapel which is still functioning.

The only structure surviving from the earlier Greene era is the beautiful Wren-like Bluecoat school in Brewers Green, SW1, which was built in 1709 by William Greene, partly to educate the children of employees. The whole of the location's name may refer to the endeavours of the Greene family, from whose name the final "e" was often dropped. It is believed that barrels were sometimes stored in the cellar there.

Whether the Watney company would have fared even better had it returned to its roots and called Red Barrel "Green Barrel" instead can only be guessed at, but at least Brewers Green and the Bluecoat school serve as small reminders of where it all began.

230: THE RIGHT ROYAL BACKSTORY OF 180 BOROUGH HIGH STREET

On 17 August 1554 two people met for the first time and stayed in a mansion where 180 Borough High Street, *marked in yellow*, is today. Two days later they were married in Winchester Cathedral. The ceremony was a bit awkward as the groom could not speak English. The couple got by with a mixture of French and Spanish.

This was no ordinary blind date. The groom was Phillip II, King of Spain, and his bride was Mary Tudor, eldest daughter of Henry VIII and best known as Queen Mary I or Bloody Mary because of all the Protestants that were executed during her short reign from 1553 until her death in 1558. The house had been there since the previous century and rebuilt in palatial style in 1522 by its then owner Charles Brandon, 1st Duke of Suffolk. Its name was Suffolk Place.

Mary was attracted to Philip, partly because he was a Catholic and might therefore help her with her plans to reverse the Reformation and reconvert England to the Roman faith. But her love was not reciprocated. Philip found Mary unattractive and after 14 months of marriage left for Spain never to return, though he remained King of England jure uxoris meaning "by right of (his) wife". Games of Thrones don't always have happy endings.

This wasn't the first time a Mary Tudor had had a marital link with the future 180 Borough High Street. It had previously been one of the homes of the sister of Henry VIII of that name and resulted from another example of royal intrigue and romance.

In 1514, this Mary Tudor was married by proxy to King Louis XII of France, who was more than 30 years her senior. The union made Mary Queen of France. Louis was nuts about Mary and spoiled her with lavish gifts, but Mary did not return his affection because she was in love with someone else – wait for it – Charles Brandon.

Her marriage to Louis had, of course, been a political one to bind the two often warring nations in peaceful coalescence, but the arrangement didn't last as Louis died barely three months later. This left Mary free to marry Brandon, at least in theory. Mary believed she had extracted from Henry permission to to do so in the event of Louis's death. But although Brandon was a courtier of Henry and had been his buddy for years, the king was opposed to the match.

The couple went ahead regardless and married secretly in Paris in 1515. To marry a royal princess without royal consent was potentially a head-losing offence, and Henry was furious when he found out. But he became reconciled to the union after Mary not only handed over all the lavish presents she had received from Louis but also pledged to give him £4,000 a year for the foreseeable future – a huge sum in those days.

Whether all this brought happiness to Mary is a moot point. Brandon still spent most of his time at court. Mary died in 1533 and, by all accounts, Brandon wasn't present during her last days as he was too wrapped up in preparations for the wedding of Henry and Anne Boleyn. He didn't attend her funeral either. Some husband.

Six weeks after Mary's death, would you believe it, the good Duke of Suffolk, by then aged 49, married Katherine Willoughby, a 14-year old heiress who had been his ward and betrothed to his and Mary's son Henry Brandon, whom, in 1525, King Henry had made 1st Earl of Lincoln at the age of two. Henry Brandon was still too young to marry, so his father, worried about losing Katherine's extensive lands, decided to marry her himself.

What Katherine thought about this in personal terms can only be guessed at, but she did go on to bear Charles Brandon two sons and the marriage was a triumph for her socially, as becoming the Duchess of Suffolk made her one of the highest ranking women in the country.

Suffolk Place – sometimes known as Suffolk House – might appear to be the one stable factor in this curious story, but even that didn't last for very long. In 1536 Brandon, needing money to fund his lifestyle at court, gave it to King Henry along with his numerous manor houses in exchange for some cash and the Bishop of Norwich's equally palatial house at Charing Cross, known later as York House. When "Bloody Mary" met Philip II in 1554, Suffolk House was owned by her dad.

Bizarrely, three years later the mansion was pulled down and tenements built on the site instead, which became a notorious rookery called The Mint. Today, a new office block stands at 180 Borough High Street. See photo above. Its name is Brandon House.

231: BLACK STARS OF BARE KNUCKLE FIGHTING

The Tom Cribb pub in Panton Street, Piccadilly, celebrates by its name the achievements of England's most successful bare knuckle fighter, who purchased an earlier version of this pub, the Union Arms, very close to the site, using his considerable winnings. Cribb's successful career has been justly applauded, but has a backstory which should never be forgotten.

On 18 December 1810 one of the most extraordinary bouts in boxing history took place. Tom Molineaux, a seasoned black fighter who had arrived from America the year before, fought Cribb, white and England's undisputed champion, to decide what was in effect the world title.

Molineaux's helper and manager was Bill Richmond, 47, another black American and who had himself been a bare knuckle fighter after being released from slavery thanks to military officer Hugh Percy, later the 2nd Duke of Northumberland. Percy had been so impressed by the 13-year-old Richmond after seeing him in a tavern brawl with British soldiers that he persuaded the clergyman who "owned" him to free him.

Richmond travelled to England with Percy in 1777, where he was set up with an apprenticeship as a cabinetmaker in York, but soon turned to fighting again. He has

been described as England's first black sporting superstar and was lauded by people of all classes, including Lord Byron and the Prince Regent, and reached the top rank of fighters by winning 18 of his 20 fights. He was so celebrated that, along with other boxers, including Cribb, he was an usher at the coronation of George IV. Now, in 1810, his pupil Molineaux had the chance to become Britain's first black boxing champion.

Bare knuckle fights rightly appal us today, but they were hugely popular in Georgian times. This one took place out of town at Copthall Common, near East Grinstead. In his biography Richmond Unchained Luke G Williams says of the contest between Cribb and Molineaux and the subsequent re-match: "These were arguably the two most significant sporting occasions of Georgian times, attracting huge crowds – an estimated 20,000 – and unprecedented press attention. Bill Richmond was a key figure in brokering and promoting both bouts."

The crux of the matter was that during round 28 – yes, round 28 of a fight that eventually ran to 39 – Molineaux had so battered Cribb that the latter slumped motionless in his corner and should have been counted out by the referee. Joe Ward, one of Cribb's helpers, accused Molineaux of concealing rocks or bullets within his tightly clenched fists – a ludicrous accusation which, nonetheless, bought enough time for Cribb to recover his senses and eventually win an amazingly blood-splattered fight in the pouring rain.

One aspect of this defies belief. According to Williams, the referee – yes the referee – turned out to be one of Cribb's backers and apparently said to Cribb when it looked as though he had lost: "Now, Tom, now, for God's sake, don't let the nigger beat you. Go for him, Tom, go for him; Old England forever." An exhausted Molineaux eventually lost and also lost the return match, partly because he was under prepared for it while Cribb had trained hard. That doesn't alter the fact that, although some of the details are still disputed, he should have been declared the winner of the first bout.

Molineaux and Richmond were not the only successes by black men in Georgian England. They came not long after Ignatius Sancho and Olaudah Equiano became best selling authors with books campaigning for the abolition of slavery, which was still being practised on a large scale abroad while these freed former slaves were being feted in London.

One interesting postscript is that Cribb and Richmond became close friends in later life and often conversed together at Cribb's pub. It was there that Richmond spent his last night before he died, aged 66, in December 1829. Molineaux's end was tragic. After a stretch in a debtors' prison he became an alcoholic and, aged only 34 and penniless, passed away in August 1818 in Galway. He is buried there in St James's graveyard.

232: THE BECKFORDS OF SOHO SQUARE

Of all the things that can be said about William Beckford – and there are many – one of the most intriguing is a question: what on Earth was going on inside his head?

Beckford was a prominent political figure in 18th century London – twice Lord Mayor of London, the MP for the City of London and a liberal who backed the radical John Wilkes, a journalist and fellow MP intimately associated with the catchphrase "Wilkes and Liberty".

In 1770, following the release of Wilkes from one of his spells in prison, Beckford decorated his house, 22 Soho Square, with the word "Liberty" in letters three feet high. However, it doesn't seem to have occurred to Beckford to extend the concept of liberty to the slaves on his 13 sugar plantations in Jamaica, which he'd inherited from his older brother Peter Beckford and had made him one of the richest people in England.

Though born in Jamaica, Beckford was educated at Westminster School and his headmaster, Robert Freind, would later say he was "one of the best scholars the school ever had".

Yet the hypocrisy of the man knew no bounds.

He was an active anti-abolitionist who, in 1758 during the Seven Years' War, urged cabinet leader William Pitt to attack the French colony of Martinique. "The Negroes and stock of the island are worth above £4 million sterling and the conquest easy," he advised.

Beckford was mainly an absentee plantation owner who used the proceeds of slavery to build up a vast art collection and the Fonthill country estate in Wiltshire. He gave lavish parties and fathered at least eight illegitimate children. He died in 1770, but controversy about him lives on. A statue of Beckford at the Guildhall has been at the centre of the debate about what to do with embarrassing monuments to the figures from the City's past.

In October 1772, shortly after Beckford's death, 22 Soho Square, which had been the centre of his political activities, began being used for something

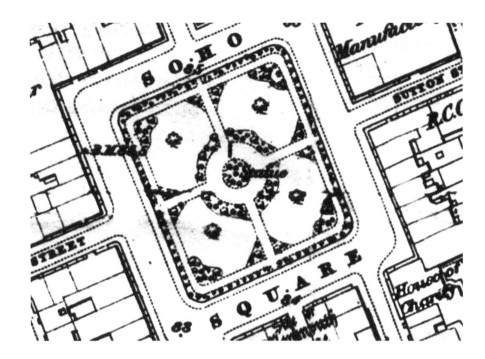

quite different when Dr George Armstrong made it the new base for his Dispensary for the Relief of the Infant Poor – an early seed of what eventually became the National Health Service. A doctor was in attendance on Mondays, Wednesdays and Fridays to give free advice to the poor (the other days of the week were for private patients).

William was not the only Beckford who resided in the area at the time. His younger brother Richard lived almost next door at 1 Greek Street – one side of which faces on to the square – and, according to the Survey of London, he improved the house considerably.

In 1811, after Richard's death, it was taken over by the Westminster and Middlesex Commission of Sewers, and in 1855 Sir Joseph Bazalgette and the Metropolitan Board of Works moved in to mastermind the construction of London's amazing sewer system. The building and its

gardens were apparently the inspiration for the lodgings of Dr Manette and Lucy in Charles Dickens's A Tale of Two Cities, which was published in 1859. The nearby Manette Street, formerly Rose Street, was later renamed in its honour.

In 1862, in another abrupt change of use, the building became the base for work to help the homeless and took on the name House of Charity (see map above), which is still emblazoned on it (see main photo), although it is now called the House of St Barnabas. A Grade I listed building, it is notable for its rococo interiors and a chute on the Soho Square side through which petty cash donations can be posted day or night. As well as hosting a worthy charity, it is home to a not-for-profit members' club – both are concepts the Beckford brothers would have found it difficult to understand.

233: EUSTON'S ROOTS AND HOW THE COURT GOT INTO TOTTENHAM COURT ROAD

Most of London's railway termini are named after the London areas they were built in, such as Victoria, King's Cross, Paddington, Liverpool Street, Marylebone and Waterloo. So is Euston, though unlike the others the origin of its name is not local. Where to begin?

In 1672 Charles II arranged a marriage between nine-year-old Henry FitzRoy – one of five illegitimate children he had with one of his favourite mistresses, Barbara Villiers – and Isabella Bennet, the five-year-old heiress of Henry Bennet, 1st Earl of Arlington.

Fitzroy is an Anglo-Norman word meaning son of a king – usually one born out of wedlock. The name was often maintained because the prestige of royalty outweighed the stigma of illegitimacy.

In 1675, when he was 12, Henry FitzRoy was created the first Duke of Grafton and – wait for it – in 1685, he and his even younger duchess wife inherited a country estate in a Suffolk village. The name of the village was Euston and at the heart of the estate stood Euston Hall, which the Grafton family still owns. Sadly, the village doesn't have a railway station but it has given its name to one.

That is because the family owned a lot of land in the area now called Euston and developed it during the late 18th and early 19th centuries. The names Grafton and Fitzroy also bear witness to this. Stroll around Fitzroy Square and its garden, built in the 1790s, and out into a maze of connections

– Grafton Way, Grafton Mews, Grafton Place, Euston Grove, Fitzroy Street, Cleveland Street – Barbara Villiers was Duchess of Cleveland – Euston Street, Cleveland Mews and, of course, Euston Road, sanctioned by Parliament in 1756 and running from Regents Park past the station and Euston Square. There was even a Duke Of Grafton pub at 278 Euston Road until it was demolished. Euston station, built by the London and Birmingham Railway company, opened in 1837.

Maybe Duke's Road is also named after Henry FitzRoy, as his family owned so much land in the area. This was augmented when the lease of the Manor of Tottenham Court "descended" to Isabella. The manor stood on, as you might expect, the very early Tottenham Court Road, at its northern end. It had previously been called King John's Palace and had multiple owners, including, in 1086, the Canons of St Paul's Cathedral.

In the Domesday Book it was known as Tottenhale.

Before its demolition in 1808 the court was for a long time the first countryside settlement reached by people leaving London from Oxford Street, as shown on the larger version of John Rocque's 1746 map of London above.

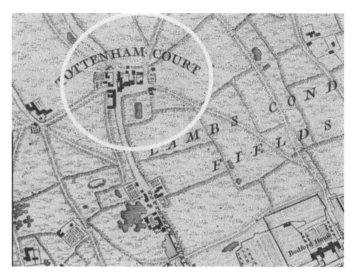

That part of Tottenham Court Road achieved a certain notoriety as the setting for William Hogarth's 1750 painting The March of the Guards to Finchley (below). You can see guards marching in the far background heading north in an orderly fashion to defend London against an invasion of Jacobite rebels from Scotland threatened five years earlier during their second uprising. But in the foreground is a typical Hogarthian scene of moral decrepitude – a bacchanalian orgy it would take a PhD to do justice to.

On the left is the Adam and Eve pub and on the right, the King's Head, a hostelrie brimming with prostitutes whose sign depicts the head of Charles II, the king in question. Extraordinarily, Hogarth had the nerve to offer the painting to one of Charles's successors, George II, thinking he would be amused.

But George was not happy seeing his glorious army depicted as ill-disciplined layabouts, and sent the painting back. It can now be seen in the Foundling Museum near Brunswick Square, which had strong associations with Hogarth, as he was involved in its creation.

If you look across the road from Warren Street station today you might be able to imagine the scene Hogarth captured. The Charles II pub was roughly where Euston Tower (main picture) now stands. Goodness knows how Hogarth would have painted how the area looks now.

234: MICHAEL DRAYTON, SHAKESPEARE'S LOST RIVAL

This is the tale of the son of a tanner who went to London and wrote celebrated poetry and plays and regularly returned to his native Warwickshire. He also acquired a share in a playhouse and is memorialised in Westminster Abbey. Meet not William Shakespeare, whose biography is so similar, but his contemporary Michael Drayton.

Drayton is little known today, but in his time he was a rival to Shakespeare and almost as celebrated. He lived in Fleet Street between St Dunstan's church and the turnoff to Fetter Lane (pictured opposite), not far from where Izaac Walton, author of The Compleat Angler, resided. His house was also close to the theatre he invested in, which formed part of the Whitefriars monastery building between Fleet Street and the Thames, some of which is still visible .

At the National Portrait Gallery there are usually paintings of Shakespeare, Jonson and Drayton displayed close together. Drayton is the one with laurels around his head, a recognition that he was once a contender for the then unofficial role of poet laureate.

William Drummond, a friend of Jonson,

said Drayton would "live by all likelihead so long as ... men speak English." One of my favourite lines of his is: "Since there's no helpe, come let us kiss and part" – a mini-story in a sentence.

Drayton was nothing if not prolific. As well as voluminous poems, he co-wrote around 20 plays but, unlike Shakespeare's canon, most of them are lost. The only surviving play to which he contributed is about the medieval solider and leader of the Lollards, Sir John Oldcastle. For a while wrongly published under Shakespeare's name, it was written as a riposte to an unflattering portrayal of Oldcastle in Shakespeare's Henry IV Part 1 (This also offended one of Oldcastle's influential descendants, which forced Shakespeare to change Oldcastle's name to John Falstaff). Meghan C. Andrews, writing in the Shakespeare Quarterly, suggests that five or six of the plays Drayton was involved in were "direct responses to or influenced by Shakespeare's work".

Drayton's magnum opus, Poly-Olbion, is one of the most extraordinary poems in the English language. That is partly because of its length (15,000 lines in iambic pentameter), partly because of how long it took to write (30 years), and partly because of the subject matter. It is a topographical epic about the history of England and Wales, which E M Forster called an "incomparable poem". Drayton began this Herculean task around 1598, when Shakespeare was in full flow. The poem may be about to get a reappraisal. Exeter University has been involved in a major study of Poly-Olbion, to be published in a year or so.

On December 23, 1631, Drayton died at his Fleet Street home almost penniless, his form of pastoral poetry having gone out of fashion. Yet he was so highly regarded by his contemporaries that, according to the antiquary William Fulman: "The Gentlemen of the Four Innes of Court and others of note about the Town, attended his body to Westminster." He was buried in Westminster Abbey next to a plaque of Ben Jonson (whose actual body is buried standing up elsewhere in the building).

Insofar as Drayton is remembered at all today, it is because of a reported binge drinking session with Shakespeare and Jonson at a tavern in Stratford-upon-Avon in 1616, as a result of which Shakespeare is said to have died. Few people have taken this story seriously, as it is based on remarks made by the local parish priest over 40 years after Shakespeare's death, albeit when some of his contemporaries were still alive.

Perhaps, then, they were unreliable recollections. But I have reached the age where although I have difficulty remembering what happened 10 minutes ago, I can much more clearly recall events 40 or 50 years in the past. I rest my case.

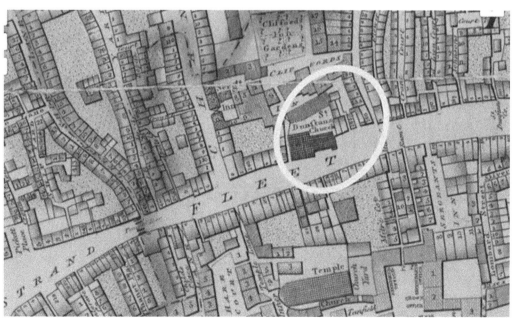

235: COFFEE, TEA AND DEVEREUX COURT

By the late 18th century London was awash with coffee houses. They were the social media of their time, doing what the likes of Twitter and Etsy do today. In an era before newspapers became popular these men-only institutions provided a forum for gossip, news and transactions – plus, of course, a cup of coffee – in return for a penny entrance fee.

Their ability to stir political discussion was regarded as so subversive by Charles II that he issued a proclamation in 1675 to suppress them on the grounds that they were spreading "malicious and scandalous reports to the defamation of His Majesty's Government … speaking evil of things they understand not".

This did not succeed, and equally unsuccessful was the Women's Petition against Coffee raised a year earlier which the historian Dr Mathew Green reminds us ranted against the abominable liquor called coffee which had "reduced their virile industrious men into effeminate, babbling, French layabouts".

The clientele of the Grecian Coffee House in Devereux Court would not have described themselves that way. Rather, they saw themselves as intellectuals. Walk down the narrow passage of Devereux Court from the Strand (see yellow line in map below) and you will come to the Devereux pub. This is the actual building in which the coffee house was located. It was built by the brilliant but notorious Nicholas Barbon in the 1670s. Barbon had a reputation as a jerry builder with scant regard

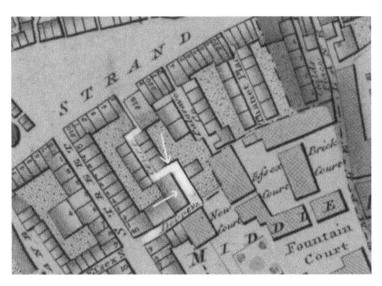

for planning laws, yet many of his buildings are still standing proud, which might explain the eerie, timeless atmosphere of Devereux Court.

If it was an intelligent conversation you were looking for, the coffee house there was the place. It was established in 1676 and patronised during its heyday by eminent men of learning, including Sir Isaac Newton, Sir Hans Sloane, astronomer royal Edmund Halley, and Joseph Addison, founder of the Spectator. Later on, that American genius Benjamin Franklin used to go there to drink with the Learned Club, a spin-off of the Royal Society.

Sometimes its debates got out of hand. A Dr. King reported that one evening a dispute between two gentlemen about the accent of a Greek word sparked such hostility that the two decided to settle it with their swords. They stepped into Devereux Court where one of them – Dr. King thinks his name was Fitzgerald – was "run through the body, and died on the spot".

There was another coffee house in Devereux Court with a less dramatic but very historic link to the present. Tom's Coffee House, established in 1702, about 25 years after the Grecian. It was pretty well where 9 Devereux Court (show in the main photo) is today. It wasn't anything special, but in 1706 it was acquired by Thomas Twining and became attached to Twining's pioneering tea shop in the same building, at the Strand end.

The emergence of tea which, unlike coffee, was easy to produce, was one of the causes of the decline of the once ubiquitous coffee houses. Another reason was that, unlike coffee houses, tea shops welcomed women.

Twinings is a remarkable company. Its shop facing on to Strand is more or less as it was 300 years ago, and although it is now owned by Associated British Foods it still prides itself on its history. It claims that its logo, created in 1787, is the oldest in the world in continuous use. It also claims to be London's longest-standing ratepayer, having occupied

216 the Strand since 1706.

Its long narrow hallway is garlanded with teas of all kinds, giving it an addictive aroma. This might at least divert our attention from the fact that Devereux Court was named after Robert Devereux, the 2nd Earl of Essex, who led a failed coup against the government of Elizabeth I and was executed for treason. He would have been better advised to have expressed his differences with the monarch in a coffee house.

236: THE WANDERING MUSEUM

The Museum of London is a wanderer among museums. It is currently situated in the Barbican but will transfer soon to a much better site at Smithfield market itself a kind of museum - of meat - which will move to an outlying location at Barking Reach.

We think of museums as staying put in the same place to give an impression of unchanging solidity but not this one. The London Museum as it was then called - and is soon to be recalled - started life on April 8, 1912 in temporary accommodation on the second floor of Kensington Palace. Its aim was to illustrate the colourful history of London. It attracted 13,000 visitors on its first day.

That arrangement lasted two years after which the collection was moved to Lancaster House on the edge of The Green Park, in a huge royal mansion - built for Frederick, Prince of Wales in 1736. It was and is a sumptuous mansion (photo below) clearly influenced by Louis 14th's Versailles and it is easy to believe the story that Queen Victoria remarked to the 2nd Duchess of Sutherland on arriving at what was then called Stafford House: "I have come from my House to your Palace."

The lease was later purchased for the nation in 1913 by Lord Leverhulme, a soap magnate and Lancastrian, who gave it a new name, Lancaster House, to reflect his northern origins. The first Keeper of the museum was

Sir Guy Francis Laking, who had shown an early interest in museum artefacts by writing an essay on The Sword of Joan of Arc when he was only 10 years old. From 1926 until 1944 the Keeper was the celebrity archaeologist Mortimer Wheeler.

During World War II, much of the museum's collection was moved underground for safety to Dover Street tube station nearby, and later to Piccadilly Circus tube station. Some of the galleries at Lancaster House reopened to the public in 1942, despite the war but in November 1943 the building was requisitioned by the Ministry of Works as a conference centre.

Having failed to establish Lancaster House as its permanent home the London Museum was once more on its pass-the-parcel manoeuvres. After the war in 1948 George VI agreed for the museum to go back to Kensington Palace from Lancaster House to be housed in the two lower floors. Another resident of Lancaster House had better luck. The Government's extensive wine collection - itself a museum of sorts - remained at Lancaster House and is still there today.

In July, 1951 the moveable museum duly reopened at Kensington Palace but was rather overshadowed by the extraordinary success of the Festival of Britain on the south bank of the Thames.

In 1975, in its biggest move, the London Museum was amalgamated with the City of London's Guildhall Museum and rebranded to form the Museum of London. In December, 1976 it opened to the public in a new building at the Barbican in the City of London. That had an air of permanence about it.

But not for long. The museum is in the midst of planning to move its collection, now more than six million objects (many in storage), to nearby Smithfield Market as long as it can raise the remaining millions.

At its new site in Smithfield - originally called Smoothfield because of the flat terrain - the London Museum will be starting a new era in its history but also bringing to an end another one as the meat market, which dates from the 10th century, has been in continuous operation since medieval times.

The new museum will be standing on a deep reservoir of history, the site of the execution of Wat Tyler, the leader of the Peasants' Revolt, and the Scottish hero William Wallace. It was also the location of Bartholomew Fair which lasted nearly 700 years before being closed in 1855. It will be fascinating to see how these memories are integrated into the new museum, hopefully before it is on the move yet again.

237: THE CENTURY-LONG WAIT FOR WILLIAM III'S STATUE IN ST JAMES'S SQUARE

St James's Square, just north of Pall Mall, was built by Henry Jermyn, Earl of St Albans and the man credited with inventing the West End of London. In 1661 he had been given a lease by Charles II to build on what had previously been mostly open land. The square was constructed, unashamedly, to attract residents of quality – the nobility and gentry – likely to attend on the king. In the early 18th century, six dukes and seven earls lived there and, over time, 15 Prime Ministers, including three in the same house (not all at the same time). The east, north and west sides of the square contained some of the most desirable homes in London.

In the centre of the square today is a statue of King William III, Protestant hero and, from birth, Prince of Orange. He became king in 1689 after the overthrow of the Catholic James II in the so-called Glorious Revolution. It was unusual but unsurprising that the proposal to erect a statue in William's honour in the square was made soon after, in 1697: unusual because he was still

alive, unsurprising because many of his strongest supporters lived there. The official notice board tells us that it was not finally erected until 1808. Could that be a misprint? Could it possibly have taken 111 years to put up a statue?

The answer is yes. Money, as usual, was part of the problem. William died in 1702 from pneumonia, which he contracted following a hunting accident. His horse apparently tripped over a mole-hill, a mishap depicted by the statue (bottom photo, opposite). But a series of attempts to fund a memorial failed. A solution seemed to have been found in 1724 when Samuel Travers MP left a bequest in his will for an equestrian statue "to the glorious memory of my master William the Third" to be built either in St James's Square or in Cheapside. However, no one was able to agree about the details.

In 1728, an ornamental basin of water 150 feet in diameter was installed

in the square, and in 1732 a pedestal followed – but still no statue. In 1739 one was apparently commissioned from Henry Cheere, his brother John Cheere, or maybe both. Made from lead, it depicted William on a horse which, for whatever reason, never managed to gallop to St James's Square.

It may be the mounted likeness of William that today can be seen in Petersfield. Other statues of William can be found in Kingston-upon-Hull, Glasgow, Bristol, Portsmouth, Ireland (north and south), Amsterdam and in Kensington Palace, the latter an ill-timed present from Kaiser Wilhelm II, who went on to lead Germany against the allies in World War I.

Lamberts history and survey of London claims that during the Gordon Riots of 1780 the mob threw the keys of Newgate Prison into the water in the square, and that they weren't found until several years later. Not until 1794 was a William statue for St James's Square at last successfully commissioned. The task was given to distinguished sculptor John Bacon Senior, who inconveniently died before he could fulfil it. However, the statue was eventually completed by Bacon's son, John Junior, using his father's design and cast in bronze.

Where the money came from is still a bit of a mystery. The antiquary John Timbs tells us it was not erected until 1808 because "the bequest in 1724 [presumably the Travers donation] for the cost having been forgotten, until the money was found in the list of unclaimed dividends".

The statue, Grade I listed, still stands serenely among the plane trees (the basin of water is long gone). Bacon Senior

was influenced by the equestrian statue of William in Bristol produced by the Flemish sculptor John Rysbrack, who also created Isaac Newton's monument in Westminster Abbey. As in Rysbrack's piece, the William in St James's Square is portrayed as if he were a Roman general holding a baton in his right hand.

No one seems to know why Bacon's work took so long to build. Perhaps there should be a special category for it in the Guinness Book of Records. It surely won't mind waiting.

238: BEAUTIFUL BRIDGEWATER HOUSE

They don't make mansions like Bridgewater House anymore. It is one of three palatial edifices – the others are Spencer House and Lancaster House – almost side by side facing Green Park from Cleveland Row in what may be the last stand of the great aristocratic residences.

The entrance to it is also one of the best-known in the country, as its facade was used as the set for scenes shot outside the fictitious Grantham House, London residence of the Crawley family in the Downton Abbey TV series.

Yet few people have seen the inside of Bridgewater House, which is owned by the Latsis family, led by Spiro Latsis, an LSE-educated Greek businessman, and not open to the public except on exceptional occasions: even the Downtown cast and crew were, apparently, not allowed in.

The building's current Palazzo-style design was by Sir Charles Barry, dating from 1840, although different versions have been on the site for much longer and Bridgewater House did not acquire its present name until 1854, when it was owned by Lord Ellesmere, heir of Francis Egerton, 3rd Duke of Bridgewater. The house had been in the Egerton family since 1700.

Ellesmere had the unusual distinction of having an island named after him, one almost as big as Great Britain.

I was lucky enough to see inside the mansion some years ago with the Thorney Island Society. Walking through the front door you are almost blown over by what you see. Instead of a hallway to a private residence you are immediately propelled into The Grand Saloon. It looks like the entrance to the Reform Club in Pall Mall, which is not surprising as Barry designed that too, as well as the Houses of Parliament. The big difference is that the Reform Club is smaller.

Standing on the million-pound carpet and looking skywards towards the glass roof, your eye is caught by a ring of domes, half of which turn out to be mirror images.

At one end of the ground floor is a set of murals by Jakob Götzenberger depicting scenes from Comus, a masque in honour of chastity commissioned

by the Egerton family from the celebrated poet John Milton and performed in 1634 at Ludlow Castle before John Egerton, the 1st Earl of Bridgewater to celebrate his appointment as Lord President of Wales. Part of the mural depicts the Earl talking to Milton, who lived for part of his life in nearby Petty France. To make sure posterity did not forget him, Ellesmere left dozens of sets of his initials at strategic points throughout the house.

The first dwelling on this site was called Berkshire House and built around 1626 for Thomas Howard, second son of the Earl of Suffolk and later Earl of Berkshire. In the 1670s it was given by Charles II to Barbara Villiers, one of his most notorious mistresses, who became the Duchess of Cleveland. She rebuilt and extended the property and called it Cleveland House.

It is sometimes claimed that the outline of the foundations of the Cleveland mansion can still be seen in the front garden of Bridgewater House, if the climatic conditions are right. The photo of the garden below was taken during this year's drought. Whether it bears out the claim is left to your imagination.

Bridgewater House once hosted the biggest private art collection in London with over 300 works, including masterpieces by Raphael, Titian and Palma Vecchio, some of them from the famed Orleans collection. The gallery was opened in 1803 and could be visited on Wednesday afternoons during several months in the summer.

But there was a catch: you had to be recommended by friends of the family or be an artist endorsed by a member of the Royal Academy. The photo above is believed to be from around 1900. The collection was eventually dispersed, but some of the works can still be seen in the National Gallery in London or the National Gallery of Scotland.

London should be grateful that a historic dwelling like Bridgewater House has been restored at private expense, but it is also inescapably sad that a gem like this is not more open to the public.

239: MONMOUTH HOUSE

Soho Square was built during the reign of Charles II and originally called King Square, though not in honour of the sovereign. It was named after Gregory King who, in the 17th century, was mainly responsible for laying out the streets and squares in an area previously known as Soho Fields.

This was a political square. If St James's Square, close to St James's Palace, the home of Charles's younger brother James – the Duke of York and heir apparent – was Tory Town, packed with Tory supporters of a hereditary monarchy, then Soho Square was Whigsville.

It was intended to be a safe haven for the nobility, particularly the Whig nobility, who wanted a Protestant successor to Charles, not James, who had converted to Catholicism. Noble Whig families, such as the Bedfords, controlled much of the land in the area.

The most important building in Soho Square was Monmouth House. It was big, occupying the whole of the south side (arrowed opposite) and the land between what have been known since that time as Greek Street and Frith Street, which was named after Richard Frith, one of its builders. This extravaganza was created for James Scott, otherwise known as the

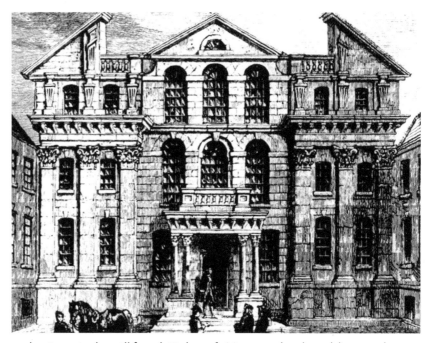

charismatic but ill-fated Duke of Monmouth, the eldest and most senior of Charles's 14 illegitimate children.

Scott was very rich, a successful soldier and very popular, at least with Whigs and the populace at large. If the Whigs had succeeded in preventing James from succeeding Charles II – they failed, as in February 1685 he became James II – then Monmouth, though he never said so in public, would have been a candidate for King, or at least for the role of the most dominant noble despite his illegitimacy. He owed his wealth to lavish gifts bestowed on him by his father.

The Duke rarely lived at Monmouth House. He and his wife Anna had plenty of other places in which to linger, including Colman Hedge Close, a large estate nearby which was his domain as King Charles's Master of the Horse. His main London residence was the original Palace of Westminster, off today's Whitehall.

Further afield there was Windsor Castle, which he greatly expanded, plus Chiswick House and Moor House at Rickmansworth 14 miles away, which he restored. Oh, and he also bought a house in Bishopsgate in order to promote the Whig cause among the City's businessmen.

Why on Earth with all these homes did he need Monmouth House as well, even though he got a surprisingly good deal out if it? The architectural historian Sir Simon Thurley points out that the house contained several large rooms that were constructed not as reception rooms but as meeting places for Whig sympathisers. It was all part of the geography of politics at that time.

After James's accession it was all downhill for Monmouth. Having been linked to plots to seize the throne he'd been forced to flee abroad. Now, he did indeed attempt to become King. His small army landed at Lyme Regis with a handful of supporters. He attracted several thousand more as he marched hesitantly towards London, but they were poorly trained and on 6 July 1685. He was easily defeated by the Crown's forces at the Battle of Sedgemoor near Bridgwater.

The captured Monmouth was brutally executed without trial on Tower Hill on 15 July 1685, Parliament having passed an Act of Attainder sentencing him to death as a traitor. His followers were also sentenced to death or transported to distant lands by the notorious Judge Jeffries.

After Monmouth's death his house in Soho Square entered a period of slow decline. Its various owners included his wife the Duchess who bought it outright in 1698 only to sell it in 1716 to Sir James Bateman, Lord Mayor of London and sub governor of the South Sea Company.

Bateman died the following year but the house remained in his family, whose name is remembered thanks to Bateman's Buildings, which stand on the site of the great house, and Bateman Street, which crosses Frith Street.

By 1770 Soho Square was in decline as fashionable people moved westwards. Monmouth House had become a white elephant and was dismantled in 1773 for redevelopment. It might have changed the course of history – but it didn't.

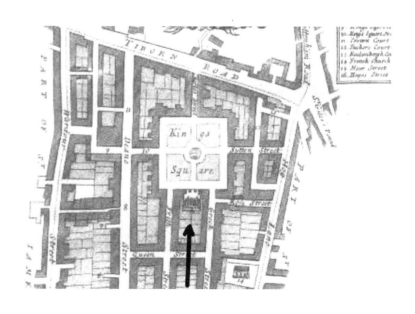

240: HENRY VIII'S PERSONAL PALACE OF WESTMINSTER

Every day thousands of people travel through a street in central London unaware that it is the site of what is almost certainly the biggest single part of Lost London.

Of all the buildings that have been disappeared from the capital none can compete – at least in size – with Henry VIII's Palace of Whitehall. He moved there in 1529 after the royal apartments of the old, medieval Palace of Westminster, were destroyed by fire in 1512.

Henry's new home occupied both sides of the street we now call Whitehall and stretched from today's Parliament Square almost all the way to Charing Cross. It became the monarch's main residence and, in historian Simon Thurley's words, "the epicentre of the main events in England for nearly two centuries".

The palace dominated the entire area, and its startling 1,500 rooms made it bigger than the Vatican and, initially, Louis XIV's Versailles. It was also much uglier although, in fairness, Louis had the advantage of planning from scratch whereas Henry's palace was assembled in a spatchcock way from York Place, which he sequestered from Cardinal Wolsey.

In addition to government offices, hospitality functions and dwellings for nobles it included a bowling green, a cockpit – located behind today's number 70 Whitehall – a tennis court and a jousting yard in what is now Horse Guards Parade.

The Victorian historian Augustus J Hare reminds us that Henry obtained an act of parliament stating that "the entire space between Charing Cross and the sanctuary at Westminster, from the Thames on the east side to the park wall westward, should from henceforth be deemed the Kings whole Palace of Westminster". Bad luck if you owned a house in the way.

And what is visible of it today? Nothing at all, apart from Inigo Jones's majestic Banqueting Hall, which was added in 1607, and the remnants of Queen Mary II's steps to the Thames (above) which are a 1691 redesign by Christopher Wren of a Tudor original.

The only original bits that have survived are out of the public eye. The most dramatic is Wolsey's wine cellar – appropriated by Henry along with the Cardinal's other property – which has been preserved, somewhat bizarrely, under the Ministry of Defence building in Horse Guards Avenue. Sadly, it is not open to the public unless you have a bit of luck. Part of the wall of Henry's tennis court has been incorporated into the wall of the Treasury building, whose bowels also contain a reconstructed cockpit.

Looking at the 1570 Agas map above you get a good idea what Whitehall was like in those days. Two gatehouses straddled the road to connect the eastern and western parts of the palace. Holbein Gate to the north was reckoned to have been more picturesque than the Westminster Gate to the south.

Historians write mainly about architecture and governance activity of Henry's Westminster palace, but rarely about the people who lived there, servicing the royal court and the adjacent Abbey. If they wanted to get to the village of Charing they would have had to walk through the palace and between the two gateways.

There was no other option, as Henry had appropriated St James's Park for his own use, including a leper hospital purchased from Eton College (which later became St James's Palace). The only alternative was to pay for a wherry to take you along the Thames.

Whitehall Palace met a sorry end in 1698 when it, like the previous royal residence, was burned down after a servant aired linen too close to a fire. Two dwellings of the monarch going up in flames looks a bit spooked. However, key parts of the first palace Henry had to vacate are still there.

The marvellous Westminster Hall, started by William Rufus and blessed with what is believed still to be the biggest hammer beam roof in the world, is still there in all its glory, as is Edward III's Jewel Tower, now home to a fine outdoor café as well as a bijoux museum.

Both stand on Thorney Island, formed by the confluence of the River Tyburn, now lost underground in the sewage system, but which still rolls down from the Hampstead hills to meet the Thames. Also on Thorney Island are the Houses of Parliament in today's Palace of Westminster, Westminster Abbey and Westminster School. It is arguably the biggest concentration of history in the country.

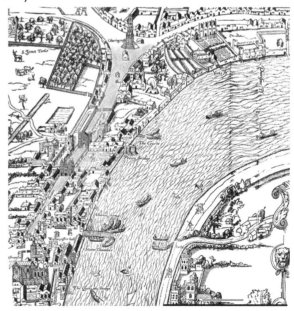

241: THE AMAZING JOSEPH HANSOM AND HIS FAMOUS CAB

Victorian London was awash with Hansom cabs. Some estimates say there were 7,000 of them in the capital, admired in fiction as well as as fact. Hansoms were Sherlock Holmes's preferred mode of transport when he was out on a case because they were fast, stable and could hold two people comfortably. And there was a bit of magic in their looks. G. K. Chesterton's novel The Man Who Was Thursday has a chase scene with all of the participants in Hansom cabs, and Robert Louis Stevenson wrote a story entitled The Adventure of the Hansom Cab.

This iconic bit of Victoriana was invented by Joseph Hansom, whose achievements are surprisingly little known today. He was born in York but lived in London for much of his life at 27 Sumner Place, off the Fulham Road, where there is a plaque to commemorate him.

The first Hansom cab journey took place in 1835 in Hinckley, Leicestershire, where the Hansom family was living at the time. The stability and relative safety of the cabs made them an international success story. They soon spread from England to Berlin, Paris and New York and prospered for nearly a hundred years until the arrival of the motor car in the early part of the 20th century.

Helen Monger, writing for Historic England, tells us that by 1927 there remained just 12 Hansoms licensed in London, and that the last London Hansom driver turned in his in 1947.

She adds, however: "One consolation for Joseph was that 'Hansom' became a household name in his own lifetime and he was able to see the impact his invention had on society. It is still remembered today as an essential part of Victorian life."

But memories don't always make money, as Hansom knew to his cost. He was a curiously doomed genius. Three of his major projects were hugely successful. but he didn't profit from any of them.

He sold the patent for the Hansom cab for £10,000 – a lot in those days – to a company that was in such financial difficulties that he didn't get paid. Maybe Holmes should have investigated. With a colleague he also designed the pioneering Birmingham Town Hall, undercutting rival designs by Charles Barry, the future Houses of Parliament architect, and Sir John Soane, designer of the Bank of England building.

Birmingham's was one of the first great municipal town halls. It is generally described as Roman revival in style, but which looks more

like the Acropolis on wheels (photo right). It was, and still is, an architectural success, but overspending on it led to Hansom's bankruptcy.

His third success was something I have been using for years without knowing who was behind it. In 1843 he founded and launched the distinguished The Builder magazine, bought by architects, builders and workmen. It is still with us today, although in 1966 its name was changed to Building. It claims to be the only journal to cover the entire building industry and has an extensive archive.

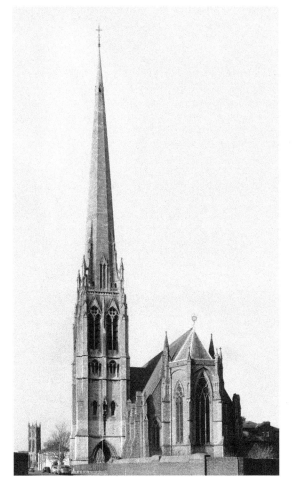

Alas, Hansom's involvement with The Builder had a sad ending. He deserves credit for devising and launching it, but he soon ran out of capital and had to give up the editorship. However, architect George Godwin, editor from 1844 to 1883, turned The Builder into one of the most successful professional papers of its kind.

These three achievements alone should be enough to guarantee Hansom's place in history, and they weren't the only ones. He designed nearly 200 buildings in all. Many of them were Roman Catholic places of worship, including Plymouth Cathedral.

My favourite, by a distance, is the Gothic revival church of St Walburge's in Preston. That is not because of its London connections – its hammer-beam roof was inspired by Westminster Hall and the bells came from the now sadly defunct Whitechapel Foundry. Nor is it because of the appealing quirkiness of its design. The church spire, according to Wikipedia and other sources – and who am I to argue? – was apparently made from railway sleepers, which had formerly carried the nearby Preston and Longridge Railway.

What amazes me is its height. At over 100 yards it is the tallest spire of any parish church in the country and seems to evaporate into the sky. I get vertigo just looking at the photo.

242: A RADICAL EXPERIMENT IN PIMLICO

Grosvenor Road in Pimlico is celebrated mainly for two things: it is where Dolphin Square, once the biggest apartment block in Europe, stands on a site which was previously the location of the works of Thomas Cubitt, the builder and developer who constructed most of Pimlico.

However, between Cubitt's death in 1855 and the creation of Dolphin Square in the 1930s, something else rather special was located there, which is in danger of being forgotten – a huge clothing factory and warehouse complex whose workers, most of them women, were employed under far better conditions than had been usual.

The Royal Army Clothing Depot began to be formed in Pimlico from 1859, when the War Office moved its storage facility there from its previous base in Northamptonshire. In 1863 this was joined by a new factory for manufacturing military uniforms, which by the end of the decade had fully replaced one established in Woolwich in 1856. In 1887, the complex was renamed the Royal Army Clothing Department. It operated until 1932 as its lease came to an end.

Prior to 1855, clothing for the British infantry and cavalry was, bizarrely, supplied by army Colonels who, along with agents, took a commission – basically a rake-off – for supplying uniforms for their men. It was a system designed to generate large profits for the Colonels and misery for the workers producing the clothes.

In 1849, Henry Mayhew, the great social reformer who collected testimony from the workers involved, commented, "I have seen people so overwhelmed in suffering, and so used to privations of the keenest kind, that they had almost forgotten to complain of them". Mayhew concluded: "If the Government would take it into their hands, and give the clothes out themselves, the poor work-people might have prices that would keep them from starving."

The Queen newspaper observed that before 1857, "all the clothes for the British army were made by contractors, whose first thought seemed to be how to amass a fortune at the expense of the makers and the wearers of the clothes primarily, and of the British public indirectly".

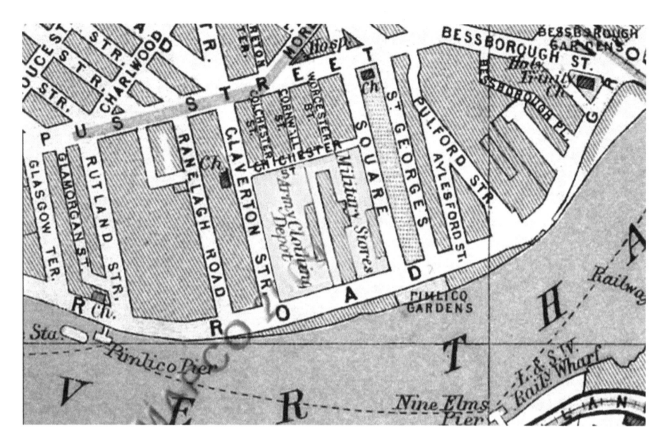

Around 2,000 people were employed at Pimlico, of whom 1700 were women, in premises that covered about seven acres. An 1871 Factory Inspector's Report by Alexander Redgrave described the factory in glowing terms, saying it was "in many respects one of the most remarkable factories in the country" and of a totally different kind from "those grand establishments upon which money has been lavishly spent by a merchant prince."

Redgrave pointed to the huge improvement in conditions compared to the contract system: "One cannot help feeling what an enormous amount of happiness this establishment has promoted in rescuing hundreds of women from the miseries and trammels of the contract system, under which they starved for so many years." In 1884 one commentator (unspecified) went even further, describing the factory as a model employer "being the largest and best of its type in the world".

The principal aim of the factory, according to Redgrave, was "getting the most for your money." Everything, he said, had to show that clothes made in a government establishment could be produced better and more cheaply than elsewhere. This was quite an achievement considering the notoriously low wages in the private sector.

The closure of the factory and depot also marked the end of a remarkable experiment – to make way for a block of luxury flats.

243: ST STEPHEN WALBROOK, THE CHURCH OF ENDLESS INNOVATION

If ever a church was built on superlatives, it is this one. One architectural historian, Sir John Summerson, described it as "the pride of English architecture". Another, Nikolaus Pevsner, listed it as one of the ten most important buildings in England. And the great Italian sculptor Antonio Canova, creator of The Three Graces, apparently told English architect Lord Burlington, "We have nothing like this in Rome."

The man who built the church took particular care, because it was in his parish. He lived in the same street, just yards away at 15 Walbrook. He also used it as a dry run for a much bigger project he was working on at the time – St Paul's Cathedral.

The masterpiece that is St Stephen Walbrook is well-loved by devotees of Christopher Wren but surprisingly little-known to Londoners at large. It is hidden behind the Mansion House and a shade unprepossessing from the outside apart from its spire, which was probably added by Nicholas Hawksmoor.

However, once you negotiate the steps, put there because the church had to be protected from the waters of the River Walbrook – which still runs underneath the pedestrianised street outside, past Cannon Street Station to the Thames at Dowgate – you are in for a surprise.

The domed splendour of the interior has a near-mesmerising effect, and Henry Moore's sculpted stone altar of travertine marble (below), framed by Patrick Heron's colourful kneelers, brings a subtle note of modernism into this historic setting.

That is no surprise. St Stephen and its antecedents have always moved with the times. An earlier church was built on the other side of the Walbrook at least as far back as the late 11th Century on the ruins of the Roman Temple of Mithras. This was in keeping with a custom of the times – an attempt to smother the site's heathen heritage.

In 1428 a new and bigger church was built 20 metres away on the other side of the river where Wren's St Stephen stands. Past one end of it ran Bearbinder Lane, the source of the Great Plague of 1665. There is a plaque inside the present church honouring Nathaniel Hodges, the only doctor in the area who stayed with his patients during the pestilence. The following year the 15th Century church was completely destroyed by the Great Fire of London. The only benefit of that terrible tragedy was that Wren designed its successor.

A more recent move with the times occurred in 1953 when Chad Varah, the church's Anglican rector, founded The Samaritans, the world's first

crisis helpline for those in suicidal distress. The bakelite phone used when the service started is kept in a glass case at the back of the church.

The church's most recent innovation came in 2006 when the London London Internet Church, a global community that meets online, was founded there. Although an integral part of the Diocese of London, it is based at St Stephen. Before that, the church allowed a branch of Starbuck's to be attached to it. This is not unique – there is another one adjoining Hawksmoor's St Mary Woolnoth a few hundred yards away – but it is certainly unusual.

The decision was taken by Varah, who died in 2007, because he needed the money to finance the expansion of The Samaritans. Who can argue with that? It was a controversial move at the time, but turned out to be a marriage made in Heaven. The Samaritans have collected lots of stars and the church has brought in bucks.

244: THE HIDDEN HISTORY OF CLERKENWELL'S RED BULL THEATRE

If you stroll along St John Street in Clerkenwell near its junction with Aylesbury Street, there is an archway that leads to an alley called Hayward's Place. Tread nostalgically, for this is the site of the Red Bull theatre that flourished, not without controversy, from the reign of James I in 1606 throughout the Civil War and its aftermath, a period which saw the complete closure of most of the other London theatres until the Restoration in 1660. A recently-installed plaque high up on a wall reminds passers-by of the Red Bull's hidden history. The arch may well be where the original entrance to the theatre was.

We have been living through an extraordinary period of archaeological discovery, which has seen the buried remains of Shakespearean theatres such as the Rose Playhouse on Bankside and the Curtain in Shoreditch revealed. But no one has yet got round to unearthing the Red Bull. That is largely because it has been completely built over, but also because it was never considered to be in the same league as the others – its performances and its audiences were thought too rumbustious and even vulgar.

The Red Bull's reputation may have had something to do with being situated along St John Street, where cattle were driven to Smithfield market through an area as famous for its brothels and prisons as its religious houses. Its reputation is in the process of reappraisal though, thanks mainly to research by Dr Eva Griffith, whose book, A Jacobean Company and its Playhouse, argues convincingly that the theatre's low status was during its later period, following ten years of being the home of Queen Anne of Denmark's Men, a parallel group to Shakespeare's troupe The Kings' Men. Anne was the wife of James I, and therefore unlikely to have lent her name to anything too unsavoury.

Griffith also claims that the Red Bull had a larger capacity than the famous Globe theatre, which could hold nearly 3,000 spectators. It was a converted inn yard in the open air rather than a purpose-built theatre like the Globe or the Rose. Anne's men also performed for a while at the new indoor Cockpit theatre in Drury Lane, which opened in 1616, though with mixed results.

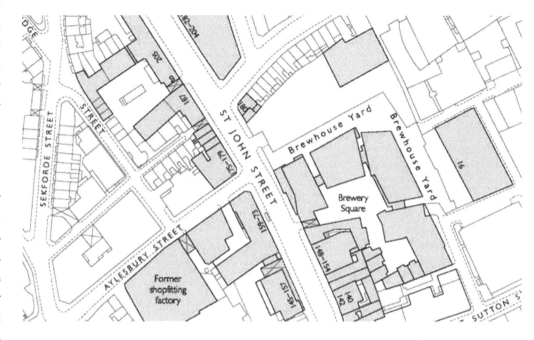

Shakespeare didn't write for the Red Bull, but many of his still-esteemed contemporaries did, including Thomas Heywood, John Webster and Thomas Dekker, and it is clear that his plays were performed there, because history records that in 1627 this was ordered to cease.

With the monarchy back on the throne, the theatre reverted to putting on crowd-pleasers such as William Rowley's All's Lost by Lust. Samuel Pepys observed (in March 1661) that it was "poorly done, with...much disorder". Things got even worse when the Red Bull started staging prize fights and fencing in a forlorn attempt to woo punters back. It petered out in the mid-1660s, outliving the Globe and the Rose, but only by morphing into a parody of its former self.

Are there any remains waiting to be dug up? Heather Knight, a senior archaeologist at the Museum of London, who has been heavily involved in the excavation of other theatres, thinks the Red Bull site is interesting. The buildings now on it are, she says, 18th or early 19th century: "It is possible remains exist beneath them, but it also depends on how the Red Bull ended its life. Was it demolished to ground level or was it re-used in a later building?"

Some Elizabethan and Jacobean playhouses have been lost without trace, such as the biggest of them all, the Swan by Blackfriars Bridge. That is because office blocks with deep foundations were built on top of them at a time before regulations required archaeological surveys to take place after old buildings were demolished. There are no plans for an office block on the site of the Red Bull theatre, but, who knows, maybe it would make a tempting investment for a drinks company of the same name.

245: WHERE TO FIND SOME REAL OLD HOLBORN

The timbered building on the south side of High Holborn known as Staple Inn, famous for being pictured on Old Holborn tobacco packets (below, right), is often presumed to be an intact survivor of Tudor London. Not really. Though listed and of Tudor origin, it has become an example of what archaeologists call "virtually modern fakes", with the beams and woodwork put in comparatively recently as part of a reconstruction following wartime bomb damage.

If you want to see a bit of really old Holborn, walk a few yards down the road towards Fetter Lane to a small doorway marked Barnard's Inn (below, left), which dates back to at least 1400. It sports signs on either side saying "Gresham College", revealing it to be the home of a unique educational institution which is still going strong after over 400 years.

Barnard's Inn, like Staple Inn, was one of the old Inns of Chancery – sort of prep schools for lawyers wanting to join one of the Inns of Court, such as Lincoln's Inn. Within, stands Barnard's Inn Hall, whose structure today is much as it was in the 15th century.

Bernard's Inn hall interior circa 1400

The hall is all that remains of the mansion of John Mackworth, the Dean Of Lincoln who died in 1451. Archaeologist John Schofield describes it as "the only surviving medieval secular timber structure of domestic scale in the City". The roof timbers contain the last crown posts, a specialised wood structure, in the whole of London.

Mackworth left the whole of the property to the Dean and Chapter of Lincoln, which subsequently leased it to a man called Lionel Barnard, from whom it takes its name. It was converted into an Inn of Chancery soon after, attached to Gray's Inn. Not everyone was an admirer. Charles Dickens allowed his character Pip to lodge at Barnard's Inn in Great Expectations, where it is dismissed it as "the dingiest collection of shabby buildings ever squeezed together, in a rank corner, as a club for Tom-cats."

Gresham College was founded separately in 1597 under the will of the amazing Sir Thomas Gresham in order to provide free public lectures for anyone who wants to hear them and has continued to do so throughout its long and distinguished history. It is, though, a recent arrival at Barnard's Inn – lectures began there in 1991. The college was originally in Bishopsgate, where Tower 42 – formerly the Nat West Tower – was later built, and it had a number of other homes before arriving at its present one.

If you want to see Barnard's Hall, one of the ways is to simply turn up at a lecture, though they are sometimes moved to the Museum of London if they become too popular. These days, they are also live streamed and available afterwards from the college archive and on YouTube. It is an astonishing educational resource, which is still not widely known about.

Another venerable repository of learning, the Royal Society – whose early members included Robert Boyle, Robert Hooke and Christopher Wren – was founded at Gresham College in 1660 and also still going strong.

Gresham himself was an extremely rich and powerful man – among other things he built the Royal Exchange, London's first stock market – and although his reputation is being re-appraised in the light of how he made his money, there is no doubt about the huge contribution he made to London.

246: BLOOMSBURY'S WONDROUS CHURCH SPIRE

It is easy to mistake St George's church in Bloomsbury Way for a spire with a church hanging underneath it. Nicholas Hawksmoor's English baroque masterpiece, consecrated in 1730, was necessarily constructed in cramped surroundings, because there were already buildings on either side. That is why from most approaches, and especially from the British Museum, all you see is the spire until you arrive at the church itself.

But what spire! It is a building in its own right. Its sculptures of lions and unicorns – two of each, all recent recreations of the originals standing more than ten feet high – represent the conflict between Jacobites and the Crown. Far above them stands a statue of George – not Saint George, the founding father of the church, but King George I, the reigning monarch of the time.

The only statue of that King George in London, it looks almost like a case of product placement, as it is highly unusual to have a monarch on top of a church, let alone one dressed in a Roman toga bestriding a stretched pyramid above a mini-temple (photo right). Not even Henry VIII thought of

Photograph by Tony Hisgett.

that. Unsurprisingly, the Church Commissioners were reluctant to pay for such a frivolous work, but eventually gave way. It is, to say the least, distinctive.

Most people first come across the spire unknowingly when they look at William Hogarth's famous apocalyptical painting Gin Lane (1751). It is a picture of a city imploding under the effects of cheap gin, thanks to William of Orange's promotion of Dutch spirits. But it also shows a beacon of hope in the background – yes, it is the spire of St George's.

The church was partly built in order that the "better sort" could have a place of worship away from the nearby St Giles, which was right in the middle of the rookery of which Gin Lane was a part. This was not a convenient place for the carriages of the affluent, who were arriving in droves at newly-fashionable Bloomsbury, to linger.

One of the numerous people to be fascinated by Hawksmoor's spire was the artist J M W Turner. He used his own drawings of it to illustrate the first perspective lecture he gave at the Royal Academy in January 1811, which discussed the effect of viewing the spire from the ground at different angles.

Hawksmoor dug into an escapist past with this spire. It is based on one of the Seven Wonders of the World, the Mausoleum of King Mausolus at Halicarnassus in Turkey, or at least Pliny the Elder's description of it. The building, 140 feet in height, was not finished when Halicarnassus died, but the sculptors and masons carried on to complete the job. It dominated the surrounding area for some seventeen centuries until a series of earthquakes in the 13th century destroyed it. But it lived on in name, because Mausolous became the generic name for grandiose memorials or mausoleums.

What is less well known is that this Wonder of the World also lives on in a very physical sense only a couple of hundred yards from Hawksmoor's church. That is because, by happenstance or psychogeography – take your choice – huge statues from the mausoleum (above, right) have ended up in the British Museum, which was opened just 30 years after St George's.

247: THE MEDIEVAL GEMS OF THE LONDON CHARTERHOUSE

Hiding behind the gatehouse and wall of the Charterhouse, located between the Barbican and Smithfield on Charterhouse Square, lies one of the capital's least known and most magnificent medieval gems.

The surprise is that it is there at all. A remarkable amount of the original Charterhouse building, a monastery for Carthusian monks built in 1371 on land which had seen over 50,000 burials during the Black Death of 1348, has survived later plagues, aristocratic reconstructions, bomb damage in the Blitz and, above all, the Dissolution, which saw many monasteries sold off to Henry VIII's cronies, who often pulled them down.

All the others – such as the Blackfriars and Greyfriars monasteries and the Priory of St John, along with St Mary's Nunnery – have been lost almost without trace, leaving remnants within Westminster Abbey as the only other parts of a monastery from the medieval era above ground.

Charterhouse's longevity may be partly thanks to its being acquired in 1545 by Sir Edward (later Lord) North,

following the monastery's dissolution in 1537. North had been Chancellor of the Court of Augmentations, and was therefore responsible for selling monastic land and properties. He pulled down parts of the Charterhouse complex, including its church, some cloisters and other reminders of Catholicism, building in their place a beautiful Great Hall and adjoining Great Chamber, which are star attractions of the Charterhouse today. But he also left much of it standing.

The property's next owner was Thomas Howard, 4th Duke of Norfolk – later executed for his part in the Ridolfi plot to put Mary, Queen of Scots on the throne – who transformed the remains of the religious house to complete a magnificent mansion, fit to entertain royalty. And so it did: Elizabeth I and James I both held court in the Great Chamber.

Today, the Great Hall (right), which looks as if it has been stolen from an Oxbridge college, provides meals for the Charterhouse's community of residents – its Brothers and Sisters, single people aged over 60 in financial and social need who live in the almshouse there. The Charterhouse is still a charity and any lay person can apply to be a Brother or Sister, as long as they meet the requirements of age and pecuniary circumstances. They can then occupy a building covering most of the footprint of the old monastery.

There have, of course, been changes and additions to the original monastery fabric – including a long terrace added by Howard known as the Norfolk Cloister – but parts of the monks' quarters are just as they were, and much original stone was probably re-used when alterations were made.

The Carthusians, in a sense, lived a privileged existence. They took a vow of silence, and their clothing "consisted of two hair-cloths, two cowls, two pairs of hose, and a cloak, all of the coarsest manufacture, contrived to almost disfigure their persons". However, their cells were more like cottages – two storeys high with four rooms, complete with a garden and fresh water piped from local sources at a time when the rest of the population had to battle with polluted water.

The Carthusians were known as "good monks" as they didn't succumb to worldly temptations like some other orders (though, curiously, today's monastery is next door to a Malmaison hotel). Their goodness reached unscalable heights when they refused to recognise Henry VIII as head of the Catholic Church. The prior, John Houghton, and six others were hanged, drawn and quartered. Houghton's head was severed and affixed to London Bridge as a warning to others and a limb impaled on the gatehouse of the monastery.

The Norfolk cloister (below), which used to be twice as long as it is now, is one of the delights of the Charterhouse. It still harbours one of the original monk's cells, complete with stone serving hatch

This cloister was later used for playing football by the boys of the original Charterhouse School, built in 1611. The Charterhouse claims, with some justification, to have played a leading role in creating the rules of the game, including the offside rule and skills such as the art of dribbling, which was honed among the confined cloisters (photo below). As Simon Inglis points out in his marvellous book Played in London: "If the ball exited through one of the [cloister] openings, the first player to leap out and 'touch' it won the right to throw it back in."

It would need a book to chronicle all the famous people who have passed through The Charterhouse. They include Thomas More, John Wesley, William Makepeace Thackeray, Prime Minister the Earl of Liverpool, Simon Raven and Roger Williams, the founder of Rhode Island . There is also a rolling cast of aristocrats, but it was a member of the nouveau riches who left the biggest mark on these hallowed remains.

Thomas Sutton was the richest commoner in Britain. He purchased the Charterhouse in 1611 as a home for his almshouse and the school, which later relocated to Godalming. Sutton died soon becoming the owner, but the Charterhouse rapidly became the wealthiest institution of its kind in Europe. It aimed to prove the superiority of Protestant good works over Roman Catholic practices.

Sutton started his working life as the servant of two powerful aristocrats in Tudor England and ended up so rich he lent money to them. Where did it come from? He owned the biggest coal mines in the north-east of England in County Durham and as a moneylender charged as much as 10 per cent in interest. Nonetheless, Daniel Defoe, author of Robinson Crusoe, praised Sutton's endowment as "the greatest and noblest gift that was ever given for charity."

Following further restoration, The Charterhouse is now open for bookable tours. There is a lovely bijou museum you can visit free of charge and a learning centre.

248: BLOOMSBURY SQUARE'S BLOODY AND INTRIGUING HISTORY

It has a good claim to being the first of central London's iconic squares, though it hasn't the audacity to say it is the most picturesque. And sitting, as it does, on top of a London Underground car park hardly enriches its mystique. But what Bloomsbury Square lacks in surface charm, it makes up for with history.

The square was founded in the early 1600s by Thomas Wriothesley, Earl of Southampton, the son of the Wriothesley to whom William Shakespeare dedicated many of his sonnets. He was also the father of Lady Rachel Russell, of whom more later.

A building called Southampton House occupied the northern end of today's Bloomsbury Square. It was later renamed Bedford House after the Southamptons were joined in matrimony to the Bedford family, which still owns much of the neighbourhood's land today. It was an idyllic spot at the time. To the west it was soon joined by the grandiose Montagu House, later dismantled to become the British Museum. Beyond those two aristocratic mansions was the end of London – all open fields as far as the eye could see (see image above).

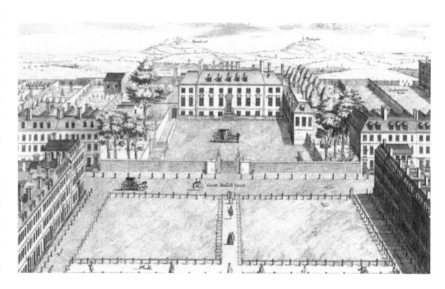

Everard Maynwaring, a distinguished physician of the time, summed up its attractions as "the best air and finest prospect, being the highest ground...a fit place for nobility and gentry to reside". Thomas Macaulay said that foreign princes "were taken to see the square as one of the wonders of England". Even the often curmudgeonly essayist Augustus Hare observed: "It is one of the most sedate and beautiful outdoor attractions in the whole of London."

Idyllic it may have been, but it was also a killing field. Like the area behind Montagu House, its remoteness made it a place for the gallants of the day to settle their debts of honour with pistols or swords at dawn. The most notorious occasion was on April 9, 1694, when the 23-year-old Scottish economist and financier John Law fought Edward "Beau" Wilson, killing him with the first thrust of his sword. Both men were smitten by Elizabeth Villiers, a society beauty and former mistress of King William. To adapt a later quip about Bloomsbury folk, they loved in triangles and duelled in squares – fatally.

Law was found guilty of murder and sentenced to death, but, to cut a long story short, escaped prison and went abroad, later becoming the Controller General of Finances for France – some say he was de facto Prime Minister – using new economic theories that were later endorsed by John Maynard Keynes.

Bloomsbury Square had already been associated with death. In 1683, Lord William Russell, husband of Lady Rachel Russell (see above), was accused of treason for his alleged part in the Rye House plot to ambush Charles II and his brother – the future James II – in order to forestall a Catholic succession. Lady Rachel stood by her husband throughout the trial, at which Lord Russell was found guilty. He was beheaded in nearby Lincoln's Inn Fields by the notoriously barbaric and incompetent executioner Jack Ketch. Lady Russell continued to live in Bloomsbury Square until she died, aged 87, in 1723, leaving voluminous letters providing insight into 17th century aristocratic life. Lord Russell was later granted a posthumous reprieve.

Prior to that, in 1642, Bloomsbury Square had experienced the whiff of warfare, when it was the site of one of the ring of forts around London constructed by Oliver Cromwell to protect against an expected invasion by Charles I's army. That didn't

materialise. But the square was badly hit during the Gordon Riots of June 1780 – disturbances on a scale at least as damaging as the French Revolution nine years later. The house of Lord Mansfield, the Lord Chief Justice – on the side of the square where Victoria House is today – was one of the chief targets. The building was all but destroyed by the anti-Catholic rioters, including Mansfield's precious library, though the Lord himself managed to escape by way of his back door.

There is an unexpected sequel to this story. Somehow, Mansfield became the presiding judge at the trial of the riots' leader, Lord George Gordon. Mansfield weighed the pros and cons with such stereotypically English fairness that Gordon was acquitted of the charges against him, even though he had set in motion the chain of events which had led to Mansfield's house being attacked.

Today, Bloomsbury Square suffers from having a main road to its south, a swanky Grecian art-deco creation to its east and that car park underneath, though it does also have a handsome John Nash-designed house at the north west corner attached to an early Nash terrace in which the celebrated architect once lived. There is a commanding statue of the remarkable Whig politician Charles Fox at the north end. His back is turned to the square itself, but we are free sit in the middle of it and contemplate its intriguing history.

249: HATTON GARDEN – FIRST HOME OF LONDON'S FAMOUS FOUNDLING HOSPITAL

In 1719, a man went to live in the maritime village of Rotherhithe by the Thames to enjoy a well-earned retirement after a career as a shipwright, running his own business in the new colony of America. Although the business was successful for most of its time, in the end it left him poor. But this was no ordinary man. It was Thomas Coram, one of the most extraordinary people in Georgian England.

On his frequent walks around London, Coram was stunned by the number of dead and dying babies, mainly illegitimate, he saw abandoned – can you believe it? – in the streets and on dust heaps. Horrifying statistics indicated that in crowded workhouses babies aged under two years died at a rate almost 99 per cent. They were described as "Britain's dying rooms". One report suggested that in Westminster Parish only one in 500 foundlings survived.

It is a sobering thought that at a time when Britain was rightly castigated for its inhuman treatment of slaves abroad, it was also allowing its own unwanted children to die on the streets of its capital. Although he was 54 years old – a good age in those days – Coram decided to do something about it. And he did. Thanks to his untiring efforts and refusal to take "no" for an answer, the Foundling Hospital became what must have been the most successful charity in the country.

The Hospital was eventually built in Bloomsbury at Lamb's Conduit Field, on the spot now called Coram's Fields (main picture). This followed unsuccessful efforts to get it located in Montagu House, where the British Museum is today. What is less well known is that Bloomsbury is not where the institution was originally based.

During its first and formative years it was located in Hatton Garden – before it became an international centre for gems – in a dwelling belonging to Sir Fisher Tench, the MP for Southwark. Tench had grown enormously rich on a range of activities including, it has to be said, the slave trade (though the Foundling Hospital was not in any way connected). William Hogarth's famous painting of Coram was presented to the Hospital while it was based at this temporary home.

Gillian Wagner says in her biography of Coram that the Hatton hospital consisted of four rooms, with two staircases to the second floor and a yard at the back, though its exact location is still a bit of a puzzle. A document in the London Metropolitan Archives recording the arrangement (see above) says it was in Hatton Street in Hatton Garden, but Hatton Street does not appear on a contemporary map. Maybe in those days it referred to the street we call Hatton Garden today, while Hatton Garden

may have been the name for the area as a whole.

There is also a contemporary reference to it being "next to the charity house in Hatton Garden", which probably refers to St Andrew's charity school, supposedly designed by Christopher Wren. The school's facade can still be seen in Hatton Garden (photo below), though the building behind it has been reconstructed as offices.

Coram's attempts to raise funds for his project were turned down successively by the government, various institutions and a number of prosperous men. He then had the bright idea of seeking the help of aristocratic women instead, and soon made such a success of it that the men felt obliged to follow.

By 1737, this humble man had signed up dozens of dukes and

earls plus the Privy Council and even Prime Minister Sir Robert Walpole. Coram won them over by walking around London from house to house to secure their signatures. It was a shining example of the golden years of philanthropy when privileged people, sometimes with ill-earned money, filled the social gap that governments recoiled from.

Sadly, Coram fell out with his fellow governors, but he retained a passion for the hospital – which, in 1935, moved to Berkhamsted in Hertfordshire – until his death in March 1751. It would never have existed without him, and for well over 100 years it was the only institution in London that took care of illegitimate children. Coram's tomb (pictured below) is at St Andrew's Church on St Andrew's Street, just below the southern end of Hatton Garden.

There was at least one unplanned consequence of all this: Hogarth, who was a founding governor of the Hospital, set up an art exhibition at its Bloomsbury home, encouraging other artists, such as Gainsborough and Sir Joshua Reynolds to show their works there too.

Visitors flocked to view Britain's first public art gallery at a time when they were almost unknown in Britain. It is reckoned that exhibitions organised there by the Dilettante Society led to the formation of the Royal Academy in 1768. The pictures can still be seen at the Foundling Museum.

250: POETRY, PLAGUE & ST GILES-IN-THE-FIELDS

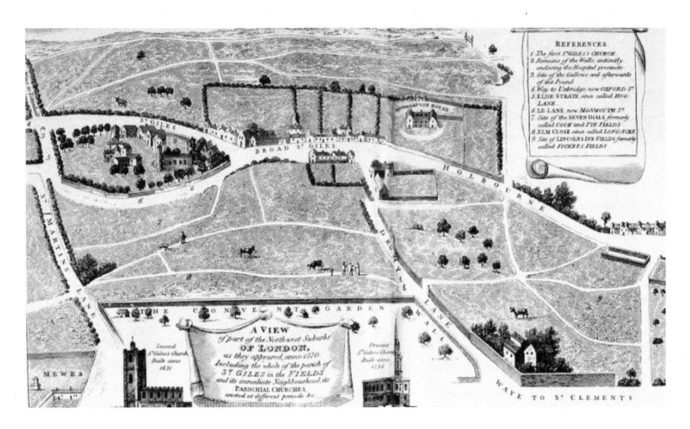

The name Matilda is best known these days as that of the hit musical staged at the Cambridge Theatre at Seven Dials, which used to be part of the decadent St Giles rookery. But it is another Matilda to whom the area is most indebted – Matilda, wife of Henry I and Queen Regent in his absence, who, in 1101, established a leper colony in what were then open fields. The chapel built there eventually morphed into the church of St Giles-in-the-Fields, following the Dissolution of the Monasteries in the 1540s, and lent its name to a St Giles district that has witnessed an astonishing series of ups and downs.

It was reckoned to have been the earliest victim of the 1665 outbreak of plague, the terrible effects of which were encountered by Samuel Pepys when he passed through the parish. The area was also badly hit by the cholera epidemic of 1848, by which time St Giles had become one of the most notorious – but by no means the only – rookery in London.

Death has also visited St Giles in a more macabre way. During the 15th century, the gallows that had been at Smithfield were moved to where today's Flitcroft Street meets St Giles High Street and remained there for well over 100 years, uncomfortably close to a church which was supposed to be saving souls.

At the Churchyard gate, the condemned criminals were offered a bowl of ale, the so-called "St Giles's Bowl", as their last refreshment in this life – one of the supposed origins of the phrase "one for the road". Anthony Babington and his co-conspirators in the Babington Plot were the last to be hanged and disembowelled there in 1586 for plotting to assassinate the Protestant Elizabeth I in favour of the Roman Catholic Mary, Queen of Scots. The gallows were later moved to Tyburn (today's Marble Arch), but those executed there continued to be buried at St Giles.

Over the centuries, St Giles had become truly cosmopolitan. Evidence of Irish immigrants can be traced to the 1620s, and of Greeks and Armenians to the 1640s. The area also attracted a large number of Huguenots escaping persecution in France. Many of these new arrivals came seeking work and protection from unrest and persecution in their homelands. In 1675, it was noted that, "the poor do daily increase by the frequent resort of poore people from several countries and places, for want of due care to prevent the same". In 1710 it was noted that "a great number of the inhabitants of St Giles's are French Protestants".

That was the backdrop to William Hogarth's 1751 masterpiece of social degradation, Gin Lane, when there were reckoned to be over 500 gin shops in an area of 3,000 houses. For this, we have to thank the accession in 1688 of William of Orange, whose government – and subsequent ones – actively encouraged gin drinking and distilling as an alternative to brandy imported from France, with which England was in continuous dispute. Around 1690, the law was changed so that – believe it or not – anyone could start a gin distillery and taxes were also reduced.

Improvements came, yet by the 19th century St Giles was still a notorious slum. A survey of the rookeries in 1849 – following fresh arrivals of Irish immigrants escaping the potato famine – revealed that between 50 and 90 people found nightly accommodation in some four-roomed houses. There was a very high death rate in the parish, with 190 burials in July 1840, and 1,856 for the year as a whole.

In 1847, the construction of New Oxford Street, joining Oxford Street and High Holborn, blasted its way through the northern end of the old slums, clearing the dilapidated houses above to the north of the church. This improved east-west communications but, perversely, at the cost of displacing more poverty stricken residents who had lost their accommodation and had nowhere else to go. It is sobering to be reminded that in 1851, when England was celebrating its global industrial success at the Great Exhibition down the road in Hyde Park, 24 people were living in a typical house in St Giles, and in some cases over 100.

One of the ironies of St Giles is that, despite being notorious in contemporary art and literature for its drunkenness, poverty and licentiousness, it also attracted creative people and aristocrats, who often lived surprisingly close to the poor. Church records dating from 1733, when the current church building was consecrated, show that there were still many aristocratic residents in the parish.

Cecil Calvert, the 2nd Lord Baltimore, is memorialised as one of those buried there. He founded the North American province of Maryland, named after Henrietta Maria, wife of Charles I, who had provided his father with the land. Baltimore didn't actually go there, delegating the governorship of the place to his younger brother Leonard.

The handsome galleried interior of the church is rich in history, including the graves of Andrew Marvell, poet and politician, who wrote the wonderful To His Coy Mistress, and of George Chapman, whose translation of Homer had John Keats in thrall yet died in poverty. The children of Lord Byron (1788 –1824) and Percy Bysshe Shelley and Mary Shelley were baptised in the font. There is also a pulpit from which John and Charles Wesley preached.

Today's St Giles in-the-Fields is Anglican and the third to have been built on the site. Flitcroft Street takes its name from its architect, Henry Flitcroft. It not only administers its religious duties but also reaches out to the street homeless, working with specialist charities such as St Mungo's, Quaker Homeless Action, Alcoholics Anonymous and Narcotics Anonymous. A café and lending library are available for these rough sleepers, together with other facilities.

Social conditions today are a far cry from the degradation the church has seen in the past, but can still be dreadful and a constant reminder of problems that never go away.

251: THE LONG BAR AND LONGER BACKSTORY OF HIGH HOLBORN'S CITTIE OF YORKE

The sign above the Cittie of Yorke in High Holborn says it all: "Established as the site of a public house in 1430." This claim and the old fashioned lettering in which it is written immediately pull you inside. And you are not disappointed. After passing through a small but comfy snug, where there was once a small garden, you enter the cathedral of taverns.

The pub claims to have the longest bar in London (pictured opposite) and it is probably the tallest as well, flanked on one sidewall by giant vats, each holding up to 1,100 gallons, and on the other by a discreet chain of cubicles where lawyers from the nearby Inns of Court – and others with different motives – can have private conversations. Camra, the real ale organisation, calls it "a truly remarkable pub" providing "a self-conscious, romantic evocation of an Olde England".

There are similar evocations nearby. The pub stands immediately next door to the

entrance to Gray's Inn, where at 7:50 pm every day, a curfew bell is sounded to warn inhabitants to put out their fires, just as in medieval times. Across the road, the site of today's Southampton Buildings was previously occupied by Southampton House, where lived the family of Thomas Wriothesley, Earl of Southampton, to whom Shakespeare is said to have dedicated many of his sonnets. Its grounds were later a location for one of the ring of forts that Parliament built around London as protection against a feared invasion by Charles I's army.

The pub has been called the Cittie of Yorke only since the early 1980s, following its purchase by its present owner, the Samuel Smith chain. The name is taken from a long-demolished 16th century pub which was situated on the other side of the road in Staple Inn. It was previously called Henekey's Long Bar: Dylan Thomas wrote an instant poem during a visit to it in 1951. It has had other names in the past, such as The Queen's Head.

Despite its appearance of being much older, nearly all the current building dates from 1923-24. Nonetheless, today's pub has a cellar dating back at least to the 1600s that is today a working bar (picture right), and its statement about 1430 is an assertion of being among the oldest taverns locations in London.

Of course, other pubs make such claims, with declared origins within a few years of each other. The Guinea in Mayfair says it has been an inn since 1423, though the present building only (only?) goes back to 1720. The Old Red Lion in St John Street, not far from the Cittie of Yorke, says it can trace its birth back to 1415 and has done some impressive research to to back that up.

There are plenty of other pubs, from the Hoop and Grapes at Aldgate to the George in Borough Market, that also have some grounds for saying they are among London's oldest. Does a pub have to have remnants of the original building to qualify as one of the oldest, a continuous record of occupation or the same name, or is being on the same site all that matters?

This fascinating question might have to be resolved by a linguistic philosopher rather than a historian or archaeologist, because all contenders have experienced huge changes, major reconstructions and been put to multiple uses. For example, during the 17 Century, the Cittie of Yorke's predecessor building hosted a coffee shop. The debate rolls on.

If retaining key parts of the original building is a requirement, there is – or was until recently – a candidate only a few hundred yards from the Cittie of Yorke, immediately on the left after passing Holborn Viaduct bridge.

There, Museum of London archaeologists unearthed substantial remains of the Three Tuns pub which had its own micro-brewery and might, in a more enlightened age, have been preserved and rebuilt. Instead, it is now buried under a new office block.

Maybe what matters in the end is whether the pub looks the part, has the atmosphere and is imbued with memories and history. The Cittie of Yorke meets all those requirements.

252: HOW CLERKENWELL BECAME THE GIN CAPITAL OF THE WORLD

Pause for a while in front of the easily missed friezes in Britton Street, pictured here. They are all that remains of the once mighty Booths distillery, which was at the centre of Clerkenwell's astonishing relationship with gin. Two other Clerkenwell gin giants, Gordons and Tanqueray, have also long since left the area.

So has J. & W. Nicholson, one of the earliest and biggest distilleries, which purchased a site on Woodbridge Street in 1808 before moving to a larger one on St John Street in 1828. Nicholson's classic London dry gin, made using botanicals such as juniper, angelica and liquorice, and said to be the Duke of Wellington's favourite tipple, was exported around the world.

It was the area's celebrated waters – which gave rise to the names Clerkenwell and Gos-well Road – that made it a magnet for these well-known gin distillers, though the area also had a bit of previous with "mother's ruin".

Turnmill Street and surrounding roads were one of the epicentres of the gin craze, which all but brought London to its knees during the 1700s. Its debilitating effects were everywhere, as most famously captured by William Hogarth in his painting Gin Lane. It is reckoned that over 6,000 houses in the capital were selling and making gin, often in sordid conditions.

It is easy to understand why the gin craze took hold at a time when poverty was rife and drinking water was contaminated. Gin offered an instant distraction from the mind-blowing misery of everyday life, but its effects were mind-numbing in more than one sense. Henry Fielding, author of Tom Jones and a Bow Street magistrate, warned that if nothing was done to tackle the problem of excessive gin drinking, there would soon be "few of the common people left to drink it".

Magistrates in Middlesex lamented that gin was "the principal cause of all the vice and debauchery committed among the inferior sort of

people". Some estimates suggested that an amazing 50 per cent of the country's annual wheat production was given over to gin production – a nice little earner for farmers, which they were reluctant to lose.

From 1729, the government introduced a succession of laws to curb gin drinking, but it was not until the 1751 Gin Act, which put small unlicensed gin shops out of business, that consumption dropped dramatically and the nation woke up from the biggest hangover it had ever experienced. The Act paved the way for bigger "respectable" corporations to move into the market, which they did. Lured by the magic of its clean waters, they made Clerkenwell the gin centre of the world.

The Booth family, which claimed to have been in the wine business since 1569, relocated to London from the north-east of England. In 1740, they established their first distillery at 55 Cowcross Street, within a neighbourhood where many of the backstreet gin shops had flourished and expanded into Britton Street in 1770. With the help of another distillery, based in Brentford, Booths became for a while the biggest distiller in England.

Alexander Gordon, a Scot, built a

distillery in Southwark in 1769 before moving to Clerkenwell in 1786. In 1898, his company merged with Charles Tanqueray & Co, which had originated in Bloomsbury just below the British Museum at 3 Vine Street (today's Grape Street. Photo above).

All production by the new Tanqueray Gordon company was eventually moved to Gordon's Goswell Road site in 1899, setting the stage for it to consolidate its position as the biggest gin company in the world, thanks largely to huge sales in the US. The building that housed Gordon's distillery can still be seen at Goswell Road's corner with Moreland Street. Charles Gordon, the last of the Gordon family to be associated with the business, died in 1899,

The whiff of gin has long evaporated from Clerkenwell, just as its watch and clock businesses have largely gone. Today, it has been colonised by media industries, work units and architects, together with restaurants and supportive companies. Tomorrow? Who knows. The economic outlook is as misty as ever, but the resilience of Clerkenwell is not in doubt. It knows how to re-invent itself.

253: THE TWO SIDES OF BLOOMSBURY'S SIR HANS SLOANE

In 1689 Hans Sloane, from Killyleagh, Northern Ireland, set up a successful medical practice at 3 Bloomsbury Place in London. This was a couple of hundred yards from Montagu House, later to become the British Museum. In between was the palatial Bedford House (see map). Not a bad address for an aspiring doctor. Among his clients were Queen Anne, King George I and King George II. He succeeded Sir Isaac Newton as President of the Royal Society in 1727.

Sloane's huge life-time collection of books and artefacts – 71,000 items in all – became the main foundation donation to the British Museum and the Natural History Museum. He had to acquire 4 Bloomsbury Place next door to accommodate it all, a source of wonder for visitors from home and abroad. He also left the wonderful Chelsea Physic Garden to the Society of Apothecaries at a peppercorn rent, without which it might not exist today. A statue of him still stands proud in the Garden's grounds. Sloane Square is named after him.

It is, however, necessary, to think of Sloane as two men. There was Hans Sloane 1, the collector and benefactor almost without peer, and there was Hans Sloane 2, whose benefactions were linked directly or indirectly to the slave trade and so have become a key part of the current re-appraisal of Britain's post-Imperial legacy. The British Museum is in the midst of just such a re-appraisal.

Sloane visited the Caribbean in 1687 a couple of years before settling at Bloomsbury Place as personal doctor to the new Governor of Jamaica, the 2nd Lord Albermarle, a

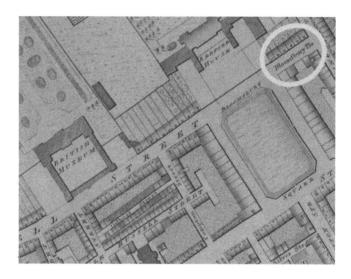

former politician and soldier who had become dissolute.

However, his main interest was in studying the island's flora, fauna and artefacts. With the help of inhabitants of the island, English planters and enslaved Africans alike, he collected an astonishing 800 plant specimens as well as curiosities and animals. His findings were written up in his Natural History of Jamaica, which was published in two volumes from 1707 to 1725, over 100 years before Darwin's Voyage on the Beagle in 1839.

One reason Sloane gave for writing it was "to teach the inhabitants of the parts where these plants grow their several uses, which I have endeavoured to do, by the best information as I could get from books and the inhabitants either Europeans, Indians or blacks". He listed around 125 diseases he found among whites and blacks and possible remedies, along with the results from applying them.

Sloane was not a typical slave owner directly trading in human beings, and he hoped his findings would benefit both blacks and whites. But that does not exonerate him.

On his return from the Caribbean he married Elizabeth Langley, the widow of wealthy planter Fulke Rose. She inherited both her merchant and MP father John Langley's Jamaican estates and a third of the income from Rose's extensive properties, which became available to Sloane. He received regular shipments of sugar during the following years, which went into his pioneering efforts to market chocolate under the brand "Sir Hans Sloane's Milk Chocolate". He also imported the bark from Peru from which quinine is made.

Rose had, like Sloane, been a physician but he was also one of the main purchasers of slaves from the Royal African Company. This inheritance was to be hugely important in financing Sloane's later collections. Although not an active slave trader he was unquestionably a beneficiary.

In 1742 Sloane started moving his books and curiosities from Bloomsbury Place to Henry VIII's former manor house in Cheyne Walk, which he had purchased in 1712. It was his earnest desire that both the building and its contents be bought at a bargain price by the government to start a national collection. This didn't happen. However, the collection was purchased and, together with the manuscripts of Sir Robert Cotton and the treasures of Robert and Edward Harley, the 1st and 2nd Earls of Oxford, became the foundation of the British Museum.

The British Museum Act, which became law on 7 June 1753, was expressly "for the purchase of the Museum or Collection, of Sir Hans Sloane, and of the Harleian Collection of Manuscripts and for providing One General

The British Museum has moved Sloane's statue to a more secure place as it starts its own inquiries

Repository for the better Reception and more convenient Use of the said Collections; and of the Cottonian Library, and of the Additions thereto". The money required was raised by lottery.

Sloane died in 1753 having donated his collection to the nation at a greatly reduced valuation and on condition that Parliament create "a new and freely accessible public museum to house it". This it did and it has been a phenomenally successful initiative until now, when fresh questions are being asked and will have to be answered.

254: THE CLERKENWELL PRIORY & THE PEASANTS' REVOLT

If you stand in the middle of St John's Square off Clerkenwell Road you will see part of a circle of cobblestones. They trace the position of the nave of the Priory Church built by the Order of St John and consecrated in 1185. The square was the northern precinct of a 19-acre priory site which reached as far as Smithfield before it was split asunder when Clerkenwell Road was bulldozed across it in the late 1870s.

The extent of the priory's property can be seen from the Agas map. It was bounded by today's Turnmill Street and Cowcross Street, their names almost unchanged since medieval times, with the River Fleet (now covered over, shown in blue) flowing to the west. From its foundation in 1144 until the Dissolution of the Monasteries it was the English headquarters of an international military order – also known as the Knights Hospitaller – which conveyed knights, monks and money to a pilgrim hospital in Jerusalem, all under the ultimate guidance of the Pope. The St John Ambulance charity is descended from it.

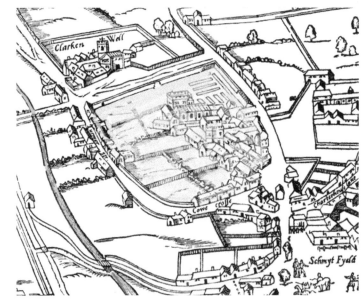

The nave no longer exists – hence the cobblestones. But next door to where it used to be survives one of the oldest crypts in London, perhaps the very oldest, dating back to the 1140s. It is beautiful, in almost pristine condition and open to the public on certain days (photo right).

There is a small stained glass window in the crypt depicting a youthful Robert Hales, a former Grand Prior of the Priory of St John. This would not be worthy of mention except that Hales had another day job: he was the Treasurer of England under King Richard II. In that position he did something whose consequences still reverberate: he was responsible for collecting the poll tax which sparked the Peasants' Revolt of 1381.

If ever there was an example of political

chickens coming home to roost it was this. The poll tax, which everyone had to pay irrespective of income, sparked an insurrection, as would another one introduced centuries later by Margaret Thatcher's government. There were multiple other grievances, such as the tenant farmer state of "villeinage" – effectively serfdom – under the lords of manors, whose actions peasants lacked any legal or political right to challenge.

The revolt was led by Wat Tyler's army of peasants, mainly from Kent. They were inspired by the radical preacher John Ball, whose iconic slogan "When Adam delved and Eve span, who was then the gentleman?" was the poetic inspiration behind the uprising. The rebels stormed the Clerkenwell priory, inflicting enormous destruction which wasn't fully repaired until over a century later under Thomas Docwra, who as Lord Prior from 1501 to 1527, also oversaw the construction of St John's Gate.

The fate of the rebels has been well documented. Representatives of the king met them at Blackheath, but failed to persuade them to return home. With most of the royal forces otherwise engaged abroad or – like Richard's uncle John of Gaunt – in the north of England, Richard, then only 14 years-old, retreated to the safety of the Tower of London. On 13 June 1381, swollen by local support, the rebels attacked the gaols and destroyed the hated Gaunt's Savoy Palace in the Strand

The following day, 14 June, Richard met the rebels in person at Mile End and conceded all their demands, including the abolition of serfdom. But in the meantime, others stormed the Tower, killing several dignitaries including Hales, who was beheaded. On 15 June Richard met Tyler himself and his supporters, this time at Smithfield, only a few hundred yards from the Priory. William Walworth, Mayor of London, killed Tyler, but Richard, after again pledging reform, persuaded the rebels to disperse. He

later reneged on his promises and took lethal revenge on the rebels, who had very nearly brought about a revolution.

The Priory survived the peasants but not Henry VIII 150 years later. In 1540, under the dissolution, all the wealth and properties of the Order of St John were transferred to the Crown and used for keeping the king's tents and hunting equipment. It was the final religious order to be disbanded by the king. Henry later gave the Priory to his daughter Mary – the so-called "Bloody Mary" – who, as queen and a Catholic, briefly restored the order in 1557. But when her Protestant sister Elizabeth came to the throne, it was again dissolved.

Worse was to come. Henry's son Edward VI was crowned in 1547. As he was only nine-years-old England was effectively ruled by the rapacious Edward Seymour, 1st Duke of Somerset, also known as the Protector. He pillaged the Priory, pulling down the church and its mighty bell tower and using the bricks to build his extravagant palace, Somerset House in the Strand. But Nemesis was waiting in the wings. Somerset died before his Xanadu was completed. He was executed for treason on Tower Hill and is buried in the church of St Peter ad Vincula within the Tower.

Almost all traces of the Priory have disappeared apart from the crypt, the gate and a reproduction of the church which stands today on the same footprint as the original, to the side of the square. From its herb garden you can see bits of medieval bricks and tiles embedded in its wall. But St John Ambulance is still based at St John's Gate and despite Clerkenwell Road running through the middle of the original site it is still possible to imagine what it was like when knights gathered here to celebrate the start of their long and ultimately fruitless journeys as crusaders to the Holy Land.

255: LINCOLN'S INN FIELDS – ITS WEST SIDE STORY

Lincoln's Inn Fields is the biggest garden square in London. It was long said that Inigo Jones, who designed it in the 1630s, had planned it to have the same dimensions as the Great Pyramid of Giza in Egypt. You don't have to believe that to be impressed by not only its size but also the fact that it has resisted all attempts to build on its considerable vacant space, apart from a restaurant and some tennis courts.

During Charles II's reign (1660-1685) there were moves to have an Academy of Painting dominating the centre of the square. Christopher Wren drew up plans for a church near the same spot. Later, in 1842, Sir Charles Barry, architect of the Houses of Parliament, designed a "magnificent structure" for new law courts to occupy the centre of the fields, including a great central hall surrounded by 12 courtrooms.

Mercifully, all of that was resisted. What has changed is the type of people who occupy the square and the buildings around it. Its early character was succinctly summed up by the novelist Walter Besant when he wrote: "The history of Lincoln's Inn Fields is a curious combination of rascality and of aristocracy. The rascals infested the fields, which were filled with wrestlers, rogues and cheats, pick-pockets, cripples and footpads; the aristocrats occupied the stately houses on the West Side."

Part of that classic poem Trivia, written in 1716 by John Gay whose later blockbuster musical The Beggars's Opera broke records at the theatre on the south-east side of the square, is devoted to ways of avoiding being

mugged or conned in the fields. Yet in its heyday the square was the place of choice for "people of worth" and most particularly Roman Catholic ones, because they could attend mass at the chapel of the nearby Sardinian embassy.

Following the Reformation, the celebration of mass was banned except in foreign embassies, which were not subject to British law. The Sardinian embassy was one of the most popular. You had to enter through the ambassador's private residence. It became a target during the Gordon Riots of June 1780. Sparked by resistance to quite modest concessions to Catholics in the Catholic Relief Act of 1778, they exploded into sustained attacks on many buildings that ended up doing more damage to London than the French Revolution did to Paris a few years later. The chapel was demolished in 1909 and is now the site of the Church of St Anselm and St Cecelia.

Number 58 Lincoln's Inn Fields is believed by Dickens devotees to be where the sinister solicitor Tulkinghorn in Bleak House lived and number 66 has been the home of Farrer & Co, the Queen's solicitors, since 1790. This is an example of aristocrats moving out of the square and lawyers moving in. The current building dates from

Newcastle House, scene of lavish prime ministerial parties

the late 1600s. When owned by Lord Powis it was called Powis House. Subsequent owners included Thomas Pelham-Holles, 1st Duke of Newcastle, who was twice Prime Minister and held lavish parties there in what was by then called Newcastle House. A passageway connecting Lincoln's Inn Fields to Kingsway passes beneath it.

The west side of the square also contains Lindsey House at numbers 59 and 60, which has had its name since the 4th Earl of Lindsey moved in there early in the 18th century. Historic England says the mansion's design is sometimes attributed to Jones. It has a remarkable history. Number 59 was the home of the Society for the Diffusion of Useful Knowledge, a fascinating Victorian experiment for spreading knowledge to the masses – a kind of pre-internet Wikipedia. Number 60, whose front door is reached by the same steps, was the home of the square's other Prime Minister resident, the ill-fated Spencer Perceval, who was assassinated in May 1812 in the vestibule of the House of Commons by a deranged businessman.

Lindsey House also features in the story of Lord William Russell, who was beheaded in the square in 1683 for his part in the Rye House Plot, an attempt to assassinate Charles II and his brother, the future (Catholic) James II, to ensure a Protestant succession. After the execution Russell's body was taken to Lindsey House where his head was apparently sewn back on. The bandstand in the middle of the square today has a plaque on the floor memorialising this macabre episode, a fitting reminder that the tranquillity of the square should never be taken for granted.

256: MARGARET CAVENDISH, SINGULAR SCHOLAR OF CLERKENWELL

Clerkenwell was the home of William Cavendish, the first Duke of Newcastle-upon-Tyne (1593-1676), where he lived in a mansion called Newcastle House (main image) which stood in today's Clerkenwell Close except for a period of 18 years when, as a Royalist commander for Charles I, he fled to the continent to avoid the wrath of Oliver Cromwell. In Paris Cavendish met a remarkable woman, born Margaret Lucas from St John's Abbey in Essex, whom he married there.

History has until recently been wantonly unkind to Margaret Cavendish who was a remarkable woman. She has been described as extravagant, flirtatious and obscene and a bluestocking "of the deepest dye" and was known as "Mad Madge" because of her eccentricities. These included requiring her footman to sleep in a closet in her bedroom so he could be summoned to write down any thoughts she had during the night.

She certainly had a lot of them.

Newcastle House

After returning to London with her husband following the Restoration, the duchess became a prolific author. She produced ten volumes of what have been described as "learned trifles and fantastic verses", many of which were so short they might have come straight from her footman's notes. Cavendish often sent copies of her work to distinguished people, sometimes receiving extravagant praise from them with their tongues in their cheeks. She also wrote plays, one of which, The Humourous Lovers, was described by diarist Samuel Pepys in 1667 as "the most silly thing that ever came upon a stage".

But what was thought silly then is looked at differently today. Cavendish was an an early feminist, whose poems, plays and literary critiques are nowadays pored over for signs of deep insights. Her works and observations about natural science are today highly thought of. Her book The Blazing World is thought to be the first work of science fiction by a woman and a pioneer of the genre itself.

A long article in the Stanford Encyclopedia of Philosophy written in 2009 admits that although Cavendish's philosophical work was not taken seriously in the 17th century "it is certainly relevant today". The duchess, it claims, laid out "an early and very compelling version of the naturalism that is found in current-day philosophy and science". Among numerous other things she offered important insights that are relevant to recent discussions of the nature and characteristics of intelligence. The encyclopedia adds that she "anticipated some of the central views and arguments that are more commonly associated with figures like Thomas Hobbes and David Hume".

Cavendish undoubtedly suffered from being a woman at a time when the scientific establishment didn't take women seriously, but she had married into the Cavendish scientific dynasty which may help explain why she was invited to attend a meeting of the all-male Royal Society in May 1667 despite protests from many of the fellows. Pepys, who was present, recorded in his diary that her dress was "so antic and her deportment so unordinary" that the fellows were made strangely uneasy. They would have been, wouldn't they? It was a couple of centuries before the experiment was repeated.

The Cavendishes divided their time between Clerkenwell and another property, Welbeck Abbey in Nottinghamshire. Newcastle House – not to be confused with the mansion of the same name which still stands on Lincoln's Inn Fields – was built on, and indeed from, the ruins of St Mary's Nunnery, which had passed into the ownership of the Cavendish family during Henry VIII's dissolution of the monasteries. The duchess died at Welbeck in 1673, aged 50, and the duke three years later at Clerkenwell, aged 84.

Margaret Cavendish's legacy is honoured at Westminster Abbey. If you enter it using the north (tourist) entrance, on the left there is a tomb (pictured below) by Grinling Gibbons which is the resting place of the duke and duchess. Of Margaret it says: "This Duchess was a wife, a witty and learned lady which her many books do well testify." She is shown holding an open book, a pen-case and ink horn to reference her literary output.

257: WHAT HOLBORN GAVE TO FOOTBALL

Football in London can be traced back at least as far as 1170 when a visitor, William FitzStephen, noted that "after dinner all the youths of the city goes out into the fields for the very popular game of ball" and that every trade had its own football team, and also its own rules about the size of ball.

Over 500 years later football was being played in London streets as well as its fields, apparently without any rules or any care for property or people. John Gay's classic 1716 poem Trivia, about walking in London, vividly recounts a wild game in Covent Garden.

"I spy the furies of the foot-ball'd war:
The 'prentice quits his shop to join the crew;
Increasing crowds the flying game pursue.

Thus, as you roll the ball o'er snowy ground,
The gath'ring globe augments with every round. . . . .
But whither shall I run? The throng draws nigh!
The ball now skims the street, now soars on high;
The dext'rous glazier strong returns the bound,
And jingling sashes on the penthouse sound."

The game as described by Gay would almost certainly have rumbled and tumbled its way on past the site on Great Queen Street just south of Holborn where, in 1775, the Freemasons' Tavern was built. Unknown to the contemporary players, that pub (pictured below) would be the place where the game of football was changed forever.

It was there on 26 October 1863 that an embryonic Football Association (FA) met to begin drawing up rules for the game, which eventually led to football being the most popular sport in the world. After half a dozen meetings, the association, which included a number of teams and one school – Charterhouse, a football pioneer – agreed the first comprehensive rules.

There was one important dissenter. As Simon Inglis records in his magisterial Played in London the first FA treasurer, the representative from Blackheath,

Freemasons' Tavern Great Queen Street Lincolns Inn Fields.

withdrew his club from the association over the removal of two draft rules: "the first allowed for running with the ball in hand; the second for obstructing such a run by hacking (kicking an opponent in the shins), tripping and holding."

Other English clubs followed this lead by not joining the FA. Instead, in 1871, they formed the Rugby Football Union. Two sports that became global phenomena had been spawned in the same Holborn hostelry. Who says you can't have a productive debate in a pub?

Would the inaugural FA rules work? What was regarded as the first "unified" match played in accordance with them took place on January 9, 1864 at Battersea Park between Sheffield FC, one of the first clubs to draw up its own rules, and a team called London City.

Reports suggest that the game's scoring system included "touchdowns", a feature later limited to try-scoring in rugby. It also appears to be the first time that "butting" the ball with the head took place, a practice of the Sheffield team that apparently prompted laughter among the London players. It doesn't seem so funny now.

Thus began one of England's greatest gifts to the world. Shame we didn't take out a patent. The Freemasons' Tavern was demolished in 1909 and replaced by the Connaught Rooms which still grandly stand today. But there's a substitute pub, the Freemasons Arms, complete with football memorabilia, in nearby Long Acre.

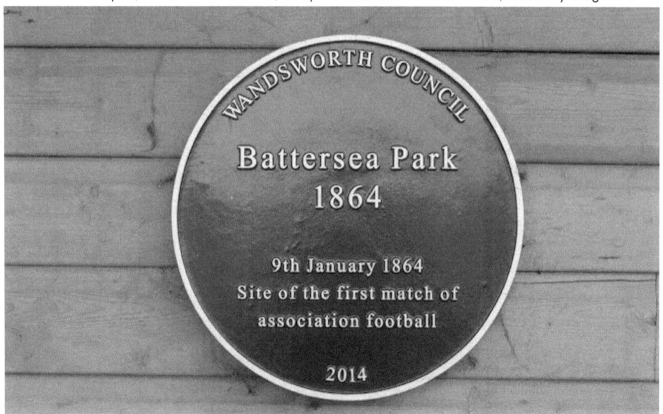

258: GAMAGES – HOLBORN'S PIONEER DEPARTMENT STORE

In September 1930 a big new department store opened in Oxford Street with a frontage over 100 yards wide. The Observer reported that it received over 100,000 visitors on its first day and was "immensely popular", but within a few months it had closed down, making it one of the biggest retail failures on record. The surprising thing was that it was a branch of Gamages, which for many years had run a highly successful department store of a very different kind well away from the West End in Holborn.

Gamages was started by Albert Walter Gamage who, in 1878, at the age of 21, rented a small hosiery shop at 128 Holborn and ended up owning most of the block from Leather Lane to Hatton Garden.

From the very start, his policy was to sell everything cheaper than anyone else, offering practically everything a typical customer would need for less than competitors could afford. A good early example was a hair brush with wire bristles, which was priced at one shilling and sixpence (0.09 pence) when at other places they were two shillings and sixpence (0.13p).

Gamages had a large number of departments assembled, it must be admitted, in a rather ramshackle way. They included hardware on the ground floor, photography, camping, pets, a huge toy area and lots of sports equipment. By the end of the 19th century Gamages purported to be the "world's largest sport and athletic outfitter". They were particularly proud of their horology section, claiming that each timepiece for sale had undergone rigorous testing at every stage of production.

You could buy a car in the motor department – where the body of Albert

Gamage apparently lay in state upon his death in 1930 – or choose a cheap bicycle from the dizzying number on display or from the Gamages catalogue that sometimes had as many as 1,300 pages, with a lion's share devoted to bikes. The store had a conjuring section too, which I remember visiting as a boy.

The Holborn store continued trading despite the disastrous Oxford Street venture, where the accent was on premium fashion and women could talk to their friends by telephone while having their hair done. Afterwards, they might go to the store's 400-seater restaurant or to its roof garden to play miniature golf. But it was launched at the start of the Great Depression and Simon Marks of Marks and Spencer next door decided to keep all his prices below five shillings – a killer blow.

The final irony is that the site of that stillborn West End Gamages is now occupied by – wait for it – Primark, a hugely successful latter day iteration of the cut-price model the Holborn Gamages pioneered. That original Gamages finally closed in 1972. It was one of the first real department stores and a revered household name.

COMING DOWN!

DEATH TO ABSURD AND INFLATED PRICES!!

Gamages, of Holborn

CHEAPEST AND BEST HOUSE IN THE WORLD FOR ALL MOTOR SUNDRIES.

LATEST AND BEST NOVELTIES.

British, Parisian, German, and American.

The "Dietz" Lamps, enamelled	**10/3** each.
" " " 1st grade	**14/9** "
Plated	**24/6** "
Brass, polished	**20/6** "
The "Automobile" Lamps, nickel mounts	**49/-** pair.
Brass " "	**48/-** "
All polished brass	**79/-** "
All nickel-plated	**89/-** "
The Bleriot Lamps	**£4 10s.** and **£6 10s.**

De Dion Sparking Plugs, genuine, **2/11** each.

All BEST goods at lower prices than CAN BE OBTAINED ELSEWHERE.

Trembler blades for De Dion, **6d.** each. The new "Ratchet" Jack, only **10/6. PETROL, 1/-** gallon. Minerva and Werner parts at lowest prices.

The new **MOTE-OIL** (guaranteed best), **4/3** gallon (tins included).

Rear Lamps—Eye Protectors—Ear Guards—Foot Warmers—Rubber Mats—Leather Clothing, and **everything for Motists.**

Write for List, post free to any address,

A. W. GAMAGE, Ltd., Holborn, E.C.,
and at Dublin and Aldershot.

259: ST MARY'S NUNNERY AND THE WELL THAT GAVE CLERKENWELL ITS NAME

The remains of the Clerks' Well, marked by a plaque at 16 Farringdon Lane, are one of the smallest yet most remarkable bits of medieval Clerkenwell still visible above ground, and the spring water source of the area's name. You can see what is left of the well through a window of the offices of Well Court.

The well got its name because it was the location where, for centuries, parish clerks performed so-called miracle or mystery plays of a moralistic or liturgical nature. These increasingly came to feature more light-hearted "interludes" performed by actors, which helped pioneer the emergence of early English dramas. It is easy to see that plays such as Christopher Marlowe's Faustus owed much to the centuries of the miracle plays preceding them.

Nearly 900 years ago the well became an essential part of St Mary's Nunnery, one of a necklace of religious houses that dominated an area now characterised by pubs, offices, car parks, the London Metropolitan Archives and a Peabody estate. St Mary's was built in 1144 close by the River Fleet by Jordan de Bricet, a Norman knight and Lord of Clerkenwell manor. Its layout was designed so that the well could be incorporated into its western wall, as shown by the blue circle on the Agas map below.

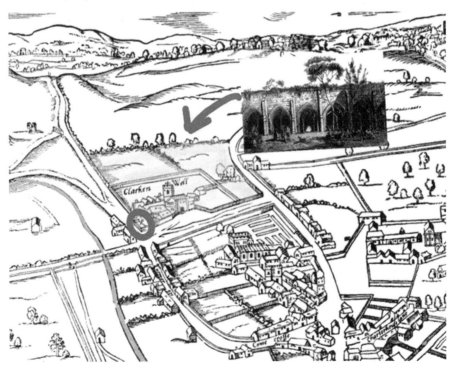

The nunnery was curious in that it rarely had more than 15 nuns in residence, yet its land (highlighted in yellow) covered 60 acres, which would have amounted to four acres per nun. It was adjacent to the Priory of St John, also built by de Bricet. Soon to come nearby was the first Blackfriars monastery, built in 1224, where the Goldman Sachs building is today. A walk down to the river would have brought you to the Greyfriars monastery. A later and nearer addition was the Charterhouse, built in 1372, a richly preserved medieval building not far from the Priory Church of St Bartholomew.

That was an astonishing number of monastic institutions for one part a city with a population of around 20,000 in the year 1200. London also had a huge number of churches, especially in the City. If you walked in London in medieval times you walked with God. How times have changed.

If you stand at the edge of Clerkenwell Close next to the Crown pub – where Vladimir Lenin, who worked from 37a Clerkenwell Green, is supposed to have had a drink with a young Joseph Stalin in 1903 – you can get a good idea of how large St Mary's was. It extended right along Farringdon Road and Lane to Town's End, a road so called because it was where London suddenly ended and became fields. On a modern map, Vineyard Walk marks where the nunnery's vineyard would have been.

Also from Clerkenwell Close you can see St James church, which is on the site of the nunnery's original church, also called St Mary's. It survived the dissolution of the monasteries in the 1540s and today, although reconstructed, still contains one or two pieces of the ancient wall (photo p.206).

The dissolution saw the area's land divided up among

Henry VIII's cronies. Mansions built there included Challoner House, later known as Cromwell House where Oliver Cromwell is sometimes said to have had a residence. On the opposite side of the road stood Newcastle House, where the intriguing Margaret Cavendish lived with remnants of the nunnery in the garden.

St Mary's had its ups and downs financially but prior to the dissolution it was drawing rents from 64 parishes plus dowries from outside London and rents from nobles and others renting property within the confines of the nunnery itself.

Rents accounted for over 60 per cent of the institution's gross revenue, making it more like a property company than a priory. But that doesn't erase its history, which still permeates Clerkenwell and enables us to conjure up images of what it looked like in medieval times.

260: OLAUDAH EQUIANO, SLAVERY SURVIVOR AND HATTON GARDEN SCRIBE

In Baldwin's Gardens, just off Gray's Inn Road and set back from the street, there is an apartment block called Equiano Court. It takes its name – displayed on the grey tile panel in the photo below – from Olaudah Equiano, a former slave who, for a brief but important part of his 18th century life, lived in this this part of Hatton Garden. He was soon to become a best selling author and leading light of the anti-slavery campaign.

Equiano resided in a variety of places in London, from Westminster to Fitzrovia, but it was at 53 Baldwin's Gardens, where he lived during 1787 and 1788, that he began writing letters to newspapers and is believed to have embarked on his best-selling book The Interesting Narrative of the Life of Olaudah Equiano, or Gustavus Vassa, the African, published in 1789. Gustavus Vassa was a name given to him by one of his slave masters.

The word "interesting" is an understatement for a book this reader found difficult to put down. In it, Equiano writes: "I was born, in the year 1745, in a charming fruitful vale, named Essaka," which was part of today's Nigeria. And he reveals: "My father, besides many slaves, had a numerous family, of which seven lived to grow up, including

myself and a sister." He describes how his father usually ate alone, with his wives and slaves having separate tables.

It will be surprising to some that Equiano was brought up in a family that kept slaves, albeit he stressed that those in his home were treated like other members of the community. Equiano became a slave himself after he and his beloved sister were kidnapped from their home by an African gang of two men and a woman when he was 11 years-old and sold to English traders. He somehow survived years of horrendous experiences on slave ships in the West Indies

and elsewhere before, in 1766, using his trading skills to earn enough money to buy his freedom from his final owner, an American Quaker called Robert King.

Equiano came to England in the late 1760s. He was surprised when he reached London that there was no obvious trade in people, something he had become used to in his original home. Although operating an abominable trade in slaves abroad, Britain was more liberal towards black people living here, even before the celebrated judgment of Lord Mansfield in 1772, which granted escaped slave James Somerset his freedom. It enshrined into law the principle that "no master ever was allowed here (England) to take a slave by force to be sold abroad because he deserted from his service, therefore the man must be discharged". The judgment had a profound effect on slavery's eventual abolition.

Equiano is honoured with several plaques in London, including St Margaret's Church, Westminster, where he was baptised, and Tottenham Street and Riding House Street in Fitzrovia, where he also lived and worked. But it is particularly fitting that a whole block has been dedicated to him in the place where his public life got underway.

By the 1780s , having lived in London on and off for a decade, Equiano was a seasoned speaker at anti-slavery rallies. He wrote letters to the Public Advertiser from Baldwin's Gardens, drawing attention to the "millions of my African countrymen who groan under the lash of tyranny in the West Indies". Another letter, written in 1788, accompanied a petition of signatures that was sent to Queen Charlotte, wife of George III, although to no avail.

His book was an instant success, attracting over 300 subscribers including the Prince of Wales, abolitionists Josiah Wedgwood, and Granville Sharp, and the Duke of Montagu. Others were William Sancho, the son of another best-selling former slave Ignatius Sancho, and Ottobah Cugoano, an active abolitionist who wrote his own successful story of his experiences as a slave. It is quite extraordinary that at a time of mass white illiteracy in late Georgian London, Equiano, Sancho and Cugoano, three self-educated black men from backgrounds of slavery wrote successful books in enviably good English that were subscribed to by leading men of letters and aristocrats.

In 1792, Equiano married an English woman, Susan Cullen, from Soham in Cambridgeshire, where they lived for a while. He died in 1797 aged 52. Recent research has established that he was buried in a cemetery next to the former Whitefield's Tabernacle in Tottenham Court Road, where the Whitfield Gardens children's playground is today.

PS: There is a puzzle about Equiano's origins. Vincent Carretta, a leading scholar of black Georgians in London, points out that both his baptismal certificate in St Margaret's Church next to Westminster Abbey and a 1773 muster list on a ship in which Equiano served gave his birthplace as "South Carolina". At the same time, Equiano's own story, full of detailed local knowledge, has a strong sense of authenticity.

261: HIDDEN HISTORIES OF A BLOOMSBURY HOTEL

The Kimpton Fitzroy Hotel stands imperiously in Russell Square displaying its thé-au-lait ("tea with milk") terracotta frontage, including statues of four queens – Elizabeth I, Mary II, Victoria and Anne.

From 1900, when it was opened, until 2018, when it was relaunched under new owners, it was known by its original name of Hotel Russell, where early meetings of the Russell Group of universities took place. But the Fitzroy part of its present name is a nod to its architect, Charles Fitzroy Doll, from whom the term "dolled up" is derived due to his liking for decorative facades – in this case using material from the Doulton potteries in Lambeth.

Behind that facade lies a sumptuous interior with a story of its own. A feature of the Kimpton is its dining hall (see photograph on page 210), which looks copied from that of the Titanic. Actually, it is the other way around – the dining room of the Titanic was copied from the hotel's by its designer, Fitzroy himself. The hotel also contains a small bronze dragon called Lucky George, which is identical to one lost on the Titanic. A further connection is that some Titanic passengers spent the night at the hotel before boarding.

The site of the hotel has a previous, now buried, history thanks to Frederick Calvert, who, upon his father's death in 1751, became the sixth Baron Baltimore (an Irish peerage) at the age of 20. As a result of this – would you believe it – he inherited Maryland in the United States, which had been in his family since Charles I gave it to his ancestor George Calvert, the 1st Baron Baltimore. The Mary in Maryland refers to Charles's wife Henrietta Maria. It was a British colony the size of Belgium, which produced income from rents and taxes worth the equivalent of many millions today.

In 1759 the young Calvert used some of this income to build a mansion called Baltimore House in the gardens of the palatial Southampton House – later renamed Bedford House – in Great Russell Street, next door to Montagu House where the British Museum is today (see map below). Beyond lay open fields, marking the end of London. Baltimore House stood where the future Hotel Russell would later appear.

Frederick Calvert was an extraordinary man for whom sin might have been invented. An old Etonian, he presided over Maryland with almost feudal powers but never actually set foot there, preferring instead to squander his riches, which were mainly derived from tobacco and the slave trade. Unlike some contemporaries, who salved their consciences with good works, he blew it on often public debauchery.

And how! Calvert led what has been described as "an extravagant and often scandalous lifestyle" culminating in 1768 with an accusation of abduction and rape by Sarah Woodcock, a local beauty who ran a milliner's shop in Tower Hill. An all-male jury acquitted him, but not many believed the verdict.

He fled the country soon after and travelled around Italy and then Constantinople, which he had to leave after being accused of keeping a private harem. It wasn't so very private, as he was known to parade his entourage of five white women and one black one brazenly in public.

Calvert was so fascinated with the Ottoman Turks that on his return to England he pulled down part of Baltimore House in order to reconstruct it in the style of a Turkish harem. Following his death in Naples, Maryland was inherited by one of his numerous illegitimate children, Henry Harford, aged 13.

After that, Charles Powlett, the 3rd Duke of Bolton and a Whig politician, took a lease on Baltimore House and renamed it Bolton House. This restored its prestige, but only a little. Historian Edward Walford described Bolton as "equally eccentric" as Baltimore.

Powlett did some good deeds – in 1739 he was one of the founding governors

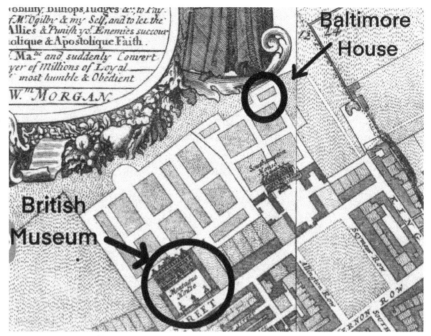

of the nearby Foundling Hospital, which did sterling work for orphaned children. But he is mainly remembered for a long standing affair with the actress Lavinia Fenton, which started in 1728 and lasted until 1751, when his wife Lady Anne died. He then married Fenton, who by then had already borne him three children.

This relationship has been immortalised by William Hogarth, whose famous painting of John Gay's Beggars Opera (below) shows the Duke, sitting on the right of the stage, eyeing Lavinia during a performance. Goodness.

262: EDWARD CAVE, THE MAGAZINE TRAILBLAZER OF CLERKENWELL

In January 1731 the seeds of a breakthrough in journalism were sown in the unlikely setting of the gatehouse of an old priory in Clerkenwell. It was from there, at St John's Gate, that Edward Cave launched a monthly publication called The Gentleman's Magazine, which has a good claim to being the first of its kind in the English-speaking world.

There were other periodicals around, but they limited themselves to particular subjects. The Gentleman's Magazine broke new ground by covering a wide variety. Cave actually invented the very word "magazine", which was derived from a similar one in French, meaning "storehouse". The Gentleman's Magazine lasted until 1922 – nearly 200 years, 50 of them while based at the gatehouse – and spawned numerous imitations across the world.

The very first issue was a hit, despite being a bit hard to digest. Stories, obituaries, appointments and many other items were vacuumed up from other sources and packed like sardines into 50 pages with no pictures.

ST. JOHN'S GATE, CLERKENWELL.

It contained items lifted from specialist journals such as the Craftsman, the London Journal, Fog's Journal, the Grub Street Journal and the Weekly Register. There was a poem by Poet Laureate Colley Cibber accompanied by a panegyric to Cibber himself – sample line: "Sing a floreat to the laureate" – written by Stephen Duck, an agricultural labourer from Wiltshire who had been taken up by George II's wife Queen Caroline. (In 1733 Caroline revived the post of governor of Duck Island in St James's Park and gave it to Stephen, who became Duck of Duck Island).

Why was Cave able to do this? Because he exploited the weak copyright laws of the time by paying hardly anyone at all for their work. He had form for this sort of thing: the son of a cobbler, he attended Rugby School but was expelled after being accused of stealing from the headmaster.

But The Gentleman's Magazine was also a major innovator in a different way. It began reporting what went on in Parliament at a time when – can you believe it? – it was illegal to do so. His reporters would sit in the public gallery and later write up whatever they could remember. Being one of Cave's House of Commons reporters, from 1741 to 1743, was among Samuel Johnson's first regular jobs. He even had a small room or garret of his own at the gatehouse.

The gatehouse building was already associated with illustrious figures. Richard Hogarth, a classical scholar, school teacher and father of legendary painter William Hogarth, set up a coffee shop in its east tower in around 1704. He conceived it as a haven for gentlemen to meet and converse in Latin. Such institutions were often called "penny universities", as you paid a penny for entrance and enlightenment. But enlightenment didn't pay in Richard's case and the enterprise, sadly, folded in 1707.

However, the greatest of all of the literary worthies who graced the gatehouse came earlier – William Shakespeare. He would have been a frequent visitor in his time, as the gatehouse contained the office of the Master of the Revels, who vetted every play performed in London in case any contained criticism of the monarch, Elizabeth I, or other seditious material.

The gatehouse, steeped in history, is well worth a visit. Dating from the 1540s, since the 1870s it has been the headquarters of the admirable English Order of St John, which is rightly proud of its medieval origins and monks who cared for sick pilgrims on their way to Jerusalem. Today, as well as offices, it has a fascinating museum and puts on guided tours. No Latin required.

THE

Gentleman's Magazine:

JANUARY, 1731.

A View of the Weekly DISPUTES *and* ESSAYS *in this Month.*

Craftſman, *Jan.* 2. N°. 235.

MR *Oldcaſtle* having begun his Remarks on the Conduct of the Kings of *England,* to ſhew how the Spirit of *Faction,* and the Spirit of *Liberty* had exerted themſelves at different Times and Occaſions, had brought his Obſervations down to the Reign of Q. *Elizabeth.* He begins N°. 234. with an Eulogium upon her prudent Conduct in the moſt arduous Difficulties that attended her acceſſion to the Throne. Theſe Difficulties he explains at large, and goes on N°. 235. to ſpeak more largely of the means whereby ſhe eſtabliſh'd her Glory and confirm'd herſelf in the Affections of her People. Her firſt Principle was to be neither *fear'd nor deſpis'd* by thoſe ſhe govern'd. He mentions ſome inſtances wherein ſhe diſcover'd her Wiſdom in both theſe reſpects, particularly in maintaining her *Prerogative*; which altho' ſhe was fond of, yet took care it never ſhould be grievous, or if it ſhould happen ſo to particular Perſons, that it ſhould appear ſpecious to the Publick. The Effects, he ſays, of a bare-fac'd *Prerogative* are not ſo dangerous to *Liberty* as the Attempts which

are made to ſurprize and undermine it. Wherefore Q. *Eliz.* never kept up a *ſtanding Army,* but placed her ſecurity in the Affections of her People. With reſpect to *Parties* he extols her moderation and equity, by which conduct ſhe ſtood on firmer Ground, and had leſs to fear from the Spirit of *Faction.* She neither haſtily eſpouſed the Party which ſhe favour'd, nor inflam'd the Spirits of the adverſe Party. The *Papiſts* and *Puritans* ſhe uſed with lenity 'till their evil Practices made it neceſſary to execute rigours, and even then ſhe diſtinguiſhed *Papiſts in Conſcience from Papiſts in Faction, nor condemn'd the Zeal of the Puritans, but ſometimes cenſured their Violence. He ſays from* Cambden, *ſhe beſtowed her Favours with ſo much Caution, and ſo little Diſtinction, as to prevent either Party from gaining the aſcendent over her, whereby ſhe remain'd Miſtreſs of her own ſelf, and preſerved both their Affections and her own Power and Authority entire.*

He proceeds to juſtify Q. *Eliz.* from the imputation of Avarice, by obſerving that ſhe neither hoarded up, nor was laviſh of the publick Money. Quotes a ſaying of the famous *Burleigh,* that; *he never cared to ſee the Treaſure ſwell like a diſorder'd Splein, when the oth*

263: TURNMILL STREET – THE CLERKENWELL ARTERY THAT CAPTURES LONDON'S REINVENTIONS

Turnmill Street in Clerkenwell is one of the oldest thoroughfares in London. It has seen it all, from high life to low life, from thriving small businesses to abject poverty and, most curiously, being lionised by the likes of William Shakespeare and Ben Jonson. The street has been there, sometimes known by its alter ego Turnbull Street, since medieval maps were invented. Its history and that of its immediate neighbourhood are a microcosm of London's constant re-invention of itself.

There was a horse and cattle market at next door Smithfield from at least the 12th century, and before the Dissolution of the Monasteries in the late 1530s the district must have been a paradigm of Merrie England. Situated near the Priory of St John, which dispatched escorted pilgrimages to the Holy Land, and the nunnery of St Mary, it lay outside the bustle of the City of London, and where Turnmill Street ended, so did the capital. Some maps even named what became the adjacent Farringdon Road "Town's End Lane".

The Dissolution created a break with the area's previous history. It threw huge amounts of religious lands on to the market to be snapped up by aristocrats and Henry VIII's court favourites. William Pinks, the chronicler of Clerkenwell, says that towards the end of the 17th century it was "a delightful place of

residence attracting nobility", yet the 1661 rate book showed 112 Turnmill Street residents assessed as poor.

Craft industries arrived, including clock and watch making by Huguenots fleeing persecution in France. Some of these trades were powered by the mill that gave the street its name and also emptied effluent into an already-polluted River Fleet. The industrial revolution brought more immigrants, this time from Italy, and also bigger industries, such as breweries, distilleries and printing. The American caramel manufacturer Murray & Co. employed 300 people in Turnmill Street and the headquarters of Booth's Gin was based in and around it for 200 hundred years.

The biggest transformation came in 1863 with the arrival of the Metropolitan Railway, the world' first underground service, which initially ran from Paddington to near the end of Turnmill Street. Butchers, bakers, candle manufacturers, coach builders, craft activities and even charcoal burners in Turnmill Street had to move as buildings on the west side of the street were demolished for the Clerkenwell "improvements", which also involved building the new Farringdon Road.

One outcome was the decline of the most notorious red light district in the whole of London. Turnmill Street might have been designed for depravity – a short road with least 20 narrow alleys or courts on either side, filled with criminals and prostitutes. What made it different from other London rookeries was the attention bestowed on it by an amazing number of great literary figures.

Shakespeare lets Falstaff (in Henry IV, Part 2) moan that Justice Shallow "hath done nothing but prate to me of the wildness of his youth and the feats he hath done in Turnbull Street". Pericles was written in conjunction with resident innkeeper and brothel owner George Wilkins, which lends an unusual authenticity to the play's brothel scenes.

In Ben Jonson's Bartholomew Fair, Ursula is indignant at being charged with frequenting Turnbull Street. A character in Thomas Middleton's Chaste Maid has twins by someone she met there. Thomas Webster's A Cure for Cuckolds features someone who comes to an inn in Turnbull Street and "falls in league with a wench". In Francis Beaumont and John Fletcher's play The Scornful Lady a character moans that the "drinking, swearing and whoring" that has been going on means "we have all lived in a perpetual Turnbull Street". And so it goes on.

Much of the surrounding area became known as "Jack Ketch's Warren," because so many people there ended up being hanged, as can be seen in the Old Bailey's online records. Jack Ketch was the common name for a hangman.

A pub at the junction of Turnmill Street and Cowcross Street, which used to form part of the southern end of Turnmill, has left a particular mark on history.

Imagine the scene. A man had been gaming at the notorious Hockley-in-the-Hole bear baiting pit, which stood on the site of today's gastropub The Coach (where you can hear the subterranean flow of the Fleet from a drain outside the front door). He ran out of money and asked the landlord of the Castle Inn if he could lend him some money to pay off his debt. As he proffered a gold watch as surety, the landlord was happy to oblige, even though the man was a stranger.

The owner of the timepiece turned out to be George IV on one of his notorious escapades. A few days later, a messenger from the King arrived to redeem the loan with a handsome amount, and, apparently, to grant the landlord a licence to be a pawnbroker.

Whether this story is true or false is for the reader to judge. But what cannot be denied is that a 19th century reconstruction of the pub, called The Castle, which stands on the same spot today, has a handsome pawnbroking sign outside, the only pub in the country to boast one. Inside there is an impressive oil painting depicting George handing over his watch (see main photo). That alone makes the pub worth a visit. Just don't ask for a loan.

264: RED CLERKENWELL GREEN

In 2017 a public consultation took place about proposals to improve Clerkenwell Green by creating "a more pleasant and greener local environment". Yes, it was finally admitted that the green was green no more and hadn't been for hundreds of years.

Indeed, if you had to assign a colour to this intriguing area of small businesses and big politics it would more appropriately be red, given that radicals have been attracted to it since medieval times like bees to a hive. And in this Clerkenwell was ahead of its time – what was radical in the past is the status quo today.

Clerkenwell's love affair with social change goes back to at least 1381 during the Peasants' Revolt, when Wat Tyler and his insurgents from Kent protested there about the imposition of a poll tax on everyone irrespective of wealth, an experiment that would remain unpopular.

Much later, the Chartists, working-class agitators, often held meetings on or near the Green. In 1816 they were addressed by "Orator" Henry Hunt, campaigning for such dangerous policies as universal suffrage (albeit just for men) and the abolition of "rotten boroughs" such as Old Sarum, which had no inhabitants yet sent two MPs to Parliament while big industrial conurbations like Manchester had no MPs at all. The Chartists continued to gather, even after 1842 when Robert Peel banned them. All of their top six demands have been met except for one: annual parliaments. Give them time.

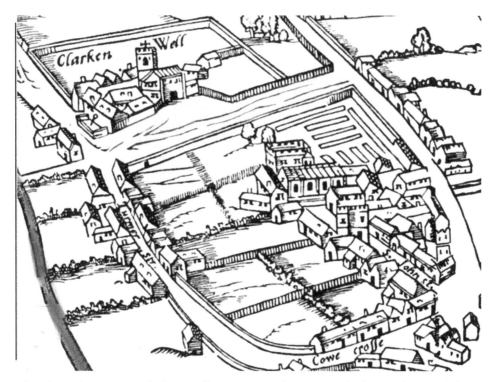

It would take a book to document Clerkenwell Green's radical vibes, which have been described by Peter Ackroyd as an "essential presence". In the late 1760s John Wilkes, the "champion of liberty" who had been born in a nearby street, addressed a meeting there. In 1826 William Cobbett spoke against the Corn Laws, which kept food prices high for the poor, to a large crowd gathered on the Green. In the 1860s the Reform League, which had particularly strong local support, held mass meetings here as did Fenian agitators both before and after the infamous Clerkenwell Explosion of 1867 .

Eleanor Marx Aveling, daughter of Karl Marx, spoke at a gathering of the unemployed on Clerkenwell Green in October 1887 before proceeding with them to Trafalgar Square behind a red flag. Soon after, William Morris addressed a crowd of some 5,000 on the Green before it headed for the same destination and was attacked by police in what became known as "Bloody Sunday".

The nearest thing to a memorial to the area's past is 37a Clerkenwell Green (on left of main photo), where the London Patriotic Society was formed in July 1872, partly by John Stuart Mill, on a site which once housed the Welsh Charity School for girls and today hosts the Marx Memorial Library.

The Patriotic Society was regarded at the time as one of the most progressive of the capital's working men's clubs, though it was not so radical or progressive that it admitted women even though in theory, despite its name, they were allowed to be part of it. Its membership and shareholders were nearly all local men, with skilled workers making up 80 per cent of them.

Number 37a is also where, in 1902-03, Vladimir Lenin edited and published a number of editions of his Iskra journal, which was smuggled into Tsarist Russia to stir revolutionary fervour. It is said that in 1903 at the Crown Tavern a few yards away, Lenin had a drink with Joseph Stalin, who was visiting London on party business in 1903, though this has never been confirmed. If only walls could talk.

The Marx Library may be sitting on a deeper secret. The building which commemorates the author of the slogan "Religion is the opium of the people" may be standing on the site of a medieval religious building – Saint Mary's Nunnery, which dates back to the 12th century. In the basement of the library are the well-preserved remains of what looks like a crypt (photo below). It may have been the cellar of one of the houses that once stood there or an outlying building of the nunnery itself.

As for the future, time will tell whether Clerkenwell Green's plan to re-green itself is a harbinger of yet another revolution still to come.

265: THE GREAT BEER FLOOD OF ST GILES

The rock musical Grease is (at the time of writing) playing at the Dominion Theatre at the junction of Oxford Street and Tottenham Court Road. It is the latest in a roll call of hits at this establishment, which includes South Pacific, which ran for over four years from 1958, We Will Rock You (12 years from 2002), Cleopatra, Porgy and Bess and, of course, The Sound of Music to name but a few. Most of the Dominion's many punters are likely to be unaware of a major incident that took place on the site many years before the theatre was there.

It would have been comic had it not been so tragic. The Great London Beer Flood occurred on 17 October 1814 at the Horseshoe brewery (pictured here), owned by Henry Meux of the Meux brewing dynasty. It happened when the corroded hoops of a vat standing over seven yards high triggered the explosive release of over a quarter of a million gallons of maturing porter, a favourite tipple of working men and street porters, whose name is derived from it.

The resulting torrent of beer did severe damage to the brewery's walls and caused several heavy wooden beams to collapse, before raging on to hit a tightly packed area of squalid houses nearby. Eight women and children were killed. It would have been much worse if the accident had happened later in the day after other residents had returned from work.

Martyn Cornell, who has researched the incident, says that most if not all of those who died were poor Irish immigrants, part of a mass of people living in the slums around the infamous St Giles rookeries, which were later cleared away when New Oxford Street was built. It is known that many of those living in cellars had to climb on to their furniture to avoid the flood.

There were stories at the time of people partying on the freak availability of free beer. Very few of these have been authenticated, although 20 years later an anonymous American visitor who had been walking along New Street, one of the most affected areas, wrote: "All at once, I found myself borne onward with

great velocity by a torrent which burst upon me so suddenly as almost to deprive me of breath. A roar of falling buildings at a distance, and suffocating fumes, were in my ears and nostrils. I was rescued with great difficulty by the people who immediately collected around me."

The construction of New Oxford Street attracted new industries to the area. One of the catalysts of change was the celebrated impresario Charles Morton who in 1852 had opened the trend-setting Canterbury Music Hall on Westminster Bridge Road in Lambeth, adjacent to the Canterbury Tavern.

Five years later, in direct response to Morton's success, Edward Weston and his father Henry opened a music hall on the site of the Six Cans and Punch Bowl Tavern on 242-245 High Holborn, close to the Horseshoe brewery. Morton responded in 1861 by taking over the former Boar and Castle pub, which stood directly opposite the Horseshoe on Tottenham Court Road.

It was called the Oxford Music Hall because of its proximity to Oxford Street. The Westons opposed this plan on the grounds that there were too many music halls in the area already, but were unsuccessful in their appeal.

Morton's new establishment became one of London's most popular music halls, featuring stars such as George Robey and Marie Lloyd, with some of the acts being moved by coach to the Canterbury between performances. The Times noted that it was "the latest development on a grand scale of a species of entertainment now in great favour with the public".

In 1922 the Horseshoe Brewery was demolished and the Oxford Music Hall closed four years later. But in 1928 the Dominion opened, as one form of musical entertainment replaced another. Over the road, the site of the Oxford is where the first Virgin megastore was briefly located and, more recently, the home Primark. That's life.

266: THE CLERKENWELL HOUSE OF DETENTION

All of London's notorious prisons from bygone days have thankfully been closed, but most have left indelible marks. Westminster Cathedral is built on the foundations of the jail which preceded it. The Old Bailey contains remnants of the walls of Newgate prison, upon which it was built. Parts of the Fleet prison have been found in Farringdon Road. Tate Britain stands on the spot once occupied by Millbank Penitentiary. But none of these remnants are as well preserved as the underground cells of the Middlesex House of Detention, otherwise known as Clerkenwell prison.

None of this is obvious when you visit Sans Walk, the narrow passage where one of the prison's perimeter walls was located. Today the site is all offices and apartments, but the remains of the cells have been remarkably well preserved, making them a popular location for fashion and design shows. However, it is difficult to think about them without conjuring up thoughts of the darkest days of the prison, which still reverberate within its sullen walls.

In December 1867 it was the scene of a reckless attempt to free two Irish republican prisoners, the Fenians Ricard O'Sullivan Burke and Joseph Casey, involving an explosion which sent shock waves across London. The authorities had learned in advance of a possible escape plot after a policeman on duty outside the prison became suspicious of a woman and a man he saw frequently conversing the previous day. Precautionary action was taken, including moving Burke and Casey to a more secure part of the building.

The blast, which was likened to a discharge of artillery, happened at a quarter to four in the afternoon. It shattered nearby houses and over 60 feet of the north perimeter wall (image below), and could be heard for miles around. Accounts of the number of casualties vary, but between six and 12 people were killed, many of them passersby, and over a hundred were reported injured.

No prisoners escaped and neither did one of the culprits – Michael Barrett from County Fermanagh.

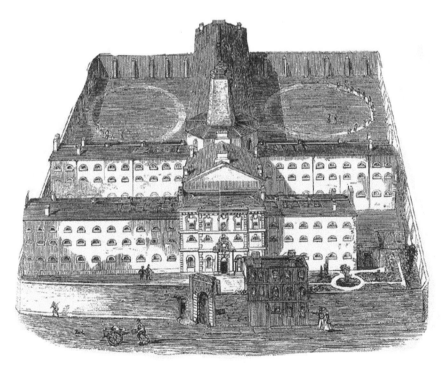

He and five others were tried before a jury at the Old Bailey in April 1868. Two defendants were acquitted on the instructions of the judge and, after sitting for 2½ hours, three others were acquitted by the jury. But Barrett was convicted of murder and hanged on the morning of Tuesday 26 May 1868 outside Newgate Prison. He was the last man to be publicly executed in that way.

The House of Detention was established on the site of two previous prisons. One of these, the Clerkenwell Bridewell, closed in 1794, with its operations incorporated by a jail at nearby Coldbath Fields, where the Mount Pleasant sorting office is today.

The other, called the New Prison, was rebuilt to become the Middlesex House of Detention, which lasted until 1886.

In its place, the London School Board built its biggest and most expensive educational establishment, which was opened by the then Prince of Wales – highly unusual for a mere school. But what to call it? Should it have a mundane name with local significance, as most schools did, or something special?

The board decided on the latter, and the school was named after Hugh Myddelton, a city grandee who had

been mainly responsible for creating the New River, which brought fresh(ish) water to this part of London from Chadwell, 28 miles away. Four hundred years later it still supplies London with nearly 10 per cent of its water. The New River was seen at the time as a kind of act of purgation, as if the link with water would wash away the site's dank memories, even though many of the original cells remained under the floor of the school. And still do today.

267: CLERKENWELL, HOME OF THE KODAK EMPIRE

If you walked along Clerkenwell Road at onset of the 20th century couldn't have missed the UK office of Kodak, the company that was once synonymous with photography. You couldn't miss it because the signs on the outside of the building, spelling out "KODAK" in bold capitals, wouldn't have let you. The small bright white ones in the picture above look as if they have been superimposed in what we would today call a photoshop operation, but there is no doubt that the frontage caught the eye.

Kodak was good with words as well as pictures. The corporate motto, "You press the button, we do the rest", also emblazoned on the building, was a brilliant bit of wordplay which any modern advertising agency would be proud of. Then there is the company name itself. That was the work of its American proprietor and creator George Eastman. It was a confected name that didn't mean anything, but it was easy to say and, unlike other brands, began with a sharp, incisive "K".

The UK's first Kodak factory was opened in Harrow in 1891, but Clerkenwell soon became the centre of its operations. In 1898 its head office and wholesale depot moved from Oxford Street into new luxury offices at what was then 43 Clerkenwell Road, which, unusually at the time, also had a swanky customer service centre. The move was partly to make use of a ready supply of skilled jewellers and watchmakers, many of them immigrants, who were well able to build Kodak's stereoscopic and folding pocket cameras.

Three years later, in 1901, Kodak also took over what was then Number 41 Clerkenwell Road from tobacco retailers Salmon and Gluckstein, which reckoned to be the biggest such operation in Europe.

One of the Gluckstein family went on to found the amazingly successful J Lyons catering empire. The Salmon and Gluckstein shop was merged into Kodak's building a year after the purchase. The street was also renumbered, as the photo shows.

Kodak left Clerkenwell in 1911 for new offices in Kingsway. Its former premises were, as shown here, taken over by another American company, Murrays, which made a wide variety of confectionery (though not Murray Mints!). The building has since been demolished.

Today, it can be hard to appreciate how dominant Kodak was. Eastman patented the process of photographic film being stored in a roll in 1884, and in 1888 perfected the first camera to exploit his invention. As recently as 1976 Kodak commanded 90 per cent of the sales of films and 85 per cent of cameras in the US.

It must have seemed to Kodak that its success would go on forever, but it hadn't planned well enough for what became its nemesis – the digital revolution. Although it claims to have developed the first self-contained digital camera, like so many other industries it failed to see the how totally disruptive to its operations digital would be. To cut a long story short, in January 2012 it filed for Chapter 11 bankruptcy protection in New York. Sadly, the second half of that famous slogan – "You press the button, we do the rest" – had become redundant.

268: THE RICH AND RED BACKSTORY OF THE WHITE HART OF ST GILES

The White Hart, squeezed into a corner where Drury Lane meets High Holborn, is very easy to miss. I missed it for decades, passing it regularly without a second thought. Apart from anything else, it looks too small to have anything interesting within. But when you go inside you find a large, friendly pub with a fascinating backstory.

It is not often you can drink in a pub once owned by Henry VIII, but that is a minor part of its heritage. Its biggest claim is that, according to what it calls "Old Bailey archives", it occupies a site where there were licensed premises as early as 1216. If that lineage of the White Hart (or Whyte Hart) is true – and it is not easy to authenticate – it would give the pub a strong if indirect claim to be the oldest in London, although none of the original building has survived.

The area known as St Giles was at that time a prosperous village, with inns, places of entertainment

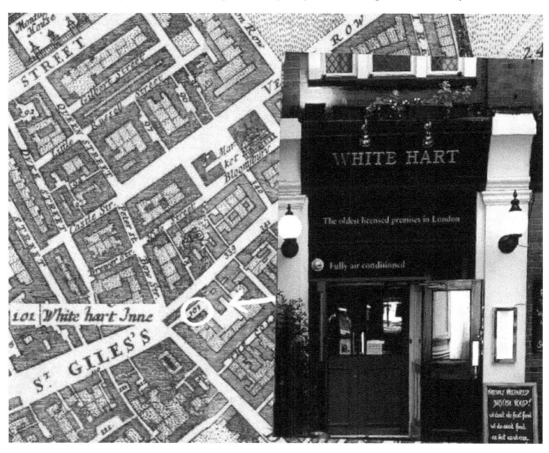

and the church or chapel of St Giles, which has been there in one form or other since 1101 when Queen Matilda, wife of Henry I, founded a leper colony there. In 1537 Henry VIII did a deal with the Master of Burton Lazars, which resulted in Henry acquiring "one messuage (dwelling) called the Whyte Harte and 18 acres of pasture".

A survey of Crown Lands taken in 1650 refers to "the White Harte situate ... in St. Gyles in the feildes ... consistinge of one small hall, one parlour and one kitchen, one larder and a seller underneath the same", and it appears on Morgan's map of 1682 as number 101, with an alley leading to Drury Lane.

Jack Sheppard (1702–1724), the romanticised thief on whom Captain Macheath in John Gay's The Beggar's Opera was based, used to drink there, as, it is said, did Dick Turpin (1705-1739) who stopped for "one for the road" on his journey to the scaffold at Tyburn.

Coincidentally, the actress Lavinia Fenton, who played Macheath's wife Polly Peachum and became the Duchess of Bolton, actually lived in a coffee house on the lane – a curious case of fact meeting fiction. Nell Gwyn, the self-styled "Protestant Whore" of Charles II sold her wares on this street for a while, though at a different time from Fenton's period of residence.

In the 17th Century Drury Lane was a fashionable street, but in the 18th it declined into one of the worst slums in London, known for drunkeness, highwaymen, prostitutes and gin addiction. Social conditions were so bad that the Great Plague of 1665, which killed 15 per cent of the population of London, is

believed to have started in nearby Stukeley Street after Flemish weavers opened goods arrived from Holland. A Travelodge hotel stands on the spot today, almost opposite the White Hart. The site also once housed stables for the brewery group Combe and Co.

In the 19th Century the White Hart played a bit part – for good or ill – in changing the world. It was there that the Communist League had its headquarters for a while. Karl Marx gave lectures there in 1847 before attending the second congress of the League. The pub was a short walk from Marx's second home, the reading room of the British Museum, then based at Montague House, (top left of the map above).

For two years Marx and his colleague Friedrich Engels, both of them young men at the time, took part in discussions at the White Hart and in 1848 presented the Communist Manifesto, just published in Bishopsgate, in its upstairs hall. The page proofs of the manifesto were apparently prepared at the pub before being delivered to the printer. The rest, as they say, is history. Communism has moved on since then, but the White Hart – maybe it should be called the Red Hart – remains one of London's most fascinating pubs.

269: LONDON STONE'S CANNON STREET HOMES

If you walk past 111 Cannon Street opposite the station you will see a protrusion at the foot of the Fidelity Investor Centre building. Don't blink or you might miss what, since 2018, has been the latest special casing for an unprepossessing lump of oolitic limestone measuring 21 inches wide and 17 inches tall.

A Stonehenge stone it is not, but the object known as London Stone has been around for at least eleven centuries and long baffled experts. All have agreed it must mean something significant, and yet they don't know quite what.

One of the earliest references to it can be detected in the name of Henry fitz Ailwin de Londonstane ("of London Stone"), the first Mayor of the City of London – from 1189 until his death in 1212 – who lived and had his business headquarters nearby.

Someone else who seemed to know its importance was Jack Cade, who, in 1450, is said to have struck it with his sword as his Kentish rebels stormed London in revolt

against Henry VI. Cade is memorialised in William Shakespeare's Henry VI – Part 2 in which he takes on the persona of John Mortimer, a claimant to the throne, and declares:

"Now is Mortimer lord of this city. And here, sitting upon London Stone, I charge and command that, of the city's cost, the Pissing Conduit run nothing but claret wine this first year of our reign. And now henceforward it shall be treason for any that calls me other than Lord Mortimer"

London Stone was originally positioned on the other side of the street, which was then called Candlewick Street after the trade that flourished there. But why was it there in the first place?

Antiquarian William Camden theorised in 1586 that it

was a Roman milestone from which distances from London were measured. Historian John Stow in the 1598 Survey of London described what was then a much larger rock, "fixed in the ground verie deep, fastened with bars of iron". Stow wrote that the stone was so hard it could break the wheels of passing carts. He added: "The cause why this stone was set there, the time when, or other memory is none".

London Stone became damaged and diminished, perhaps including by the Great Fire of 1666. By 1742, in its much reduced form, it had been moved from the south side of the street to the north side and positioned next to the door of St Swithin's Church, built by

Christopher Wren after the Great Fire destroyed an earlier church there, itself built on the remains of others dating back to the 12th Century – an excellent example of the layers upon which London is built.

The stone was later moved to a part of the church's south wall and then, in the 1820s, embedded and protected in a different part where it remained until 1962 when the Wren church, which had been badly damaged in World War II, was demolished.

By then the stone had been imbued with mystic significance, such as in William Blake's 1831 poem They groan'd aloud on London Stone. At the start of this century, London biographer Peter Ackroyd wrote: "It was once London's guardian spirit, and perhaps it still is."

An office building replaced St Swithin's, and London Stone was preserved in an alcove within it. Then, in 2016, planning permission was secured for a new office block to be constructed on the site, resulting in the stone being temporarily cared for and displayed by the Museum of London.

It was returned to Cannon Street in October 2018. Judging by the two images (left), it is now on more or less the same spot as when housed by St Swithin's.

Photo of the stone from the Museum of London

The difference is that a House of Mammon has replaced a House of God.

If you visit London Stone be sure to also wander in the adjacent Salters' Hall Court, where you will discover one of London's smallest and most secluded gardens (see above). A space that used to be the St Swithin's burial ground is now surrounded – I was going to say enshrouded – by enormous office blocks.

A curiosity is the statue (above, right) dedicated to Catrin Glyndwr, daughter of Owen Glyndwr, the Welsh nationalist who led a prolonged revolt against Henry IV. Catrin was buried in the church grounds in 1413 after being imprisoned in the Tower of London. She was married to Edmund Mortimer, who had a claim to the throne of England and was part of the same Mortimer dynasty with which Jack Cade would associate a few decades later. It is enough to give a psychogeographer collywobbles.

270: TOWER 42'S EXTRAORDINARY CITY HISTORY FOOTPRINT

Number 25 Old Broad Street, better known as Tower 42 – and even better known by its former name of the NatWest Tower – is a vertical history book just off Bishopsgate. If you know nothing about London's history except what has happened on this site over the centuries you will be acquainted with some of its key moments.

Designed by Richard Seifert, who was also the architect of Centre Point, the tower was the City of London's first skyscraper. Formally opened in 1981, it was the tallest building in London until the topping out of One Canada Square in Canary Wharf in 1990 and the tallest in the City for 30 years.

Though long since departed, the NatWest bank has left an indelible mark – the top of the building was designed in the form of the company's logo and can still be seen if you look at one of the 3D maps online, such as Apple's, or maybe from an aeroplane if you are flying by.

As with so many places in the City, Roman remains were found during archaeological digs at the time of the tower's construction. Mosaics and tessellated floors have been preserved in the Museum of London. But the real fascination of this building, with its offices, restaurants and other amenities, is what came after the Romans.

In 1466 Sir John Crosby built a mansion on the site called Crosby Place, having purchased the land from the nuns of St Helen's Priory who had been there since the early 13th century. Crosby was a City dignitary, knighted for his

role in resisting an attack on London by the so-called "Bastard of Fauconberg", a cousin and accomplice of the Earl of Warwick – known as Warwick the Kingmaker – who was trying to reinstall Henry VI as King. This was an extraordinary moment when the Wars of the Roses, fought mostly in the north of England, reached the gates of London Bridge.

Crosby's mansion, often known as Crosby Hall, was completed in 1472 but Sir John wasn't able to enjoy it fully because he died four years later. In 1483 it was bought from his widow Lady Crosby by the Duke of Gloucester, the future Richard III. Robert Fabyan's Chronicle of 1483 notes that "the Duke lodged hymself in Crosbye's Place, in Bishoppesgate Street" where the Mayor and citizens waited upon him with the offer of the Crown.

Much later on, in 1598, William Shakespeare, who we know lived nearby for a while, used the location for parts of his controversial play Richard III, such as in Act 1, Scene 3: "When you have done, repaire to Crosby place". One wonders how many people think of Richard when they enter Tower 42.

In 1519 another great figure of history, Thomas More, Henry VIII's ill-fated Lord Chancellor, purchased the lease to the property. He subsequently also bought an estate in Chelsea, which would become part of the Crosby Place story.

Later that century Crosby Place belonged to Sir Thomas Gresham, founder of Britain's first stock market, the Royal Exchange. In 1596, in keeping with Gresham's will, the Institute for Physic, Civil Law, Music, Astronomy, Geometry and Rhetoric was established in the mansion's Great Hall. Known as Gresham College, it provided

free lectures – including, over time, by the likes of Christopher Wren and Robert Hooke. Amazingly, 500 years on, today's Gresham College is still fulfilling this role, though its lectures are delivered not at Tower 42 but at Barnard's Inn or online.

Sir Walter Raleigh, another formidable intellectual, had lodgings there in 1601, two years before he was imprisoned in the Tower of London by James I. And between 1621 and 1638 Crosby Place again became a global centre, though not of science but international trade when the East India Company, then the biggest company in the world, made it its headquarters, prior to moving to Leadenhall Street. It would take a book to chart the company's amazing rise and shameful fall as it became mired in slavery and corruption.

During the 1660s another intellectual powerhouse moved in – the Royal Society. Its origins can be traced to a meeting at Gresham College on November 28 1660, following a lecture by Wren. Endorsed by Charles II in 1663, its full name was The Royal Society of London for Improving Natural Knowledge.

Crosby's mansion survived the Great Fire of 1666, but in 1672 was severely damaged by another one. Only the Great Hall and one wing survived, but these carried on through most of the 19th century partly by being turned into a luxurious restaurant. Augustus J. Hare, the Victorian author, said it was "altogether the most beautiful specimen of fifteenth century domestic architecture remaining in London".

However, in 1907 oblivion beckoned as new owners the Bank of Australia and China made plans to demolish it to make way for a new bank building. Fortunately, an outburst of public opposition saved it.

The building was pulled down and yet preserved. After considering various suggestions, the London County Council (LCC) found a new site for it and, stunningly, in 1909-10, transported the 500 year-old remains, stone by stone, five miles along the Thames to be rebuilt in Chelsea, in part of the garden of the estate former Crosby Place owner Thomas More had purchased there.

Having become in effect a council property, the hall was for years the home of the British Federation of Women Graduates. The Greater London Council (GLC), successor body to the LCC, maintained it until it was abolition in 1986. The London Residuary Body, formed to dispose of GLC assets, put the new Crosby Hall up for sale, ushering in an astonishing end to this tale.

It was purchased in 1988 by Christopher Moran, a philanthropist and sometime controversial businessman. He spent lavishly to return it to its former splendour as his private mansion and last year renamed it the Crosby Moran Hall. The picture below shows the outside of the restored Great Hall in Portland stone on the right and a recent modern addition in red brick on the left.

Sir Simon Thurley, who was involved in its restoration, calls it "the most important surviving domestic medieval building in London". It may well last longer than Tower 42. What goes around comes around.

PS: In 1993 tragedy struck when the then NatWest Tower was badly damaged in the IRA Bishopsgate bombing, which killed one person and caused extensive damage to other buildings.

271: SAMUEL PEPYS AND SEETHING LANE

London is blessed with small spaces covering up layers of history. They are often former plague pit sites, though few are as intriguing as the oasis of greenery in the City shown, right, which would fetch a small fortune if sold to developers. This was the land of Samuel Pepys, subject of the bust on the right.

Pepys lived, wrote, worked, played and worshiped in the area covered by this photo for 12 years from 1660 after he was appointed Clerk of the Acts, a position originally called the Keeper of the King's Ports and Galleys. It lies between Seething Lane and Crutched Friars. Pepys is also buried in this area, in St Olave's church, along with his wife Elizabeth. The spire of the church can be seen peeping up in the background of the photo.

"Seething" didn't mean boiling with rage in those days but "full of chaff", the chaff in question generated by the nearby corn market in Fenchurch Street. Crutched Friars is a corruption of cruciferi and referred to the

crosses sewn on the habits of the mendicant friars in the adjacent monastery, after whom the road is named.

Pepys lived in a dwelling on the left side of the newly created Navy Office, shown above (and page 236), working night and day – including the nine years he wrote his famous diary – as he steadily rose in seniority, reforming the navy as he went along, not least by opposing the rapacity of contractors. He is rightly thought to be one of the founders of the modern navy.

The Pepys diaries are a unique eyewitness account of how one man lived in an era of huge political and social upheaval, taking in the Restoration of Charles II in 1660, the Great Plague of 1665, the Great Fire of London the following year, and the Second Anglo-Dutch War.

The 1665 plague was the darkest period for Seething Lane. It is reckoned that an astonishing 300 plague victims were buried in the churchyard, which led Pepys to remark: "It frighted me indeed to go through the church…to see so many graves lie so high upon the churchyard, where many people have been buried of the plague." It also "frighted" Charles Dickens, who named the church "Sir Ghastly

Grim" because of three skulls which still hang over its side entrance.

One of Pepys's Seething Lane neighbours was Sir William Penn, whose amazing son, also named Willam Penn, was educated around the corner at All Hallows church. William Jnr went on to found the US state of Pennsylvania, which the Crown bestowed on him after Charles II's death in lieu of debts the Crown owed his father. The younger Penn wanted to call it "Sylvania" after silvia, the Latin word for wood, but was persuaded to affix his surname to it instead.

Pepys saw the first flames of what was to become the Great Fire of London from this garden on 2 September, 1666, though he had to be woken up and told twice by his maid before realising the seriousness of it. He then had a good look round and rushed by water to the King in Whitehall to tell him that "unless his Majesty did command houses to be pulled down nothing could stop the fire". Pepys added: "The King commanded me to go to my Lord Mayor… and command him to spare no houses, but to pull down before the fire every way".

On Tuesday 4 September the diarist wrote: "Now begins the practice of blowing up of houses in Tower-streete, those next the Tower, which at first did frighten people more than anything, but it stopped the fire where it was done, it bringing down the houses to the ground in the same places they stood, and then it was easy to quench what little fire was in it, though it kindled nothing almost."

When it looked as though the fire would sweep up Seething Lane, Pepys and Penn famously buried their best wine and Pepys favourite cheese, parmesan, in the garden. Who knows, maybe a bottle or two is still there.

Pepys is generally considered to be the greatest diarist in the English language, albeit accidentally, because he never intended his journals to be published, despite their containing absolutely invaluable first-hand accounts of what was happening in politics at the time. They were written in a code that wasn't deciphered until 150 years after they were written and contained graphic details of his near-serial philandering, some of which was non-consensual.

These activities took place around the town but also in Pepys's home, where he made approaches to some of the maids in his household. On one extraordinary occasion he was caught in the act by Elizabeth when having his hair combed by her companion Deb Willet. According to his diary entry of 25 October 25 1688 this "occasioned the greatest sorrow to me that ever I knew in this world, for my wife, coming up suddenly, did find me embracing the girl".

Unsurprisingly, Pepy had an often turbulent relationship with his wife, but it was also a loving one. When she died suddenly of typhoid on 10 November 1669, aged 29, he was devastated, and the small sculpture he had installed in St Olave's in her memory can still be seen today.

The Navy Office was spared the Great Fire, only to be destroyed by another one seven years later, in 1673. It was rebuilt in 1674-5 but demolished in 1788 when the Navy Office moved to Somerset House. The site was then occupied by warehouses of the all powerful East India Company, but they too have disappeared, leaving just the Pepys bust to hint at the past of this historic City green space.

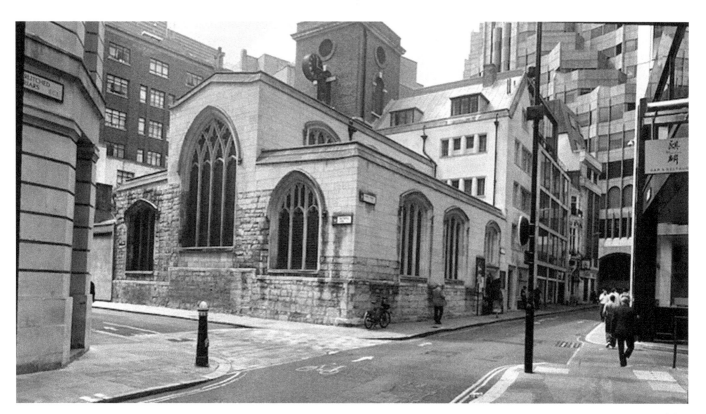

272: THE COFFEE HOUSE THAT CAME BEFORE THE GHERKIN

"This is to give notice that the House late in Threadneedle Street, near the Royal Exchange, is now open'd by the Name of the Virginia and Baltick Coffee-House, where all Foreign and Domestick News are taken in; and all Letters or Parcels, directed to Merchants or Captains in the Virginia or Baltick Trade will be carefully deliver'd according as directed."

This is one of the earliest records of what had previously been called the Virginia and Maryland coffee house, one of what eventually became nearly 3,000 coffee houses in London. It was wise to change its name to the Virginia and Baltick. Trade with the vast Baltic area, especially Russia, was booming while in America Britain's colonial inheritance, Maryland included, would later be shattered by the looming War of Independence, which broke out in 1775.

Coffee houses were of immense importance. One sometimes wonders where the City of London would be today if they had not been invented. They were where financial deals were transacted, where businessmen (rarely, if ever, women) caught up with the news. Clerks in Parliament working for the coffee houses would race each other in hansom cabs to convey outcomes of vital parliamentary votes to their clients ahead of rivals. Money was at stake.

In 1810 the coffee house company moved to larger premises at the Antwerp Tavern, also in Threadneedle Street, and in 1903 to a new and lavishly decorated Exchange at St Mary Axe – the Baltic Exchange (main picture), which provided its members with a daily guide to what was going on in global shipping markets, from freight market prices to shipping costs or the settling of freight futures contracts. It was the last of the City institutions to abandon its trading floor to do business by telephone or on screens.

Disaster struck in 1992 when it was badly damaged by an IRA bomb, which killed three people and injured many more. At first, key parts of the structure were put into storage in the hope of constructing a new building around what remained of the hall and the façade, but in 1995 English Heritage dropped its insistence on a restoration when the damage turned out to be much greater than previously thought.

So, what to do with unwanted remains and a prime building site? Enter Sir Norman Foster with plans for a Millennium Tower, a 92- storey building that would have been the tallest in Europe. That soon bit the dust amid fears that it was simply too big for the skyline and, according to Heathrow, a danger to incoming aircraft. Just when the site was starting to look jinxed a happy

ending came along. The Foster partnership submitted a different plan for a smaller skyscraper. Nicknamed The Gherkin, it became an unmistakable modern classic at 30 St Mary Axe almost as soon as it was finished.

Meanwhile, the marvellous stained glass (below), which had survived the blast, was re-installed in the National Maritime Museum in keeping with the maritime history of the Baltic Exchange.

And the rest of the salvaged material? Much of it – including stairs, marble columns, panelling, even telephone

boxes – was purchased from an online platform for £800,000 by two Estonian entrepreneurs, Heiti Hääl and Eerik-Niiles Kross. They shipped it to Estonia in dozens of containers. Parts of it were showcased in an exhibition in 2016 and they hope to eventually incorporate it into a new office block in their homeland.

There is something rather wonderful about the heart of London's historic Baltic Exchange being found a new home in...the Baltic.

273: SHAKESPEARE AND THE THEATRES OF BISHOPSGATE AND GRACECHURCH STREET

The reigns of Elizabeth I and James I saw an explosion of literary talent in London that has never been matched. Plays by William Shakespeare, Ben Jonson, Christopher Marlowe, Thomas Middleton and others created during that period are still being staged around the world today.

They were mainly associated with playhouses such as the Globe, the Rose, the Swan and later the Blackfriars, all of them deliberately situated outside the confines of the City of London, whose puritanical rulers were opposed to plays, regarding them as lewd and degrading.

It is less well known that at about the same time, and in some cases slightly earlier, playhouses did nonetheless exist within the confines of the City. They were not purpose-built but instead attached to inns, either inside or outside, which is one of the reasons detailed records about them don't exist.

There were four of them in all. Two, the Cross Keys and the Bell, both indoor venues, were close to each other in Gracechurch Street, and a third, the Bull, was further up the road in Bishopsgate. The fourth, the Bel Savage (or La Belle Sauvage), was in Ludgate Hill.

If you walk north up Gracechurch Street today – or Gratious Street as it used to be called – from the Monument you will come

to Bell Inn Yard, next to Wetherspoons. The original Bell Inn Yard, which existed from the 14th century, was destroyed in the Great Fire of London, but today's entrance to it is almost certainly in the same place as the way in to the old Bell Inn and its theatre. Confusingly, the Bell Inn Yard sign has a plaque beneath it honouring the Cross Keys Inn, but it was actually located about 25 yards away.

These theatres came into their own after 1569 when the City authorities relaxed the rules allowing plays to be staged at inns in return for a payment of £40 – a hefty sum in those days. That situation lasted until 1594 when the Lord Mayor got the Privy Council to ban all use of City inns for theatre shows.

Shakespeare would have been familiar with Bishopsgate. If his footprints could be traced they would be everywhere. He would have often strolled or ridden from Shoreditch, where his plays were put on at The Theatre in Curtain Road, to London Bridge in order to cross the river to The Globe and the Rose. Also, we know for certain that he lived for a while in the neighbourhood of St Helen's church, off Bishopsgate, because he is named in the tax records for the area for 1598. It is difficult to believe that he didn't visit the inns of Bishopsgate too.

Were his plays performed at them? Julian Bowsher, an

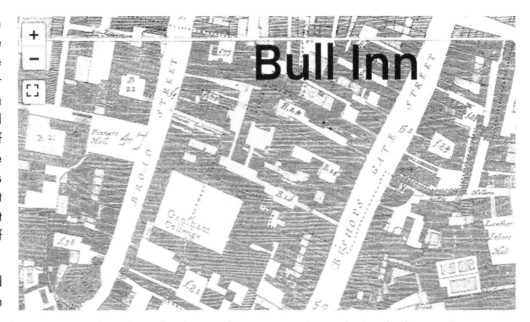

archaeologist who wrote Shakespeare's London Theatreland, says that in 1594 the Lord Chamberlain said: "My new company of players have been accustomed for the better exercise of their qualities…to play this winter time within the city at the Crosskeys in Gracious Street".

The Lord Chamberlain's Men – later renamed The King's Men after James ascended the throne – was Shakespeare's company and had exclusive rights to perform his plays. Several scenes from one of his most famous works, Richard III, were set near Bishopsgate at Crosby Place. In one scene he tells the assassins he had hired to kill the Duke of Clarence: "When you have done, repair to Crosby Place."

What was it like inside those theatres? They offered a mixture of serious entertainment and dating opportunities. A rare contemporary account by Stephen Gosson states: "In the playhouses at London, it is the fashion of youths to go first into the yard, and to carry their eye through every gallery, then like ravens, where they spy the carrion thither they fly, and press as near to the fairest as they can."

It is not clear if Gosson was thinking of classic playhouses like the Globe or the inns of Bishopsgate and Gracechurch Street. Probably both. He gives the impression that at the Bull, where the stage was in the open air, the spectators were more restrained, perhaps because of its generous dimensions. Alleys leading to it stretched all the way from Bishopsgate to Broad Street.

The explosion of literary talent in early modern England could only have happened in London, which had entrepreneurs prepared to put their money behind the new theatres, aristocratic patronage – a sine qua non – royal approval, loose copyright laws and a rising population. It all happened in a small geographical area, which enabled clusters of playwrights to meet and collaborate. Bishopsgate and Gracechurch Street played a small but very important part.

274: LEADENHALL MARKET'S ROMAN FOUNDATION – IN A BARBER'S BASEMENT

If pictures could talk, the montage opposite would have a tale to tell about 2,000 or more years of a historic part of London. The skyscrapers oiling the wheels of the City of London's prosperity today stand behind the beautiful Leadenhall Market.

The market's current form was designed in 1881 by Sir Horace Jones, who also gave the capital many other buildings, including the original Billingsgate Market and Tower Bridge. But a market has been on this site in one form or another since at least the 14th century, when it belonged to city dignitary Sir Hugh Neville.

In 1411 it was acquired by the City of London Corporation with the help of one Richard Whittington. According to Walter Thornbury's 1878 Old and New London, Volume 2, reproduced at British History Online, when Don Pedro de Ronquillo, the Spanish ambassador, visited Leadenhall in the 1600s he told Charles II he believed there was more meat sold there than in all the kingdom of Spain in a whole year.

Occupying much of the land between Gracechurch Street and Leadenhall Street, the market used to be so large that in the 1720s a part of its land accommodated the

headquarters of the East India Company, the biggest corporation in the world, as the map opposite shows.

And the age of today's market buildings is as nothing compared with that of a piece of masonry found by archaeologists in the 1880s when Leadenhall was being reconstructed to Jones' plan. Today, believe it or not,

242

it is located in the basement of a barber's shop (below) where the market meets Gracechurch Street. The staff were amazingly friendly when I dropped by unexpectedly for a peek. It is down two flights of stairs and protected by a glass partition.

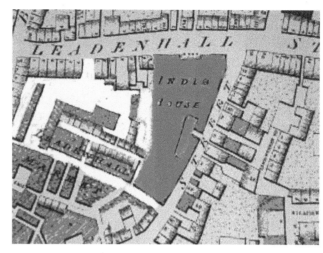

This unique artefact is a base of an arch that formed part of a basilica – a law court or assembly room – dating back to the year AD70. The basilica was the largest Roman building south of the Alps and the centre of Roman London, from where most roads to the rest of the country started. It is said to have been as tall as St Paul's.

It was constructed on a five-acre site where the foundations of many rooms have been uncovered and recorded by archaeologists before being buried forever under new constructions. It stood along one side of a forum – a market place and a public space where citizens could meet and exchange ideas. Though much larger, the forum was not unlike Leadenhall today – a location where merchants, residents and visitors trade and party.

The basilica and forum lasted for over 200 years until they were destroyed, not by an alien force but by Rome itself as punishment for London supporting the rule of the "rogue emperor" Carausius.

In the medieval period that followed, Leadenhall was the most important market in London, especially for meat and poultry and also butter, cheese, wool and cutlery. As now, it would have been a hive of noisy activities, though much more smelly.

Today you still get a sense of the medieval as you emerge from narrow alleys into the magnificence of Jones's marketplace. It is easy to see why it has found its way into films, including Harry Potter and the Philosopher's Stone.

Leadenhall invites comparison with the even older Borough market on the other side of the Thames, which began at least as early as 1014. It has more sculpted charm than Borough, but is heavily dependent on commuting City workers. This ensures a lot of spending during the week, but Leadenhall almost goes to sleep at weekends.

That is a problem but also an opportunity. The City Corporation and the EC BID are seeking to attract more visitors from home and abroad. The infrastructure is already there and a huge reservoir of history remains to be fully exploited – from its Roman foundations upwards.

275: THE MANY MYSTERIES OF MARK LANE IN THE CITY

Mark Lane in the City, near the Tower of London, has always been a bit of a puzzle to me. It sounds to me as if it was named after a bookmaker, but as historian John Stow pointed out in the late 16th century it was actually so called because of a "mart" or cattle market once located there. If you walk down it today, starting from the Great Tower Street end, it seems to offer only a conglomeration of overcrowded office blocks.

However, a couple of its newish buildings bear the name Corn Exchange – a reminder that an actual Corn Exchange existed in the area from 1747 for nearly 250 years, selling oats, beans and grain on behalf of farmers. From 1826 it had rival, also on Mark Lane, and between them they generated so much chaff it is easy to see why a street running parallel to Mark Lane, which bore the brunt of it, was called Seething Lane – "seething" means constantly agitated. Continue along Mark Lane and find a surprise on the left hand side: a Grade I listed church tower with no church attached.

It is what remains of a church called All Hallows Staining, an earlier version of which was recorded on the site in the late 12th century. All Hallows means

"all saints" and "staining" means stone, which distinguished it from other All Hallows churches in the City, which were made of wood. It is situated next to its benefactor, the Worshipful Company of Clothworkers, one of the City's livery companies. This helps explain the tower's Grade I status.

Beneath the tower and slightly to one side of it there is crypt (shown in the engraving opposite). But the crypt wasn't part of All Hallows Staining church. It was originally situated in Monkwell Street, which ran through where the Barbican estate now stands, and formed part of an ancient hermitage known as the Chapel of Saint James in the Wall, the wall being London Wall.

Following King Henry VIII's dissolution of the monasteries in 1543, the chapel was given to local man, William Lambe, who is best known for, in 1577, building a conduit to carry water over 2000 yards from near the junction of what is now Lambs Conduit Street – named after Lambe – and Long Yard in Bloomsbury to a conduit head at Snow Hill in Holborn.

This brought fresh spring water to the inhabitants of Holborn long before the New River company started supplying it almost 40 years later. Lambe was also a longstanding member of the Clothworkers company, and when the

chapel was pulled down in 1872 its crypt was moved, stone by stone, to All Hallows Staining. Every year, the adjoining Clothmakers' Hall hosts a service to commemorate Lambe, who has been described as "a person wholly composed of goodness and bounty".

There are plans for a major redevelopment scheme which envisages incorporating the tower and crypt as the focal point of a new public open space, which would bring a largely lost part of the City to renewed prominence. It may come as a surprise to City commuters that there was once a Mark Lane London Underground station. It was actually on Seething Lane, but not named after it because it didn't sound soothing enough for a station.

You can still see the former entrance to it in Byward Street (above, left) and if you peer through the gate the top of the stairs leading down to the platform is visible. You can also, apparently, still see one of the Mark Lane platforms during the Tube ride from Monument to Tower Hill, but the train I took for that journey was travelling too fast for me to spot it or photograph it. Unless you happen to be a Tube driver, it remains a lost bit of London.

276: THE WAYFARERS AND BAPTISED OF ST BOTOLPH-WITHOUT-BISHOPSGATE

The churchyard of St Botolph-without-Bishopsgate, near Liverpool Street station, is like no other in London. Where else in the middle of this frenzied city can you find a relaxing garden, a tennis and netball pitch, a converted Turkish bath, a church hall that once hosted a City livery company and, of course, a working church?

And then there are the people.

In 1556 Edward Alleyn, one of the great actors of the Elizabethan Age and the founder of Dulwich College whose father ran a pub across the road, was baptised there.

Three years later so was Amelia Bassano who, in 1592, married Alfonso Lanier in the same church, taking her husband's surname. Several members of the Bassano family were influential court musicians, but Amelia became one of the most interesting women of her age. You don't have to believe she was the "dark lady" of Shakespeare's sonnets, as some think, or that she was the real author of his works, as a recent book claims, to appreciate her importance.

Amelia was indisputably among the very first women to publish a book of poetry,

and also a pioneer of proto-feminism through her emphasis on social and religious equality for women. She even dared to suggest in her verses that it may not have been Eve who tempted Adam in the Garden of Eden, but the other way round.

There is no evidence that Shakespeare had associations with the St Botolph church although, as he lived nearby, he might have. His friend and rival Ben Jonson was certainly acquainted with it, as his infant son is buried here.

In 1650 Sir Paul Pindar, a great City dignitary was interred in the graveyard. He is remembered as not only a successful merchant and benefactor, but also because the facade of his house, which stood where the Bishopsgate entrance to Liverpool Street station is today, is preserved in the Victoria and Albert museum. It is just about the only example of the front of a London house from that era to survive.

In October 1759 Mary Wollstonecraft, author of A Vindication of the Rights of Woman and surely a soul mate of Amelia Lanier, was baptised at St Botolph's. It is an extraordinary coincidence that two giants of feminism should have been baptised in the same church, albeit 150 years apart.

We should also mention that amazing business woman of the late 18th century Eleanor Coade, whose statues of school children fashioned from Coade stone adorn the outside of the church hall (below). And on top of all that, if you go into the church you will see the very font where another literary giant, the poet John Keats, was baptised in 1795.

But pride of place in St Botolph's history should arguably go to William Rogers, who was appointed its rector in 1863. He was appalled by the squalor and poverty around him and also by the disturbing fact that much of the money accumulated by the church over the centuries from bequests was used to fund jollies for the great and good. Rogers was determined to put these funds towards improving the lot of the labouring poor instead.

As the Bishopsgate Institute records: "He enabled families to get access to clean drinking water by fund-raising for new drinking fountains in local streets. He was involved in the construction of bath and wash-houses, and he campaigned to establish play areas, schools, and picture galleries in his community." The opening of the Institute in

1895 was Rogers's crowning achievement. It was devoted to the education of those who most needed it in his parish and elsewhere, and it is still flourishing today.

St Botolph's is also unusual in that for 40 years until 1992 its church hall hosted a livery company – the Worshipful Company of Fan Makers. This was a rare example of the co-existence of God and Mammon, but the fortunes of the company have a familiar ring about them.

Fan making was brought to Britain by French craftsmen in the late 1500s. Their numbers received a huge boost in 1685 after the Catholic King Louis XIV of France revoked the Edict of Nantes, a measure introduced by a predecessor in 1598 granting rights to the country's Protestant minority, known as Huguenots. Many Huguenots found sanctuary in London and renown as East End silk weavers. They were fan makers too.

Since then, domestic fan making has had its ups and downs. In the early 1700s the East India Company, just down the road from St Botolph's, flooded the market with hundreds of thousands of cheap fans made by untrained workers in China, who were paid a pittance. Sound familiar?

Fan makers in England continued to produce high quality fans and still do, but there were no home manufactured

fans on display at the Great Exhibition of 1851. Much later, in April 1998, a company called Fan Enterprises Ltd was launched to sell a Millennium Fan. That was a good idea, but sadly the product was made in Spain as no English fan makers good enough to do the job could be found.

And what of St Botolph himself? A revered East Anglian noble, he died in 680 after a long life of Christian endeavour and became known as the patron saint of wayfarers, of whom many interesting examples have left their imprint on this fascinating church and its surroundings.

277: THE GREAT COFFEE HOUSE FIRE OF 1748

If you walk from Gracechurch Street along Bishopsgate to Liverpool Street it is easy to feel overpowered by the gigantic office blocks that have blotted out much of the skyline. They are there for a reason, of course – to maintain the City of London's position as one the world's leading financial centres.

This may look like a triumph of money over history. Yet if you find your way into the area between Cornhill and Lombard Street you may be surprised. It is like falling into a time warp – a network of alleyways that have hardly changed since medieval times.

To find your way around, forget GPS and mobile phones. Instead, use the 18th Century map reproduced above. All the buildings it shows were destroyed or damaged in a fire which began in what was then called Exchange Alley on Friday 25 March 1748, but the serpentine lanes are still much as they were. Here, history has triumphed over height.

It is fashionable today to talk about clusters of like-minded companies or start-ups as catalysts of change, yet that is exactly what was happening in these streets around 300 years ago in the form of an agglomeration of coffee houses, from which a direct line to the success of today's London's financial district can be traced.

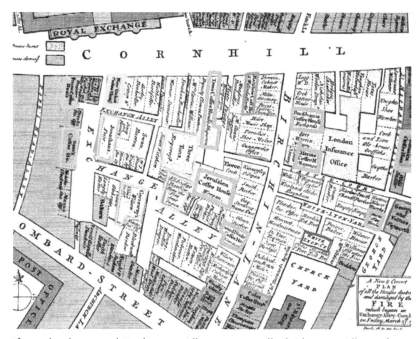

If you had entered Exchange Alley – now called Change Alley – from Cornhill you would first have passed the New Union and Drapers coffee houses. A few yards on you would have had a choice between two of the most famous, not to say notorious, of them all: on your left Jonathan's and on your right Sam's, both of which played crucial roles in the emergence of stockjobbing or the trading of stocks and shares.

After paying the customary one penny entrance fee – there was no class distinction if you had the money – you were free to gossip with acquaintances and newcomers about news and rumours of companies here or abroad. Both kinds were involved in one of the great financial frauds of the time, the so-called South Sea Bubble, which burst in 1720, leaving hundreds of people deprived of savings they had invested. At school we learned about how South Sea Company attracted speculators on an industrial scale, though hardly anything about the slave trading that lay behind it.

Even after that scandal Sam's continued be the go-to place for the get rich quick dreamers of the day. If crypto-currency had been around back then, Sam's would have been in the thick of it. Jonathan's is often thought to have been the inspiration for Thomas Rowlandson's famous cartoon *A Mad Dog in a Coffee House* (below, from New York's Museum of Modern Art), which shows posters of ship movements on the wall.

Following Exchange Alley round to the left brought you Garraways (opposite). Its name was derived from that of its original owner, Thomas Garway, who, among other things, is credited with being the first person to sell tea in England on a retail basis, beginning in 1657. Garraways (pictured below) claimed to have dramatically brought down the price of tea in leaf form from upwards of six pounds per pound in weight.

Garraways began to serve coffee too after the pioneering initiative of Pasqua Rosée, who established the Jamaica Coffee House on the other side of Birchin Lane – the very first such establishment in London. At Garraways you could buy and sell anything from books and paintings to South Sea Company stock. It lasted for over 200 years.

A MAD DOG IN A COFFEE HOUSE.

Still further along Exchange Alley, a left turn would have brought you to the Eldridge Barber shop – where the Great Fire of 1748 actually started – and the Jerusalem Coffee House, the most powerful of them all, not least because it was owned by the East India Company, the biggest corporation in the world before its ignominious fall from grace. The Jerusalem was a popular meeting place for traders and shipowners, particularly those with an interest in the east, and an early rival of the Lloyds coffee house on Greater Tower Street, or just Tower Street as it was then known.

Also in the area was Tom's Coffee House, which had artistic as well as business vibes. David Garrick, one of the greatest actors of his age, was known to frequent it and Colley Cibber, the actor manager, was a customer. The poet Thomas Chatterton, who died tragically young, told his sister that he needed to be writing at Tom's because "my present profession obliges me to frequent places of the best resort".

The family home of Thomas Gray, author of Elegy Written in a Country Churchyard, one of Britain's best-loved poems, was in Cornhill, around the corner from Birchin Lane. Gray's father Philip, a scrivener and broker, would have been familiar with some of the almost 20 coffee houses crammed into this small space.

Had those who started and ran them known that the cluster of coffee houses that thrived in this part of the City would lead to the giant skyscrapers that dominate the area today, they would have been astounded. From little acorns…

278: DICK WHITTINGTON'S VERY LONG LAVATORY

On or around 1 May 1421 a public toilet built over a dock on the Thames by the mouth of the River Walbrook opened its doors. Called the Longhouse, it had an amazing 128 seats – 64 for men and 64 for women, something you might only see at big pop concerts these days. Its contents were discharged through a gully underneath and carried downstream at high tide. Homes were built above it to utilise the space created.

This "house of easement" was unusual for two reasons: one, it was the first convenience of its time to have separate facilities for men and women; two, it was built or bequeathed by someone not normally associated with that sort of thing – Dick Whittington.

You don't hear much about this side of Whittington in the pantomimes that have made him and his supposed cat so famous. As John Schofield says in his book The Building of London from the Conquest to the Great Fire, the real Dick Whittington was a man of even greater stature than his legend.

"Born not into poverty but into a well-off family, he rose to be what has been called a 'merchant Prince' by trading in the risky but profitable north and Mediterranean seas," Schofield writes. "He supported three successive English kings with loans and left a fortune equivalent to the wealth of a medium-sized kingdom."

The Longhouse, though innovative, was among the least of Whittington's benefactions. These also included the rebuilding of the Guildhall, schools, drainage systems around Billingsgate and Cripplegate – which the great Victorian engineer Joseph

Bazalgette would have approved of – and a ward for unmarried mothers at St Thomas's Hospital.

That is not to mention the rebuilding and extension of his local parish church, St Michael Paternoster Royal (main photograph) where, in 1423, he was buried (the church was destroyed in the Great Fire of 1666 and later rebuilt by Christopher Wren). Whittington also built an almshouse (or "college") there, though that endeavour was relocated first to Highgate in 1808 and then, in 1966, to its present location in Felbridge, East Grinstead. He lived on College Hill, where a plaque marks the spot.

Whittington died childless but left a fortune that has been estimated at around £7 million in today's money. Some of it was used to rebuild Newgate Prison with accommodation in it for sheriffs. It can be viewed as a forerunner of the Old Bailey, which was constructed on the site of the prison after it was pulled down.

Whittington's fortune also helped build the first library in the Guildhall, which eventually led to today's Guildhall Library. The Whittington Charity still disburses money each year to the needy through the Mercers' livery company. Not bad for one man, even though how he made his fortune is not completely clear.

None of this will do anything to stop – and nor should it – all the wonderful pantomimes based on the romantic tale of a poverty-stricken Dick and his cat leaving London to return to his birthplace in Gloucestershire.

Along the route – the folklore usually says it was at Highgate – he was summoned back to London by the sound of the bells of St Mary-le-Bow in Cheapside and eventually became the City's Lord Mayor four times. Who is surprised these days when fact fails to dislodge fiction?

279: THE CHURCH OF THE BEHEADED

If death is the great leveller there are few more macabre examples of it than the church and crypt of St Peter ad Vincula. The church – its name means "St Peter in chains" – is one of two situated within the Tower of London, and an earlier version of it was probably there before the Tower was built.

It is a macabre place because it contains the decapitated bodies of a Who's Who of powerful people executed at the Tower for alleged acts of treason – many sanctioned by an Act of Attainder, which meant they didn't have a proper court trial. It would fit perfectly into Game of Thrones. Lord Macaulay, in his 1848 book The History of England, said there was no sadder place on earth, and it is easy to see why. If there is life after death, goodness knows what those laid to rest there might be talking about.

Here lies the headless body of Anne Boleyn, the second wife of Henry VIII, executed with a sword on 19 May 1536 on Tower Green in front of the church for alleged adultery. The green, now a bizarre tourist attraction, is much as it was back then, although without the scaffold. Anne's brother, George Boleyn, had met the same fate as his sister two days earlier. He was beheaded in public view on nearby Tower Hill, but was buried in the same place.

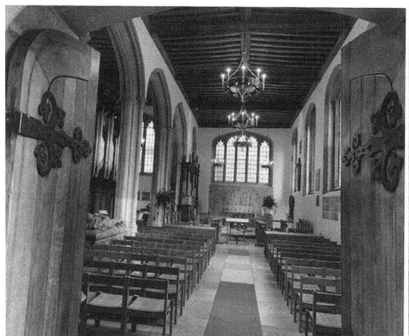

Anne was killed on the authority of Thomas Cromwell, Henry's chief minister, who was later blamed for the King's ill-fated marriage to Anne of Cleves. What happened to Cromwell? He was beheaded on Tower Hill 28 July 1540, which was the same day – can you believe it? – as Henry married his fifth wife Catherine Howard. She in turn lost her life two years later, on 13 February 1542, because of her alleged promiscuity, a subject Henry was a bit of an expert on. Like those of other nobles her beheading took place on Tower Green and her corpse added to the St Peter ad Vincula collection.

Even before Anne Boleyn was despatched the church was where the headless corpses of distinguished traitors were laid to rest in Henry's time. Thomas More's was put there after he was executed on Tower Hill on 6 July 1535 – he is buried at the far end of the crypt (main photo) – for refusing to acknowledge that Henry, rather than the Pope, was head of the Church in England. His friend John Fisher, Bishop of Rochester, had met the same fate on 22 June of that year, though his body didn't get taken to the church until the same time as More's. Both men were later canonised.

To list all the executions connected to this church would be to risk decapitation fatigue. One of the most bizarre was that of Thomas Seymour, the brother of Henry's third wife, Jane Seymour, and the husband of his sixth, Catherine Parr, whom he married after Henry's death. Seymour was a ruthlessly ambitious man who was beheaded on Tower Hill in March 1549 for treason on the authority of his older brother, Edward Seymour, who was Lord Protector of England while the boy king Edward VI, the son of Henry and Jane Seymour, was growing up.

Edward's reward? He was himself decapitated on Tower Hill for treason nearly three years later, in January 1552. The Lord Protector didn't even last long enough to enjoy the ludicrously palatial residence, Somerset House (not the present one), he built from stone pillaged from other buildings, including the nearby church of St Mary's in the Strand and the

Priory of St John in Clerkenwell. He even tried to demolish the wonderful St Margaret's church next to Westminster Abbey, only to be repulsed by armed parishioners. Both brothers are buried at St Peter ad Vincula.

It goes on and on. In 1553 John Dudley, first Duke of Northumberland, who succeeded Edward Seymour as chief minister under King Edward, was executed on Tower Hill on August 22, 1553 in front of thousands of people following his role in helping his Protestant daughter-in-law, Lady Jane Grey, very briefly on to the English throne. He was buried in the church as well.

How did this come about? The young king, a Protestant, who was terminally ill, hadn't wanted his half-sister "bloody" Mary Tudor, a Catholic, to be Queen and in his will had nominated Grey – who was married to one of Dudley's sons, Lord Guildford Dudley – to be his successor.

It is not clear how much the elder Dudley influenced Edward's decision, but it was clearly in his interest and, ahead of events, he marched to East Anglia to capture Mary, only to surrender when the Privy Council in London proclaimed Mary Queen.

The upshot was that Jane Grey spent her nine-day reign in the Tower with her husband, a fellow teenager, in a different part of it until on 12 February 1554, they, like Dudley senior, were beheaded, Dudley junior on Tower Hill for public consumption, Grey in private on Tower Green. Two more decapitated bodies for St Peter's.

Later execution victims buried there include Robert Devereux, 2nd Earl of Essex, a former favourite of Elizabeth I, who became the last person to be beheaded on the green on 25 February 25, 1601 for, in the words of his indictment, conspiring "to depose and slay the Queen, and to subvert the Government." His executioner was one Thomas Derrick, whom Essex had previously pardoned after Derrick was convicted of rape.

The one condition for this let off was that Derrick became an executioner. He went on to put over 3,000 people to death, including, eventually, Essex himself. Gratitude, as they say, belongs to history. The word "derrick" became the name for the frame from which a hangman's noose was supported, and is today the term for a type of crane or the frame above an oil well.

It is a great shame that its macabre history has distracted attention from the attractions of this small but rather wonderful church, which still functions as a Chapel Royal, run by the Crown, and holds regular services which are open to the public and free to attend, as long as you don't also visit the rest of the Tower.

280: BISHOPSGATE, FISHER'S FOLLY AND THE 'REAL' WILLIAM SHAKESPEARES

It could be argued that Bishopsgate should be renamed Shakespeare Street because of William Shakespeare's associations with it. The great writer would have walked along it regularly, as it was the main road north of the Thames on the journey between the south bank of the river, where the Globe and the Rose theatres were, and Shoreditch, where the Curtain and the Theatre playhouses were.

We also know that Shakespeare lived for a while in the parish of St Helens church, close to where the Gherkin now stands. As a previous piece in this series has documented, his plays were staged at City inns such as the Crosskeys in Gracechurch Street. And several scenes from Richard III were set at the nearby Crosby Place mansion whose location now forms part of the footprint of Tower 42.

It is less well known that Bishopsgate also has links with people claimed by some to have been the true writers of works attributed to Shakespeare. Competing accounts of the source of Shakespeare's canon form the longest who-done-it in

literary history, one that refuses to go away despite being virtually ignored by those – known as Stratfordians – who firmly believe that the output attributed to Shakespeare was indeed created by the glovemaker's son from Stratford.

For a long time, beginning with the work of John Thomas Looney in 1920, the foremost candidate among the dozens of alternatives proposed has been Edward de Vere, the 17th Earl of Oxford. And guess what? It was this

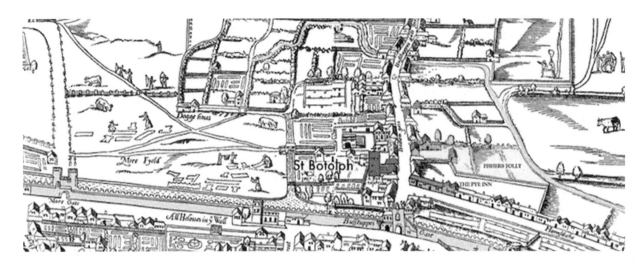

same Earl of Oxford who, in 1580, purchased a palatial home (main picture) in Bishopsgate opposite St Botolph's-without-Bishopsgate church. It was a magnificent dwelling, built by a man called Jasper Fisher in the late 16th Century. Fisher must have been reasonably well off, as he was a member of the Goldsmiths' livery company, but constructing a mansion on this scale was beyond his means.

John Stow, the 16th century historian, called it "a large and beautifull house with Gardens of pleasure, bowling Alleys and sumptuously builded". He reported that Fisher spent all his funds building it and owed money to many people, leading locals to refer to the result as "Fisher's Folly". Fisher died in 1579, heavily in debt.

The Earl of Oxford's tenure lasted from 1580 until 1588, so it would have coincided with the period when Shakespeare was thinking about his early plays, such as The Two Gentlemen of Verona and The Taming of the Shrew, both of which were written or first performed at the turn of the decade.

Oxford was certainly a deeply literary person. Charles Wisner Barrell, an American art critic and a supporter of the view that Oxford was the "real" Shakespeare, suggested in 1945 that Oxford acquired his impressive home "as headquarters for the school of poets and dramatists who openly acknowledged his patronage and leadership."

Fisher's Folly was sold by Oxford to Sir William Cornwallis, and Stow's The Survey of London, in a section published in 1603, says of the property, "It now belongeth to Sir Roger Manars", by whom he is assumed to have meant Roger Manners, the 5th Earl of Rutland.

This is curious because in 1907 German author Burkhard Herrmann argued that Rutland was the real author of Shakespeare's works. Rutland was ranked seventh in a top-ten list of "the most notable possible authors of the works of Shakespeare" as determined by TopTenz.net in September 2011.

That makes two would-be Shakespeares living in the same mansion, albeit separated by a few years. It gets curiouser when we learn that Rutland was friends with Henry Wriothesley, the 3rd Earl of Southampton, who was Shakespeare's patron. When Rutland undertook the Grand Tour of Europe he studied at the University of Padua where The Taming of the Shrew was set and where two of his fellow students were apparently called Rosencrantz and Guildenstern, as if they had stepped out of Hamlet.

It gets curiouser still. St Botolph's – shown in blue in the map above – is where the poet and writer Amelia Lanier was baptised and married. She is thought by some scholars to have been the "dark lady" of Shakespeare's sonnets and by others to have been the actual Shakespeare. That makes three people alleged to have been the real authors of works accredited to Shakespeare living within a few hundred yards of each other – four if you include Shakespeare himself.

Lanier came from an Italian-Jewish background, and a recent book contending that she was really Shakespeare describes a litany of Jewish imagery in Shakespeare's work, which I found impressive. I would have been more impressed had I not read another book a few months earlier arguing that Shakespeare must have been a Catholic because of all the Catholic imagery he deployed.

From 1620 until 1670 Fisher's Folly, as it continued to be known, was taken over by the Earls of Devonshire to add to their collection of palatial residences and was renamed Devonshire House.

In 1678 that fascinating and controversial speculator Nicholas Barbon purchased what was by then called Old Devonshire House and proceeded to pull it down to make way for the profitable construction of small houses instead.

Barbon had a track record of demolishing aristocratic residences, such as Essex House and others in the Strand. He also designed Devonshire Square in the space where the Fisher mansion had stood before selling it, largely undeveloped, in 1682. But Devonshire Square is still there and well worth a visit. Today, it leads to an impressive glass-roofed entertainment and eating centre.

The best way to get there is to take a right turn off Bishopsgate along Houndsditch and then a left up a tiny street called, unsurprisingly, Barbon Alley, which leads you into what little remains of the site's 450 years of history.

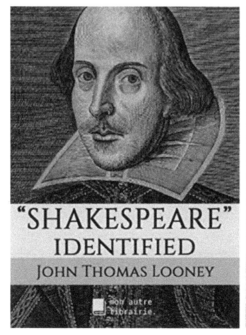

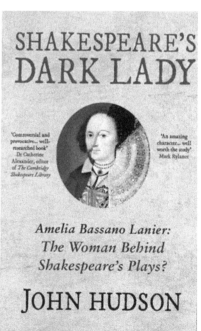

281: THE MISSION HALL OF LAMBETH WALK

Some parts of London have been lost forever because new buildings have replaced old ones. Others are lost in plain sight because not enough people know about them – such as the former Pelham Mission Hall on Lambeth Walk.

Built in 1910 to a design by architects Waring and Nicholson, it was a church with an open air pulpit – still there at the front of the building – named after Francis G Pelham, rector of Lambeth from 1884 to 1894. It was constructed on the site of the earlier Star Mission Hall, which was originally what has been described as a "beerhouse" about which little is known. The foundation stone of the Pelham hall was laid by the Archbishop of Canterbury of the time.

It is almost the last physical trace of a bygone era of poverty-tinged Cockney pride. In those days, Lambeth Walk had over 100 market stalls run by costermongers who sold surplus food and other things at discount prices. The song that glorified the street, The Lambeth Walk, was once a global hit.

But like the pawn shops that used to temporarily ease the hardship of local residents, there is no longer a call for the hall's original purpose. It has moved on from saving souls and today is the home of Morley College's Henry Moore Sculpture Studio, which describes the building as "well equipped to provide a creative space for our sculpture courses including metalwork, clay life modeling (kiln fired), wood and stone carving, bronze casting and mould-making".

There is a palpable buzz of creativity as you enter this extraordinary building. The outside looks slightly faded but its attractions have increased as others on the street have, aside from the base of the King's College London Maths School, become commodified. The pulpit now houses an outlet for the fumes from the kiln (the interior pipework can just be seen in the right hand photo above).

I recently posted the photo of the hall at the top of this article on Twitter. I was astonished that it attracted well over 150,000 views, which is rather more than I usually get. Many who commented on it were in awe of the beauty of the building, which I often pass during my walks around London, even if they thought it was in need of a wash and brush up. Thanks to social media it is getting more of the attention it deserves.

282: LLOYD'S OF LONDON AND THE CITY'S HISTORIC LAYERS

The coffee house opened in 1686 by Edward Lloyd in Tower Street – today's Great Tower Street – near the Tower of London soon became a popular place for seafarers, merchants and shipowners to exchange information of mutual interest about the movements of ships, trends in world trade and maritime insurance and more. Anyone from a docker to ship owner could join in, as long as they paid the penny entrance fee.

Lloyd's tiny establishment gradually expanded into the global insurance colossus we know today as Lloyd's of London. Over the years it developed linked businesses, such as Lloyd's Register and Lloyd's List, which provided daily news about everything from stock prices to high water times at London Bridge, along with news of ship arrivals, departures and accidents. Lloyd and his successors were among the first people to realise the importance of data to business and to make money out of it.

Small wonder that Samuel Pepys would frequent places such as Lloyd's to get news that was often more reliable and up-to-date than what he learned in his day job at the Admiralty. Small wonder also that in 1675 Charles II had tried without success to shut down all the hundreds of coffee shops that already existed in London because they spawned too much criticism of the government. They were the mass media of their day. In this digital age we are used to companies such as Google, Facebook, Apple and Microsoft springing up from backstreet premises to become all-powerful global forces. But how many of them will still be with us in 300 years' time?

Lloyd's is one of the great financial success stories of our age. However, as the company has recently acknowledged, there is also a shameful side to its past because of its links to slavery from insuring an industry that transported an estimated 3.2 million Africans across the Atlantic. In a statement on its website Lloyd's apologises for its involvement in slave trading and adds: "Prompted by the anti-racist activism of Black people and allies following the murder of George Floyd, Lloyd's is on a journey of research and reflection as we acknowledge our historical connections to slavery, as well as the lack of ethnic representation – particularly at senior levels – that still exists within the Lloyd's market."

By a somewhat bizarre coincidence Lloyd's iconic head office (right), designed by the Richard Rogers partnership, occupies exactly the same site today on the corner of Lime Street and Leadenhall Street as another, even bigger, organisation that was also besmirched by links to repressive colonialism and slavery.

For over 130 years, from June 1729, this location housed the rebuilt head office of

the East India Company (main image opposite, and location shown on map pg264), which in its time was the biggest company in the world. In its earliest days, around 1600, it was based nearby in the house of its first governor, Sir Thomas Smythe, which stood – would you believe it? – where the Walkie Talkie skyscraper is today.

Roger Williams in his book London's Lost Global Giant recalls that the East India Company – known as the "Monster of Leadenhall Street" – had a startling 200 metre frontage decorated with statues that reinforced its view of itself as, in Williams's words, "the controller of world trade with a monopoly everywhere east of the Cape of Good Hope". It also had a private army of 260,000 men to enforce its rule of India, which lasted until the 1857 Indian Rebellion (or Mutiny) against it. The company was then de-privatised and brought under Whitehall's command as the British government assumed direct control of India.

There is a further twist to the story. The site on which Lloyd's and the East India Company built their head offices has another link with colonialism, though of a totally opposite kind. It was not the result of Britain engaging in colonial expansion but being the victim of it when the Romans invaded.

Research by Museum of London archaeologists on the site of the Lloyd's building has confirmed that it was the scene of successive phases of Roman building from the late first century. Finds at the eastern end of the five-acre forum built in Londinium included a basilica said to be the tallest building north of the Alps.

Other interesting features included the foundations of several rooms and evidence of a small stream which provided fresh water and, according to the archaeologists, may have been a stimulus to development. The stream was later blocked up as the city expanded and so became one of the earliest of the lost rivers of London.

No one, as far as I know, has suggested that Rome should apologise or compensate for its invasion which, for all its ills, left a positive legacy of buildings. London has many lost layers whose implications we are still coming to terms with.

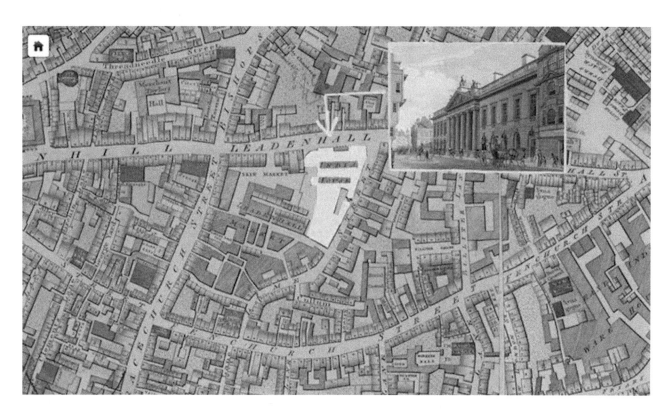

283: THE MEDIEVAL SPELL OF ST MARY-LE-BOW

If you wander around Cheapside guided by its street names you will be transported back to medieval London. Milk Street, Bread Street, Wood Street, Ironmonger Lane, Old Fish Street and Garlick Hill are all named after the trades that did business either side of Cheapside itself, although the traders had to sell their wares in that main City street as it was the legally designated trading area.

Some of them are shown on the 1561 Agas map below. Highlighted in yellow on "Chepefyde" are the last of the series of Eleanor Crosses erected by Edward I in memory of his wife and, to the right of it, a smaller structure which was one of the conduits that brought fresh water to the locals. The big building highlighted is the church of St Mary-le-Bow which can trace its origins back to 1080, though after the 1666 Great Fire of London it was reconstructed by Christopher Wren.

If you want a genuinely ancient experience at the church, go downstairs where you can have a coffee and something to eat in a crypt largely unchanged since medieval days (photo next page). It is one of the very few places in London where such gastronomic time travel can be done. The monks' cellarium in Westminster Abbey is another.

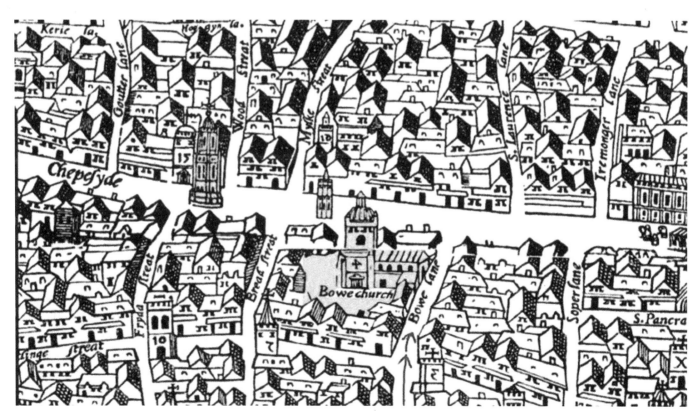

If the crypt seems to be lacking a couple of stones this could just possibly be because in 1912 two of them were removed and given to Trinity Church in New York, situated on the corner of Wall Street and Broadway. This was in recognition of William of Orange granting it the same privileges as St Mary-le-Bow.

The New York church had been designed by a British immigrant from Shaftesbury, Richard Upjohn, and until 1869 was the tallest building in the United States. Trinity Church confirmed to me that they had received the stones, but they don't know what has happened to them. Lost in time.

St Mary's is, of course, famous more for its bells than for its stones, not least because of the unproven tale that Dick Whittington when leaving London turned back when he heard the sound of Bow bells and went on to become Lord Mayor. The bells also feature in the nursery rhyme Oranges and Lemons:

"I do not know,

Says the great bell at Bow."

If you lived within the sound of Bow Bells you were, by tradition, defined as a cockney. How this went down with the rich goldsmiths and merchants who lived nearby is not obvious. Nor is the implication that entitlement to being called a Cockney could depend on which way the wind was blowing. However none of this has prevented the story being

embedded in global folklore.

Less well known is the fact that Bow's bells were also used as a curfew (from the old French "cuevrefeu" meaning "cover fire") to tell householders to put their fires out as a precaution against a conflagration. The custom has long since died out at St Mary's but to keep the tradition going a curfew, albeit electronic, is still sounded each evening at Gray's Inn.

The church has Wren's signature all over it, especially its tower. As David Crawford notes in his book The City of London, it contains all five of the classical orders of columns (Tuscan, Doric, Ionic, Corinthian and Composite) and it apparently cost as much to build as the whole of the rest of the church. The tower is a monument in its own right and represents money well spent because only it and the walls of the church survived a World War II bomb.

The church is best accessed from Mansion House Underground station along Bow Lane, a road built to convey goods from the ancient port of Greenhithe to the Cheapside markets. As you walk up Bow Lane the spire of St Mary peeps out and then disappears in the grand manner of London's unfolding townscape.

Turn left before reaching the church and you enter its forecourt where there is an imposing statue (above) of Sir John Smith, a local parishioner who led a quite extraordinary life before playing a key role in establishing the first British outpost in America at Jamestown, Virginia in the early 1600s.

Smith was reputedly saved from the death penalty after a plea from the native American Pocahontas, who subsequently made a highly successful trip to London on behalf of the Virginia Company, though she tragically died at the very start of her return journey and was buried in Gravesend.

St Mary-le-Bow is a successful working church which also runs a project that takes young homeless people into safe flats and young ex-offenders – often ex-prisoners – into its office for training. This is run in association with the Pret a Manger Apprenticeship Scheme and often leads to permanent employment.

284: THE MIXED CITY IMPRINTS OF KING WILLIAM IV

King William IV only reigned from 1830 to 1837 but he was honoured in the streets of London in several significant ways. Some of that legacy endures. Some has been lost. And some of it never happened at all.

One tribute to William that has lasted to this day is King William Street, built in the City of London between 1829 and 1835 linking Lombard Street with what was then a brand new London Bridge. Designed by the great Scottish architect John Rennie and completed by his son of the same name, the bridge was formally opened in 1831 by William and his wife Adelaide of Saxe-Meiningen. They sailed down the Thames together to perform the ceremony, never suspecting that in 1968 the Rennies' creation would be bought and moved to Arizona to become a tourist attraction.

Adelaide was celebrated during her time as Queen by having a new hotel named after her. In the 1850s it was converted into offices, but retained Adelaide's name. The new block that replaced them in 1925 was called Adelaide House and stands on King William Street next to London Bridge to this day, having been listed Grade II since 1972.

A monument to William himself appeared on the street named after him in 1844, seven years after his death – a large granite statue erected at the point where King William Street crosses Cannon Street (photo right). But William was later remembered with a far more substantial tribute – a railway station. And no ordinary one.

Opened in December 1890, the King William Street station was the northern terminus of the capital's first functioning deep-level underground railway. The City and South London Railway connected the City with Stockwell via Borough, Elephant and Castle, Kennington and Oval, eventually

forming part of the future Northern Line. However, ground-breaking though the station was, in didn't last. It was closed in 1900 when the line's new Moorgate station was opened.

William's memory suffered a further indignity in 1936 when the statue of him was moved to Greenwich Park to help relieve traffic congestion. Yet this was not the greatest misfortune to befall the late King's heritage.

Trafalgar Square's Fourth Plinth has been famous throughout this century as the stage for a series of modern artworks, but it was originally intended to form the base for a statue of William astride a horse. Indeed, the

CORPORATION OF LONDON

SITE OF
KING WILLIAM STREET
UNDERGROUND STATION
FIRST CITY TERMINUS
1890 – 1900

entire square was initially to be named after him. But, oh dear, the money for the equestrian tribute was not forthcoming and the project was abandoned.

There has, though, been a more recent recognition of William brief tenure as monarch. Today, a building called Regis House stands at 45 King William Street on the site where the underground station used to be. Constructed in 1994, its name alludes to the link with William – "regis" is Latin for "of the king".

Extensive pre-construction excavations by Museum of London archaeologists revealed a wealth of London history on and around the site. They found evidence of a Roman-period well and oven, waterside quays and, amazingly, a street front wall which they say probably supported the side of a causeway leading to the original London bridge, built by the Romans across low lying water between Southwark the Forum and Basilica in the Roman walled city. Several timbers were dated by dendrochronological analysis to AD 52.

To this mixed collection of William IV imprints on London could be added one little known fact – the City and South London Railway was probably the first "subway" in the world. A map from 1885 refers to it as the "City of London and Southwark Subway". That was 12 years before the word was first used in America to describe the new underground railway in Boston.

285: THE SOUTH SEA BUBBLE'S THREADNEEDLE STREET HOME

If you walk along Threadneedle Street in the City of London towards its junction with Bishopsgate you will find on your left at Number 38 a handsome Grade II listed building which houses, among other things, the Piazza Italiana restaurant. The building went up in 1902 as the London office of the Scottish-owned British Linen Bank, which later became part of the Bank of Scotland. But long before that the site was occupied by South Sea House – pictured below and opposite – headquarters of one of the most controversial companies in British financial history.

The South Sea Company, despite its romantic-sounding name, is known only for its association with the South Sea Bubble of 1720, a classic example of the madness of crowds blindly buying into get-rich-quick schemes. Its collapse is on a par with the Dutch Tulip scandal and the recent crypto-currency boom as history we didn't learn at school. Comparatively recently its involvement in the slave trade has also become apparent.

The company began as a clever scheme organised by Chancellor of the Exchequer Robert Harley (later the Earl of Oxford) in 1711 to establish a consortium of public and private investors, including merchants and senior politicians, to relieve the government of its – in those days – huge debt of £10 million.

A big part of that debt was the cost of financing the Royal Navy in its long war with France and others. In exchange, the South Sea Company was issued with government stock paying interest of six per cent a year (which the government tried to recoup by imposing "sin" taxes on wine, tobacco and luxury goods). It seemed like a good deal for both sides and was entirely legitimate. However, the company soon realised it needed income from other sources to sustain it.

The government provided this in 1713 when the South Sea Company was granted a monopoly

to supply slaves from Africa to the Spanish colonies in the Americas. It didn't have much success at first as Spain, which controlled the ports, was reluctant to let the ships   But, helped by its close links with the Royal African Company, Britain's biggest slave trader, the South Sea Company gradually became a big slave trader in its own right.

Britain's involvement with the slave trade was a horror story that was not fully realised until all the details of the voyages were put online. Professor Helen Paul of Southampton University,

an authority on the Bubble, recalls one of the worst examples: in 1713/14 a South Sea ship, the St Mark, took 280 enslaved Africans aboard but only 261 arrived in Kingston, Jamaica.

The financial outlook for the company received a boost in 1718 when King George I, already a shareholder, became its governor, creating more confidence in its future. Many of the investors were buoyed up by unfounded stories that it would be able to exploit gold and other riches in the Americas, not least from the gold and silver mines of Peru and Mexico. Rumour fed on rumour and in 1720 the boom took off only to collapse in a single year, with shares rising from £128.5 in January to more than £1,000 in August before collapsing back to £124 in December.

The apparent success of the South Sea Company inevitably spawned lots of imitators. The most notorious took deposits for a "Company for carrying on an undertaking of great advantage but nobody is to know what it is". Crowds of people gathered to invest but on the third day the fraudster disappeared and, according to Professor John M. Pick in a Gresham College lecture, took the money and "lived a life of a gentleman in Paris for the rest of his days".

Although many were ruined by the South Sea Company's crash, others made money, such as John Guy who founded Guys Hospital on the proceeds. His statue still stands in the forecourt of the hospital today. At the time the Bubble was seen as a catastrophe, but these days economists can't find any evidence that it caused severe dislocation to the economy as a whole. For instance there wasn't a significant rise in bankruptcies.

Are there any lessons today? The evils of Britain's history of slavery have been accepted and taken on board by companies in the City and elsewhere, even though they have yet to agree what exactly should be done about it. In a curious way the lessons of share booms, being rooted in a desire to make money, have been harder to learn as can be seen in the recent crypto-currency bubble. Even people who didn't believe in it were prepared to invest in the hope they could bail out before the collapse. There is sometimes a method in the madness of crowds which is hard to extinguish.

286: SIR THOMAS GRESHAM, THE CITY'S FIRST "TRUE WIZARD" OF GLOBAL FINANCE

In prime position in the charismatic church of St Helen's Bishopsgate lie the remains of Sir Thomas Gresham, one of the most influential and enigmatic figures the City of London has ever produced.

Gresham, who lived from roughly 1519 until 1579, was hugely rich, with a palatial home in Bishopsgate where Tower 42 is today, yet he died heavily in debt. The story of his grave just about sums him up. Gresham manoeuvred to have his tomb located in what was his home parish church by promising an endowment to build a steeple – a promise Professor John Guy, one of his recent biographers, says "he never made good".

It is easy to see why Gresham wanted to be buried in this singular church. It is beautiful and exceptional in that it incorporates the remains of a nunnery, which was once next door and became part of the church after the dissolution of the monasteries – hence the dual naves seen in the photo opposite.

A little later, in around 1598, it was the parish church of William Shakespeare who for a while lived close to where the Gherkin is today, and is honoured with a stained glass window. It went on to become one of the few churches to survive both the Great Fire of London and the Blitz.

Gresham had an astonishing career by any standards. He was an effective banker to three monarchs, segueing between the fiercely Protestant Edward VI, the fiercely Catholic Mary I and back to the Protestant Elizabeth I. He bailed Edward and Mary out of their financial difficulties by halving the government's overseas debt through shrewd manipulation of interest rates and interventions in the foreign exchange markets. Small wonder Guy calls him "the first true wizard of global finance".

Gresham was also involved with bullion and arms smuggling on the government's behalf. He even had his own intelligence network which he bequeathed to Sir Francis Walsingham, Elizabeth's spymaster. He was the inspiration for Gresham's Law, the monetary principle that "bad money drives out good".

Most of Gresham's financial and diplomatic activities were conducted in Antwerp, when the Belgian city was Europe's financial capital. But he had long wanted to set up a rival centre in London, an idea first put forward by his father, Richard. An opportunity to do this arose after Philip II of Spain forced his Roman Catholic Inquisition on the Protestant

Netherlands. This led to thousands of skilled Flemish people, fearing persecution, moving from there to London.

Gresham offered to build the Royal Exchange with his own money if the City and others, such as the Mercers' livery company to which he belonged, would provide the land. The Exchange building was designed by a Flemish architect helped by a Flemish carpenter and, to the consternation of London brickies and labourers, was constructed mainly by Flemish workers. In 1839 John William Burgon, an early biographer of Gresham, claimed that, apart from wood from Suffolk "nearly all of the materials of which the edifice was composed were brought from Flanders."

The building was officially opened in January 1571 by Queen Elizabeth, who gave permission for use of the Royal title and a license to sell alcohol. The Exchange had 150 shops on an upper floor – mainly catering for well-off women – which gives it some claim to have been Britain's first shopping mall. It was said you could find more coaches parked there than outside church doors.

At least half of the traders and others who operated there came from Holland, France and Germany, wresting financial supremacy from Antwerp. This transplanting of a major industry laid foundations for London's future dominance. Perhaps the City would have prospered anyway, but it is difficult to believe all the successes of subsequent centuries would have happened without Gresham's vision.

The second great thing Gresham did can be appreciated today by anyone. After his only son died in a riding accident in 1564 he decided to leave a lasting legacy in the form of Gresham College, an institution of higher learning providing Londoners with free educational lectures.

It was eventually opened much later, in 1597, by the executors of his will on the site of his grand mansion (shown on page 274) which stretched from Bishopsgate to Broad Street. Early speakers included Robert Hooke and Christopher Wren.

Initially, lectures were given once a week on subjects including divinity, astronomy, music, geometry, law, medicine and rhetoric.

The amazing thing is that the college is still giving free lectures today, despite higher education having become a paid-for luxury practically everywhere. They are delivered in person, usually at the college's main building at Barnard's Inn Hall in Holborn, and anyone can attend. Since going online in 2001 the lectures have received over 40 million views and there is still scope for growth as lots of people simply don't know about them.

How was it financed? By another bit of Gresham chicanery. Shortly before he died, to the surprise of the Mercers' Company which had been expecting to be the beneficiary of his will, he decided to leave his assets and income from the Royal Exchange and Gresham House to fund the college.

For all Gresham's brilliance there is a darker side to him which has only come to light comparatively recently and challenges Burgon's assessment that Gresham died "with unsullied honour and integrity". Questions have arisen about the extent to which his activities were linked to the slave trade.

In his Gresham lecture John Guy described plenty of duplicity and a controversial private life but no mention of slavery. Yet in another Gresham lecture Professor Richard Drayton of King's College argues, among other things, that the Antwerp model of finance Gresham imported into London had close links to the slave trade. If this is proven it will change attitudes to Gresham's otherwise stunning achievements.

London's links to the slave trade are part of a wider inquiry the City is engaged in about its past and what should be done about it. It is entirely appropriate that Gresham lectures should contribute to that exercise.

LOST LONDON 1

This is the map from the first Lost London book, which is available from most online retailers, or you can get a discounted copy from the author, if you can collect from central London.

Contact Vic Keegan - victor.keegan@gmail.com

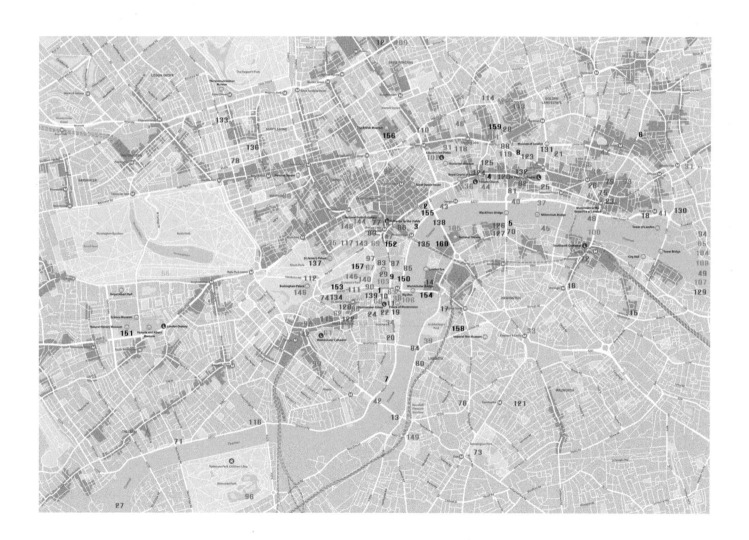

ABOUT THE AUTHOR

Victor Keegan is inescapably a Londoner. He was raised in outer suburbia, first in a leafy road in Raynes Park (SW 20) and then a council flat in Wimbledon (SW19) until he left university to join the Guardian newspaper and ended up in a flat in Victoria (SW1) where he lives with his family.

His hobbies include writing about English wine, football - AFC Wimbledon of course - and tramping the streets of London with his iPhone for relaxation and enlightenment. Also, occasional quirky excursions such as walking from Trafalgar Square to Islington - without crossing a road.

He believes poetry to be the most creative form of writing. Poems can be as long as a book or as short as a text message. They can rhyme or not rhyme and can be about anything under the sun (and beyond). He has written six poetry books on subjects ranging from the origin of the universe to a Nun on a Train.

Victor was educated at Wimbledon College and Brasenose College, Oxford. He had dozens of jobs, from road sweeper to barman until he joined the Guardian where he stayed for nearly 50 years doing numerous things including a column about industry and economics for almost 25 years, and later one on consumer technology ranging from mobile phones to virtual worlds. He is married to Rosie with two children, Dan and Chris.

Milton Keynes UK
Ingram Content Group UK Ltd.
UKHW050450030823
426155UK00003B/61